SENTENCING

As I See It

The Honorable Richard L. Nygaard

United States Court of Appeals for the Third Circuit

COPPERHOUSE PUBLISHING COMPANY

930 Tahoe Blvd. #602
Incline Village, NV 89451
775.833.3131   Fax 775.833.3133
e-mail info@copperhouse.com
www.copperhouse.com

Your Partner in Education
with
"QUALITY BOOKS AT FAIR PRICES"

SENTENCING
As I See It

Copyright© 2000 by Copperhouse Publishing Company

Library of Congress Catalog Number 00-106368
ISBN 1-928916-03-1 Paper Text Edition

2 3 4 5 6 7 8 9

Printed in the United States of America

Dedication

To my wife of thirty-five years,
and eternal friend,
Martha Jean.
"Just us."

and

To my parents,
Leo Bernhard Nygaard,
and Amanda Zelma Nygaard,
who taught me all I needed to know
about morals and their consequences.
All the philosophy and law I have learned since
are merely footnotes to the lessons I learned at home.

Richard Lowell Nygaard

About the Author

When I was a boy, I had but one lasting ambition in life—I wanted to be a judge. Other ambitions came, but they just as quickly left. When an evangelist came to town with tent and sawdust, I hoped God would call me to be a preacher. When the rodeo came, with ropers, clowns, and bronc riders, I wanted to be a cowboy. Then, as I approached my teen years, my Norwegian seafaring heritage inspired in me a desire to run away and go to sea. Each fleeting fantasy either faded away as some other childhood excitement took its place or was thwarted by maturity, and these ambitions quickly passed. But, my dream of becoming a judge was always there.

My interest in the law was kindled early when my father took me to visit the Pennington County Court House in Thief River Falls, Minnesota, the town where I was born. My father was the most honorable, honest, and fair man whom I have ever met. He epitomized the Norwegian concept of *snill*.[1] That trait, and his profound sense of intellectual piety, provided me with an exemplar from which I developed my compassion for others and a sense of fairness that still cause me great angst when the law requires that I do something that does not reach the threshold level of my convictions. My belief that firm, gentle, and fair treatment is required for others has also caused me to rethink both the traditional foundations of America's sentencing philosophy and its practices.

Years ago in that courtroom, I stood hand-in-hand with my father in great awe of the cathedral-like atmosphere, afraid to speak louder than a whisper, and experienced something I have never forgotten—it was the overwhelming impression that great people moved through, and great things happened, in that courtroom. This was a place where "good" would triumph, even for poor people such as we were. Even today when I enter a courtroom—any courtroom—I experience the same sense of awe, a respect for the majesty and the traditions of the law, and a belief that it is a place where the good, and "good," *must* triumph.

I am Richard Lowell Nygaard, born of Norwegian ancestry in 1940, the fourth in a family of five children. My father was a butcher, and my mother did "day work" (cleaning houses and doing laundry for others). They lived by, and taught us, the creed that success came to those who work hard and play by the rules. We were raised in the Scandinavian tradition—doses of discipline by my father and overdoses of love from my mother.

At the age of ten, my family moved from northern Minnesota to the Antelope Valley in the Mojave Desert of Southern California, where I spent, or perhaps misspent, my youth. There, beginning at the age of eleven, I worked at such jobs as shoe shiner, paperboy, dishwasher, soda jerk, bus boy, stocking clerk, ranch hand, school bus driver, and salesman. I attended the Antelope Valley Joint Union High School, and in 1958 I shared the dubious distinction of graduating 496th out of a class of 500, with my classmate, Frank Zappa. After high school, I served a tour of duty with the United States Navy, where military discipline and maturity gave me a measure of focus, self-discipline, and self-confidence. I mustered out as a Petty Officer Second Class. I then enrolled in a junior college and began the task of correcting my numerous high school grade deficiencies.

In 1963, I went to work as a Fireman for the Los Angeles County Fire Department and spent six years fighting a lot of brush fires and a few structure fires in and around Newhall and Castaic, California. While working for the Fire Department, I continued my studies and after several years of taking correspondence courses and attending various junior colleges, was admitted to the University of Southern California.

Meanwhile, I met and married a person who is as beautiful as her philosophy, "I never knowingly do anything that *I* believe to be improper." She has lived by these words, as profound as they are simple, and instilled the same ethos in our children. If followed by everyone, her philosophy would obviate the need for this book, and indeed, for my job.

In 1969, I graduated from U.S.C., receiving a bachelors degree *cum laude* in Public Administration. Soon after graduation, my wife and I sold our home, I left the fire department, and with our two infant children in a fourteen-foot travel trailer, we moved to Ann Arbor, Michigan where I entered law school.

My experiences at the University of Michigan Law School deepened my respect for the law, and my study of Criminal Law piqued my interest in the rationale for, and philosophy of, criminal sentencing. Indeed, that course was for me the most significant in law school. There I began to question the reasons why we, (any of us) discipline, and why we (as a justice system) punish. I received my Juris Doctorate from the University of Michigan in 1971.

After law school, I considered opportunities with a couple of major law firms in larger cities, and instead we decided to settle in a small Pennsylvania borough, where I teamed up with another sole practitioner. There I was engaged in the general practice of law, representing families and small businesses, probating wills, and defending clients accused of minor crimes.

In 1980, I realized my professional dream of becoming a judge when a vacancy occurred on the Court of Common Pleas for the Sixth Judicial District of Pennsylvania, and Governor Thornburgh appointed me to fill it. On the Court of Common Pleas, I presided over hundreds of trials, pleas, and sentences. I loved every minute on the trial court. I loved jury trials. Each one was like a whole new study in group dynamics. And, I loved all my juries. Indeed, I cannot think of one jury panel that did not fulfill its obligation with great care, and with a solemn attention to its duty. It was on the trial court that the inner workings of my conscience began to clash with the reality of the law. It was there that my protective wall of ignorance and indifference to sentencing and prison conditions, was fully breached by the ordinary human beings whom I met in my courtroom, and who had run afoul of the law.

In 1988, President Ronald Reagan appointed me to the United States Court of Appeals for the Third Circuit (which comprises Pennsylvania, New Jersey, Delaware, and the Virgin Islands). On this court, reviewing sentencing issues and *habeas corpus* appeals from countless convictions, I saw the breadth of the unjust and inhumane results of revenge. On this court, my angst and distaste for the injustice of our current system of sentencing evolved into a decision to make behavioral research my life's work.

My judgeships opened up other opportunities for me as well. In 1982, I served a presidential appointment as a United States delegate to the Conference on Free Elections, sponsored jointly by the American Enterprise Institute and the United States Department of State. There, with 34 other national delegates, we helped develop plans to assist in implementing democratic governments for countries that 1) had experienced nondemocratic intervention,

2) had no experience with democracy, or 3) were struggling to establish democracy. I spoke to the conference on the necessity of a free and independent judiciary to the success of any democracy. Shortly after, Dr. Amos Sawyer, who was then a professor, asked me to assist him in drafting a judiciary act for Liberia. Dr. Sawyer later became Interim President of Liberia.

When the Soviet Union collapsed, the Central and East European Law Initiative of the American Bar Association called upon me to participate in the first Constitutional Convention in Bucharest, Romania. Thereafter, I have traveled to and/or assisted Russia, Ukraine, Kazakhstan, Albania, Lithuania, Croatia, and Azerbaijan to develop Constitutions, Bills of Rights, and other primary legal codes. As a result of my research for these countries, I developed a model *Charter of Rights and Responsibilities*[2] that is in use in varying extents in these countries. For my constitutional work in Central and East Europe, Edinboro University of Pennsylvania in 1993 conferred on me the degree of Doctor of Laws, *Honoris Causa*.

In 1995, I was invited to participate in an Ethical, Legal, and Sociological Impact study of the Human Genome Project, conducted through the University of Virginia. I spent the following two years studying genetics, and lecturing and writing about the impact this new research could have on the fields of law, criminology, and penology.

I have from time-to-time lectured at Mercyhurst College, in Erie, Pennsylvania, Edinboro University of Pennsylvania, and Pennsylvania State University, where I now lecture in law and government. In 1999, Penn State accepted my proposal to develop *The Institute for Behavioral Research*. It will be dedicated to researching causes of, and exploring remedies for, crime. I am now its director. I am on the Board of Advisors of *Crime Times*, a publication of The Wacker Foundation. And, I am a member of the Board of Visitors of Regent University Law School. My published works include essays on judicial history, philosophy and penology. I also write some music and poetry.

When I am not working on the court, teaching, directing The Institute, or writing, I enjoy playing the accordion, fly-fishing, bicycling, golf, and, my all-consuming passion, reading. My wife Martha Jean, who taught first-grade, is my constant companion. We have three children and five grandchildren.

ENDNOTES

1. *Snill* does not translate well. Strong, silent, gentle, kind, stoic, begin to capture its essence.

2. An essay adapted from a speech I delivered on Law Day 1993 entitled, "A Bill of Rights For The Twenty-First Century," is published in *Hastings Constitutional Law Quarterly*, 189, Vol. 21, No. 2, Winter 1994. It contains the *Charter of Rights and Responsibilities*.

Table of Contents

Preface

A note on the first page of the very first essay I wrote years ago reads:

> *I am not sure why I set out to write this paper. I greatly doubt that I have any significant control or influence on outcome or change. I am, I know, totally disenchanted with United States penology, sentencing philosophy, and hence, sentencing jurisprudence. So, I suppose I am writing this to flex and test my theories and positions, to develop them, and expose them to evaluation so that they may either flourish from examination in the intellectual crucible of the academy, or die as victims from exposure to the truth. So, here goes...*

Here goes indeed. Although many of the works collected in this reader have been previously published, and have drawn an interesting range of comment, it is my fondest wish that compiled in book form, they will reach a wider audience and inspire debate, searching inquiry, scientific research, and remedial action. I am not so naive as to assume that my ideas will escape without criticism. Indeed, I hope not! I am confident enough in them, however, to believe that you will be able to profit from them and build upon them to develop penal theories of your own. These essays do not purport to proffer an exhaustive range of sentencing theories. They are, however, sentencing as I see it.

This anthology is written primarily for inquiring individuals, and for use in undergraduate courses that deal with America's penal system, usually taught under some variation of "Corrections," "The American Legal System," "Administration of Justice," or "Police Science." It is intended, among others, for students majoring in political science, pre-law, criminal justice, or those who need a social science elective. Even for the non-student, however, the law, the courts, and criminal sentencing remain important topics of discussion in American society. In the news, Americans are constantly confronted with issues of crime, our reactions to it, and how governmental institutions respond to it. The ideas I express herein can help any who are interested in current events to sharpen their inquiry into crime and their thoughts about remedies therefor.

This book differs from others on the subject because it explores both the theoretical and pragmatic aspects of the sentences we impose upon our cultural offenders. The conclusions and emphasis grows out of nearly three decades of observation, empirical research, and writing. In addition to imposing hundreds of sentences as a trial judge, reviewing hundreds more on the United States Court of Appeals, and lecturing extensively on sentencing, I have had occasion to interview, discuss, and debate these topics with criminals, ex-convicts, lawyers, judges, professors, criminologists, penologists, and behavioral scientists from around the world. Most importantly, I have personally observed sentencing in theory and in practice. Through these essays I have tried to convey my passionate belief in the need for thorough policy, examination of, and scientific research into American sentencing policy and practice.

Acknowledgments

Many persons deserve special thanks for helping to edit and critique these essays, and for assisting me in preparing them for publication. First, my law clerks, all of whom have for the last two decades, constantly invigorated me intellectually, challenged my premises and conclusions, given me ideas for lectures and essays, and were always ready to give of their spare time to assist me in editing them. To specifically name a few: first and foremost, Roger Schwartz, an amazing guy, whose mind never seems to rest, Philip Abromats and Luke Dembosky, from whom I learned many lessons about writing, Steven Ted Kern and Dan Barnhizer, who always seemed to have ideas, David Fine, ex-cop and critical thinker, Matthew Duchesne, John "Sean" Heasley, former clerk and now Chambers Administrator, and "right hand man," and my Administrative Assistant, Judy Paullet, who was always willing to give of her spare time to answer my dumb questions.

For helping me understand sentencing from the perspective of an offender, and the actual workings of prison from a person on the inside, thanks to Mr. James Shields, whom I sentenced to prison (but is out now and doing fine), and Mr. Carmen Musolino (who is still serving out his life sentence).

For their help straightening out my philosophy, thanks to Professors Thomas Upton, Ph.D., Edward Peirce, Ph.D., and Robert Rhodes, Ph.D. Thanks also to Maj. Robert Marks, USAF (Ret.), my brother-in-law, who was a sounding board for many ideas. Thanks to Father John "Tex" Hilbert, whose wise counsel had a profound effect on my jurisprudence. Many, *many* thanks to Frank Hutchinson, friend, neighbor, retired English and Composition teacher, and critic extraordinaire, for his review of the manuscript and his many editorial suggestions for placing the essays in book form. Finally, special thanks to my wife, Martha Jean, who has heard my speeches and lectures, read my essays, and patiently listened to all of my ideas.

Attributions

Several of the essays that appear herein have previously been published in substantially similar form in periodicals or professional journals and are being used here with the permission of their publishers.

Essay 1, "The Myth of Punishment: Is American Penology Ready For the Twenty-First Century?" was first published in the *Regent University Law Review*, Vol. 5, Spring 1995, p. 1.

Essay 2, was first published as "On The Philosophy of Sentencing: Or, Why Punish," in the *Widener Journal of Public Law*, Vol. 5, No. 2, 1996, p. 237.

Essay 3, "Freewill, Determinism, Genetics, and Punishment," was first published as "Freewill, Determinism, Penology, and the Human Genome: Where's A New Leibniz When We Really Need Him?" in *The University of Chicago Roundtable*, Vol. 3, No. 2, 1996, p. 417.

Essay 4, "Is Prison an Appropriate Response to Crime?" was first published in the *Saint Louis University Law Journal*, Vol. 40, N0. 3, Summer 1996, p. 677.

Essay 5, "The Death Penalty and Punishment," was first published as "On Death as Punishment," by the *University of Pittsburgh Law Review*, Vol. 57, Issue 4, Summer 1996, p. 825. Abridged editions of this essay were earlier published as "Vengeance Is Mine Says the Lord," in *America,* October 8, 1994, p. 6; as "Legalized Vengeance: A View of Capital Punishment," in the *Presbyterian Survey*, May 1995, p. 10; and as "Victims of Vengeance," in *The Lutheran*, August 1995, p. 22. It was entered into the *Congressional Record,* by Senator Paul Simon (D. Ill.) on September 5, 1995.

Essay 6, "Crime, Pain and Punishment: A Skeptic's View," was first published in the *Dickinson Law Review,* Vol. 102, No. 2, Winter 1998, p. 355.

Essay 7, "The Insanity Plea, Mental Defenses, and Punishment," was first published as "On Responsibility: Or, The Insanity of Mental Defenses and Punishment," in the *Villanova Law Review,* Vol. 41, No. 4, 1996, p. 951.

Essay 10, "The Ten Commandments of Behavioral Genetic Data and Criminology," was first published in *The Judges Journal,* Vol. 36, No. 3, the American Bar Association, Summer 1997, p. 59.

Essay 11, "The Dawn of Therapeutic Justice," was first published as a chapter in *The Science, Treatment, and Prevention of Antisocial Behaviors: Application to the Criminal Justice System,* ed. Diana H. Fishbein, Ph.D., Civic Research Institute, Kingston, N.J., 2000.

The Conclusion is an adaptation and abridgment of portions of "On The Role of Forgiveness In Criminal Sentencing," which was first published in the *Seton Hall Law Review,* Vol. 27, No. 3, 1997, p. 980.

Notes To The Reader

The fundamental purpose of this book is to provide you with a knowledge of the theoretical underpinnings, political processes, and practical realities that underlie American sentencing policy. Too little is known about the foundations of sentencing theory. Too little is known about the social consequences of sentencing policy. And, unfortunately, too few Americans even care. I am encouraged at the progress being made to professionalize all aspects of corrections and the administration of justice. These wardens, corrections officers, psychologists and prison counselors are the knowledge workers closest to the real theater of penal operations. But, a wider-spread interest is necessary, because it us ultimately our politicians who control and will change our policy and that takes public interest and public pressure. Towards all these ends, I encourage your critical thinking, and would welcome and covet your thoughts about the material contained herein.

On another note, you will see that I usually refer to offenders as males. This is not a gender slip, nor am I ignoring the fact that some readers may find this politically incorrect. My reason is simple, over 90% of criminal offenders are men. And, it is the male who seems to present the greatest challenges to the public peace and to personal safety.

You will also note that there is some repetition among the essays. This is because these essays were prepared for different readers and at different times. Others began as lectures and speeches, delivered to different audiences, again at different times. I have excised most of these repeated phrases and ideas. Some, however, I have left in to emphasize and give context or background to the subject matter of the particular essay.

Richard Lowell Nygaard, USCJ
February 2000

Introduction

*"One set of people will ask what is the law,
others, what ought to be the law."*

Lord Acton

Sentencing, as I see it, is going to change. The question is not *whether* it will change, but *how* and *when* it will change? The probability of that change, and the range of possibilities of change, both alarm and invigorate me. I am alarmed that the changes, if driven strictly by economic motivations, will cause our legislatures to succumb to the temptation to take the cheapest and easiest way out; for example, by simply declaring a percentage of those who are incarcerated to be "rehabilitated," and then, by releasing them. Or, that they will economize by eliminating potentially productive practices, or by limiting research into causes of crime and corrective measures for offenders.

I am invigorated, however, when I consider that the technology that is now transforming the nature, methods, and practices in the business economy will have a profound impact upon the government generally, the courts, and the various criminal justice organizations, specifically. As the speed of information generation, transmission, and retrieval increases, even product and manufacturing industries will become more essentially service organizations. Product and market flaws can be discovered and corrected in moments, and businesses can react to issues, and correct problems in real time. The gap between discovering and realizing the potential of an organization, program, or idea has now been shortened from years, to months, to days, to minutes. Our economy and our society are well into the Tofflers' *Third Wave*.[1]

> The Tofflers conceptualize world history in three waves. The first, the agricultural wave, occurred when we were a primarily agrarian society. The second wave was represented by our shift to a manufacturing economy where employment was "massified" in factories; students massified in schools; administrators massified in offices; others in institutions, and so on. The Tofflers now visualize us as moving into the third wave — the information age — when social and cultural codes must be rewritten for a world society unfettered by first and second wave physical, emotional and mental bonds.

Penology, and the elements of our criminal justice system are not. Organizationally, they remain very much as a *Second Wave*, or massified structure, unable to compete with modern social and business systems and unable to compete with crime. These organizations and institutions are exclusively service organizations, which are as yet failing to operate as a coherent system. I see hope, however, for these multiple organizations. With digital technology overwhelming the business economy, and changing forever the way it does business, the elements of the criminal justice delivery system cannot, and I think will not, be left far behind. The public will expect more of the system, and government must respond by doing more. I am one who greets *that* change with open arms, and I hope to have a role in stimulating and directing it.

Outside of my courtroom duties, I have a very narrow, but very deep professional passion—to change the very focus of American penology. Since I became a judge in 1981, no issue has troubled me more than criminal sentencing. I felt in 1981 that in sending offenders to prison, merely to be incarcerated for a term of years, I was shoveling sand against the tide. Now, nearly two decades later, I feel the same. Something is not working well in our system. Perhaps nothing is working well. Recidivism is too high. Prison, and the other costs of crime, are too high. And even with crime rates diminishing for the present, Americans feel unsafe.

Something must be done. I suggest that *much* must be done to the various organizations that comprise our criminal justice delivery system to make it, and them, truly responsive to the needs of the victim, the offender, and society as a whole.

I fear that without cautious attention to why we are changing the criminal justice delivery system, and what we must do to change it positively, change will simply become an expedient of current political whim and accomplish nothing positive for our culture. I urge that the changes begin with the very philosophy upon which our system is based and that the changes continue throughout the system to post-incarceration supervision, continuing until the offender is finally released totally from the system and from supervision. No element of the current *non*-system of justice is free from fault, and each component must become fully accountable to the whole for the product we ostensibly desire to create — obedient citizens and public safety.

In America, punishment has become more severe and most offenders' terms of imprisonment have become longer because our legislatures have responded, indeed are pandering, to a society that is frustrated with its government's failure to prevent crime, and that wants to strike out angrily at any offender who gets caught. But society, I fear, is misinformed because the governmental organizations upon which it relies for crime response and control are not striking at all criminals or offenders, just at those who are careless or stupid enough to get caught.

Society is disillusioned with the criminal justice system because it still feels unsafe, and, it should. Most crimes do not get solved. Many do not even get reported. Hence, all the things we do to offenders and the punishment we impose upon them is only to the few who get caught committing crimes and get convicted of them. They become the surrogates for all of society's fear, frustration, and anger about crime, and they become the recipients of "tough" punishment. But, sentence severity or duration is not solving the problem of recidivism, and it does nothing to intervene in the lives of potential offenders, and does little to increase safety.

Few people would argue against programs that would permit them to live a society that *is* safe from predations by criminals, and makes them *feel* safe as well. This degree of social health is a close second to physical health among our competing priorities in life.

So, to me it just makes eminent sense that we do whatever is necessary to get society to the point where it feels, and is, safe. Impossible? Perhaps. But, sentencing policy as I see it must set that dream as its goal, whether or not it can eventually attain it. This requires *correction*-based, not *offense*-based, sentences. We must try to change offenders from what they are to what they should be while we have them under our control. As it now stands we merely punish them for what they did without regard for the social consequences of our punishment.

There is really nothing novel in trying to change the mind of others, even in a mass situation. That is what education is all about. Education is behavior modification in its most positive, culturally expansive, and acceptable role. Through compulsory primary and secondary education, and massive aid to colleges, we seek to provide a sound base of information, and, I would hope, knowledge, by which we will provide the work force and the brainpower necessary to assure our culture's continued success. Why then do we abandon hope for the incarcerated? There is no pragmatic answer. Should not the question now be, what must we now do to re-make this individual in the basic image of our culture? Should not our goal be, how best eventually to reenculturate him? Why do we not seek as a primary or even an intermediate goal to bring the incarcerated to the required threshold for positive participation in society? These questions are not being answered. These questions are not even being asked.

Rene' Descartes, 1596–1650, was one of the most influential thinkers in human history. He is known as the father of *dualism*, that a human is composed of two substances: mind and body. The body being of physical dimensions; and the mind as a conscious or thinking being, understanding, sensing, imagining, and, importantly, willing. He felt that one's life was the consequence of a series of conscious and deliberate decisions.

Thomas Hobbs, 1588–1679, was an English philosopher, scientist, and political theorist. While exiled in Paris he wrote his most famous work *Leviathan*, a philosophical/theological study of the political absolutism that replaced the power of the church. He felt that the natural state of humans was war with each other, and that from self–interest, people make peace by delegating power to the state. He felt that because individuals are free to make their own choices, a breech of that delegation is punishable by whatever penalty the government may choose to impose.

I am enough of a Hobbesian or Cartesian that I believe we must reinforce the notion of individual responsibility for the choices each one of us makes in life, and affirm the idea that we must take responsibility for, and suffer the consequences of, our actions. I do not believe we can allow the demands of the offender, or any claim of a right to treatment, whatever the etiology of the crime, somehow to shift the responsibility for correcting his behavior onto society. The offender is responsible for making the behavioral change in himself. We can no more force behavior modification on deviant individuals than we can force education on others. We *must*, however, do what is necessary to bring offenders face-to-face with the reality of their situation as cultural deviants, give them graphic notice that they must make a positive behavioral change, and then provide them the opportunity for change.

We *must* be unequivocal about our demand that offenders change or face the consequences. Our society is not sophisticated enough, nor is it cohesive enough, to assume responsibility for the actions or transgressions of others. Society has the right to demand from its offenders that they account for their actions. It has the right to demand from the criminal justice delivery system that offenders be corrected. In turn, the system has the right to demand positive change from the offender before his release and societal reentry.

All this, of course, is complicated by the fact that America is pluralist, multi-cultural, multi-religious, multi-racial, multi-lingual and diverse almost beyond comprehension. Regardless of our complicated culture, from this vibrant, but potentially volatile mix, we must maintain a cultural order. On matters of culture, race, religion or language, and many other individual desires and interests, we are required to set aside our differences and obey the law. The law is by us — it, collectively, *is* us. Our culture lives by values that the whole nation accepts. That is the social contract. If some among us do not accept these values, although I care greatly, I state with equal emphasis they must not drag the rest of us down. We must assist all segments of society to attach themselves to our basic values, and obey the contract. Then, if they are not willing to commit to our civilization, and further signify their unwillingness by committing crimes against it, we must detach them from us.

Obedience and disobedience are incompatible social patterns. We cannot coexist with those who operate below the legal threshold of order that our culture has established. Nor can they coexist with us. The patterns will clash, and human nature dictates that one must emerge a victor. Moreover, we will be unable to cope with the rapidly developing new world order if we are preoccupied with domestic disorder. National defense is traditionally recognized to be the first concern of any state. But unless a country insists upon civil order, what it, or any civilization, defends from assault without, it will lose by incremental decay from within. The results are the same. Whether we lose to belligerent international or disobedient intranational foes, it matters not. Our culture will have succumbed to the enemies of it.

Obedience to the law is not something to be complacent with. It is the basic element of a free society. Society cannot hold together unless, at minimum, its members adhere to the requirements of its law. But even obedience to the law is insufficient. Developing the moral qualities we desire of each other in a civilized society requires more than simple attention to a basic legal obedience. Of course, the threshold level of behavior by members of any civilized society is that which is demanded by the law. More is necessary. Built first upon obedience; culture and civilization come next. And all this determines what is required of us, beyond the mere threshold of obedience to the law, to promote social development.

Next, the liberty we wish to possess and protect is a moral quality. Liberty is the ultimate level of a culture. This is the level we operate on when we have met the first two predicate thresholds. First, obedience to the law to control us; then the development of culture to civilize us; then the blessings of freedom to enrich us. The ideal in a constitutional democracy is universal participation, not just theoretically, but actually.

> *Although a democratic government is founded upon a very simple and natural principle, it always presupposes the existence of a high degree of culture and enlightenment in society.*[2]
> *Alexis de Tocqueville*

This is the basis for our free society, of our republican form of government and must, I submit, be factored into our criminal justice delivery system's scheme of corrections. To me that is the essence of justice. Obey *and* grow, or face the consequences. Unfortunately, justice has yet to face what it must do to assure obedience. And cultural growth is not even a gleam in penology's eyes.

To do *justice* to everyone requires that the sentencing scheme not only encompasses but also proceeds from the idea that the sentence an offender receives upon conviction is simply a matter of *fact*, and what happens to that offender is nothing more than a *consequence*. The sentence should be a consequence of the fact that the offender violated the law. It should be a consequence of the offender's personality. It should be, simply stated, a consequence of what must necessarily be done, within humanitarian and constitutional strictures, to contain him or bring him up to society's civil standards. And, all that must be accomplished before he is released.

My position is plainly and simply that criminal justice must be rehabilitative, not because I believe offenders are driven to their crimes or are ill, although some may be. Nor is it that I believe that crime is some form of personal, emotional or biological disorder, although the crime may indeed result from such a disorder. Nor, as I have said, do I favor any system that does not advance the notion of personal responsibility, for we are all, no matter our level of intelligence, responsible in some degree for our actions. Neither do I believe that all offenders have committed their offenses freely and intentionally. I have no doubt that we all face environmental forces that are beyond our control, and which impinge to varying degrees upon our behavior.

I am a rehabilitationist. Viewed from utilitarian and humanitarian concerns, I believe that the primary function of sentencing must be to produce positive behavioral change. I am a rehabilitationist because I believe that most offenders are capable of positive behavioral change. I am a rehabilitationist because it is my opinion that for those capable and desirous of making such a change, rehabilitation is the least expensive and most productive method, both in human and economic terms. Finally, I am a rehabilitationist because I view America as "stronger, gentler, and kinder" than how it currently treats its criminal offenders.

But, change is tough. It will be tough on the system because the sentence must separate from society all those offenders considered to pose a danger to it. That will take a massive effort by the system to separate those who deserve incarceration from those who would be corrected by something less. It will also initially be expensive to keep offenders separated economically and humanely until they see the error of their ways, are willing to account for their transgressions, and make a positive change. Finally, the system must devise new programs to do all this in a way that facilitates positive change in all offenders who earnestly want to change. All of this takes more work than mere containment and a "lock 'em up and throw away the key" mentality.

Change is also tough on the offender because it is the ultimate "put down." He must face his own failure, his mistakes, and be stripped of all the macho myths and defense mechanisms by which he has maintained his sense of self. He has to admit to himself that wherever he is in life, he must start over. Change is the toughest sentence that the criminal justice delivery system can demand of an offender!

It is not enough that we arrest an offender in only a minor percentage of crimes; fewer than 50% of homicides, and fewer than 10% of property crimes result in arrest and conviction. It is not enough that legislatures require, and courts impose, tough sentences upon convicted offenders. It is not enough that the prison be an efficient keeper, if it is merely warehousing humans for a period of time. More is needed—from pre-arrest to post-conviction. We in government must rethink, research, and remodel all components involved in criminal justice, into a fully integrated criminal justice delivery system. I would require that every arrest become part of a longitudinal study of the offender and the crime. I propose that all sentences have a correctional goal for the offender, a plan, and a process for reaching that goal. I would require, too, that such a fully integrated criminal justice delivery system become fully accountable, both as a shared responsibility with the rest of the system for its collective success, and a shared culpability for its failure.

Sentencing is now based upon little more than myths: myths that punishment will ameliorate the pains that crimes cause, myths that law enforcement can control crime, myths that prison is the appropriate medicine for misbehavior, and myths that criminals are somehow different from us. These myths create an infirm formula for criminal justice. Our _non_-system must be rejected, rethought, and restructured into, what I prefer to conceptualize as, a _criminal justice delivery system_—a system that delivers justice to all parties. What I attempt to do in the following essays is to unwrap these sentencing myths to their centers, and rethink, and redescribe a productive and pragmatic _system_ that truly confronts the problem of individuals who, for various reasons, disobey the law.

Currently no one element of the criminal justice delivery system truly operates as if it were a part of a _system_. Indeed, I hesitate to use the word _system_, even loosely. (But for want of another word, I have occasional lapses and use it anyway.) You will see, however, that I do not believe we really have a criminal justice delivery _system_. Instead, we have a confusing patchwork of individual functions, most operating separately; some not coordinating, or even cooperating; or worse, some are even competing with the coordinate components thereof. Legislators who write the laws, and, in some instances all but control sentencing by their sentencing guidelines; police officers who are called upon to enforce the laws; prosecutors who try the offenders; judges who sentence them; prisons who house them; probation and parole who supervise them; all compete with each other for the glory in times of success, and blame each other in times of failure. Currently, our *system* is like a perversely designed jigsaw puzzle: no two pieces of which fit precisely together, but which forms a recognizable image nonetheless. I would like to see that image clarified.

In my essays, I opine that at least a part of the solution to correcting this puzzle lies in what I call "correction-based sentencing," or "CBS." I suggest that a change to a CBS system from an offense-based system, (sentencing an offender for what he has done with little regard for who the offender is), will help to transform our entire corrections scheme. A focus upon correction will provide profound improvements in the way criminal justice, (lawmaking, crime prevention, arrest, into the trial, through execution of a sentence, and following the offender's re-integration into society), is designed and managed. If a definitive penal history of the twentieth century is ever written, offense-based sentencing will be viewed as one of penology's colossal failures. A change to a CBS approach, on the other hand, will be viewed as a watershed event in criminal law.

I suggest that *all* criminal sentences should be correction-based, that correction become the primary goal and theory for *all* offenses and offenders, and that all other philosophical justifications (retribution, containment and deterrence) be reduced to a secondary or tertiary role. It matters not to culpability, under a CBS scheme, whether criminals are made or born, nor for that matter why one erred—*why may provide a reason for the behavior, but not an excuse. Why* may explain, but simply will not excuse, the behavior. Why one erred, however, is of *paramount* importance to the remedy. To fashion a remedy we *must* find out why one behaved as one did, and respond to the reason.

The clock of *now* is always ticking. No person or system can simultaneously stand still and keep abreast of events, attitudes or mores. Events happen. Attitudes change and mores evolve. Almost without thought our responses to them change, too. We adjust our emotional reaction to words we hear in daily conversation that would have appalled us had we heard them used in casual conversation a decade ago. We accept behavior that earlier would have evoked a strong negative reaction and, perhaps have drawn a stern rebuke. We have realigned our reactions to events, actions and attitudes to accommodate a society whose members have grown increasingly less compassionate towards each other. In our personal and business decision making, we can alter our responses to social and economic stimuli because as the clock ticks on we have not cast our social, commercial, or moral feet in concrete at one moment in time.

Sentencing _has_ gotten its penological feet stuck in time by treating every offense and every result the same. Crime is crime. In an offense-based sentencing scheme he who has done an illegal act is treated the same as all others who have done the same thing, with little regard given to what motivated him or why he performed the act at all. What is needed instead of this rigid conditioned response to crime is a new penological _theory of relativity_ in which each sentence must relate in a systematic and significant fashion to the correctional needs of the offender and his social milieu, and not necessarily and exclusively to the nature or even gravity of the crime.

A young man once stood before me for sentencing on charge of homicide by motor vehicle while under the influence of alcohol. It was his first offense. He was credibly contrite and obviously remorseful for what he had done. In sum, he had learned his lesson and I am sure neither I nor any other judge would see him again. He was a good boy who had made a terrible mistake of judgment and with tragic consequences. In fact, he had been designated the driver by the others because he was the least drunk among the youths who were in the car. Even the deceased victim's mother appeared, testified on his behalf, and asked for leniency. He was just over eighteen years of age and the law required that I sentence him as an adult. I looked at him, bookish, handsome, with blond curly hair, and I knew he was going to be "meat" for the prison gangs — prey for homosexual rape. There was nothing I could do. The mandatory minimum sentence was five years of imprisonment. I needed a CBS option because I had an opportunity to _salvage_ a life. All I had was the vengeful sentence our legislature had dictated, which would be likely to _ruin_ one. I want to change that.

Sentencing and the role of punishment has been given far too little consideration in the criminal justice delivery system. It has been my experience that most criminal indictments result in findings or pleas of guilt. The culpability portion of criminal proceedings—the trial or plea—is simply not as significant as the sentencing that follows. At sentencing an offender may lose his liberty, and sometimes lose his life. I think it is time that we give sentencing the prominence it deserves.

Never be a pioneer, we are told. Those of us who buck current theories and methods face darts and arrows from those who have a vested interest in the status quo. This is never more true than in the vast justice business and bureaucracy, which now includes not only political and governmental entities, but also the corporations and businesses that make their millions because we have crime. Nevertheless, we cannot continue to avert our eyes from the failures of our current practices. Although there is a waning of the crime wave for now, crime is still too expensive, economically and humanly. Too many persons are failing to live up to our culture's moral threshold. Pioneers and researchers applying scientific method to the problems of crime are what is necessary.

I have written these essays because I want to express my view of CBS, not because it is the only view. Perhaps it will not be the best view. I will be happy if I have stimulated debate, encouraged you to reach your own view, and encouraged research to improve upon our system. I am convinced that every component of the criminal justice system must change. This is sentencing as I see it, how it has been, and how it should be in the future.

ENDNOTES

1. Alvin and Heidi Toffler, Bantam (1980) p. 53.

2. Alexis de Tocqueville, *Democracy in America* 212 (Anchor, 1969) (J.P. Mayer, trans.).

ESSAY 1

The Myth of Punishment:
Is American Penology Ready for the
Twenty-First Century?

"Mythology is music we dance to even when we cannot name the tune."

Joseph Campbell

Michael Fay, an American teenager who had earlier pleaded guilty to several acts of vandalism, was *caned* on May 4, 1994 in Singapore. He was stripped, bent at the hip over a padded trestle, tied down at his ankles and wrists while a martial arts specialist lashed his buttocks four times with a four-foot long, half-inch wide stick of rattan soaked in a diluted antiseptic. Fay, eighteen, who has lived in Singapore since 1992, was sentenced to four months in prison, a fine of $2,230, and the caning after he pleaded guilty to various acts of vandalism and mischief. All were relatively minor offenses by our standards.

The corporal sentence attracted great media attention in the United States. Many Americans expressed views on the caning of Michael Fay. In a personal letter to Singapore President Ong Teng Cheong, President Clinton urged him to "spare the rod" in Fay's case and rescind a punishment that Clinton had earlier described as "extreme." In separate appeals to President Ong, twenty-four U.S. Senators said clemency would be "an enlightened decision." American public opinion, however, expressed solid support for the punishment. Indeed many Americans even wrote the Singaporean Embassy in Washington, D.C. to express their approval. The predominant reason for the support was clearly articulated—Americans are fed up with crime and consider the

1

punishment given U.S. offenders to be "too lenient." In Dayton, Ohio, where Fay's father lives, citizens supported this punishment by a 2-to-1 margin.

Apparently buoyed by an outpouring of support from crime-fearing Americans, the Singaporean courts and government stood firm against the appeals from U.S. officials and, except for reducing the number of lashes, rejected the pleas for mercy and clemency. The Home Affairs Ministry stated in response to criticism from the U.S. Embassy, "It is because of our tough laws against antisocial crimes that we are able to keep Singapore orderly and relatively crime-free. We do not have a situation where acts of vandalism are commonplace, as in cities like New York, where even police cars are not spared the acts of vandals." Singapore's Senior Minister, Lee Kuan Yew, supported the Ministry statement, stating, "The punishment is not fatal. It is not painless. It does what it is supposed to do, to remind the wrongdoer that he should never do it again. And it does work."

A Singaporean doctor who has seen the scars left by caning, corroborated this conclusion adding, "They don't forget it."

America long ago discontinued the practice of corporal punishment as a criminal sanction. Any violence incurred by a convicted offender is a byproduct of incarceration. It is not institutionalized nor acceptable in our constitutionally supervised penology; that is, of course, with one notable exception—we execute. American criminal punishment is simple: probation, incarceration, or death. Offenders are either swept from public view to prison, where few persons visit or even care to, or they are spectacularly executed. Since we abolished corporal punishment, criminal laws have come and gone. For the most part, however, the number of acts proscribed by law has expanded geometrically. We are prosecuting, convicting, and punishing greater numbers of people than even before—but we do not seem to progress.

In 1994, the United States passed a major crime bill. Among other things, Congress grasped onto a sports analogy and enacted into law the spirit of the slogan, *Three strikes and you're out*. The result of this concept is that third-time offenders of certain crimes would be put *out* of society and in prison for life. Unfortunately, this law and this concept, like their predecessors, will not control crime, will not stem the tide of lawlessness, and, unfortunately, will evade the real issue—public safety. Cicero said, "*Salus populi suprema lex esto*" (the safety of the public shall be the first law). I am deeply concerned that the safety of the public is now given insufficient attention in the calculus by which we determine how we will treat our criminals. I fear that safety is no longer America's first law. Citizens increasingly feel that America has a gun to its head and that someone else has a finger on the trigger.

FBI Director Louis Freeh at a Senate Judiciary Committee hearing testified that the level of crime in the United States is, in his words, "tragically and unequivocally high. From 1960 through 1993 . . . the number of violent crimes reported in America increased 567 percent. In the last 10 years only, it increased 51 percent."

He noted that the "level of fear in America is even higher. A recent survey showed 93 percent of those polled said addressing America's crime problem should be an absolute priority for the federal government."

Despite the many battles and wars of this century, Americans never before have been the victims of a foreign dictator. Ironically, we are now becoming the victims and prisoners of violent crime dictated by an increasing army of home-grown criminals.

Moreover, and of critical importance, citizens do not *feel* safe. Americans have, in reality, turned over to the government the right to protect us. In the interest of society, we have in a practical sense ceded to the government our right to shoot back, and in the actual sense the right to shoot first. But in doing so, we are entitled to expect that the treatment given those convicted of crimes will not only punish them, but that it will also correct them so that when released, they have not only served time, but that we will be safe when they are reenculturated. This is not happening.

Although we have experienced a recent decline in some crime rates, we do not know why. Yes, noted criminologists, politicians, and others solemnly express their views. But none of their opinions has any scientific validity; most of these experts simply are employing *post-hoc* rationalization to some theory or another, or their favorite *causes*, such as economic trends, increased rates of incarceration, tougher sentences, and the list goes on. All of these factors may play a part in this decline. But, the decline may be temporary, and we simply cannot know what works until we employ scientific method, isolating all factors and studying each to determine causes and effects.

The 30-year update of a landmark study by the National Commission on the Causes and Prevention of Violence found that:

➤ Violent crime is up 40% in major cities.

➤ The number of people possessing firearms is up 120%. We now have nearly 200 million firearms in the United States.

In the past ten years:

➤ The incarceration of women is up fourfold.

➤ One of two urban African-American young men is in the justice system.

➤ More mentally-ill people are in prison than in hospitals.

➤ There is more money being spent on prisons than on education.

Our theories of criminal law are not solely or necessarily at fault. Our trial mechanism, prosecutors, attorneys, and judges, although overburdened and underfunded, systemically work well. Our prison system does what government intends it to do—keep convicted offenders removed from society for a specified period of time. American penology, however, is in shambles. It is critically important in any omnibus approach to crime control that we examine and reconsider the theoretical underpinnings of American penology, which is now guided by a philosophy that has been parodied and condemned by writers, penologists, and philosophers since the time of Aeschylus; and, it simply does not work well. The entire belief in punishment as the sole response to crime is a myth.

Michel Foucault states that the trial and "the ceremony of punishment" of an offender is an affirmation of the government's power. Indeed it is. He refers to the process of punishment as a "political ritual," a liturgy performed to display the lack of symmetry between the weakness of the citizen and the strength of the government. He refers to punishment as a "ceremonial of triumph." That too is true. The punitive nature of the sentence we impose upon offenders has become a culturally ingrained ceremonial custom, held dear in American penology, where it has achieved near universal and unchallenged acceptance as the central component of criminal sentences. For retribution, we punish. For correction, we punish. For deterrence, we punish. The myth of punishment as a criminological "cure-all" influences, indeed controls, penology because significant numbers still believe that what the myth tells us is truth. But we are not being guided by truth. We are beguiled by a distorted image of reality. Unfortunately, our legislators and judges know the truth, but are content to sit silent, too timid to speak out against conventional theory and politically popular misperception. Some elected officials do not wish to risk being called "soft on crime." Others have turned the perceptions of crime and punishment to their political advantage, by using the offender as a popular "whipping boy." The *sentencing* is central to the ceremony. *Punishment* need not be.

In Fyodor Dostoyevsky's *The Brothers Karamozov*,[1] Fetyukovich, the defense counsel, argues to the jury that if they punish Mitya to a degree beyond his guilt, that will only give him reason to reject them and their verdict. He tells them that Mitya will say that the jury, "[d]id nothing for my upbringing, my education, in order to make me better, to make me a man. . . . I am quits with them, I owe them nothing now and shall owe no one anything until the end of the ages. They are wicked, and I shall be wicked. They are cruel, and I shall be cruel. . ."

Fetyukovich continues, "And this is what he will say, gentlemen of the jury! And I swear: with your accusation you will only relieve him, relieve his conscience, he will continue to curse the blood he spilt, and will have no remorse for it. At the same time, you will bring to ruin the man still possible within him, for he will remain wicked and blind all the rest of his days."

Dostoyevski knows that a "get tough" punitive sentencing system will not rehabilitate man. Instead it tends to harden him and render him more cruel. If someone is punished beyond what is necessary to correct, the sentence merely becomes a part of the spiral of violence as recrimination between our laws, and the rebellious escalates. Punishment, alone, does not, and will not, control crime.

Let me illustrate by referring to two individuals, two very opposite people whose pathways crossed and tragically created a textbook model that generates many, but answers few, questions about American penology. This case points out the serious and unending deficiencies in the American sentencing system.

The first person is not a member of your society and mine. He is a member of a criminal counter-culture, whose only interest in our system is to avoid it or subvert it for his own benefit. He cares nothing for our laws or morality. The second person graduated from college, became an artist, and typifies the traditional American way: law abiding and employed. She was a product of an average home. She carried no gun, knew no self-defense maneuvers, and had no "street smarts."

In 1995, handguns were used to kill:

➤ 2 people in New Zealand

➤ 15 people in Japan

➤ 30 people in Great Britain

➤ 106 people in Canada

➤ 213 people in Germany

➤ 9,390 people in the United States

In 1997, 80% of firearm homicides were committed with handguns.

Source: *A Thirty Year Update of the National Commission on the Causes and Prevention of Violence*, 1999, by The Milton Eisenhower Foundation.

The first person wanted no part of our system; the second person depended upon it. But the system failed Kristen Huggins, and she is dead. People in the Philadelphia area were shocked to learn that she had been kidnaped and brutally murdered. Not long after she disappeared, the police arrested Ambrose Harris. The newspapers reported that he, while out to conduct a car jacking, had abducted Ms. Huggins, placed her in the trunk of her own car, and when she made too much noise, put two bullets in her head. Harris was just days out of prison. He was not released by some "bleeding-heart" judge who gave him a light sentence, or who was misguided by some notion that Harris did not deserve imprisonment. He was released from prison after serving the full nine years of a four-to-nine year sentence. Indeed, between the years of 1976 and 1992, Harris spent all but ninety of those days behind bars. For fifteen and three-quarters of the last sixteen years, Harris was exactly where he belonged. He was exactly where he had been placed by the system.

But what went wrong? Why is it that after controlling his life in minute detail for the last sixteen years, we could not change him, or alternatively keep him locked up until it was safe to return him to society? The whole sentencing scheme went wrong. What was done with Harris is exactly what the law requires be done to all criminals. The American sentencing system required nothing more of him than just to "do his time." The incarcerated need not improve in his behavior—all he needs is to just do time. I do not know whether sixteen years of effort would have resulted in any positive changes in him, but this I do know: we must change our system so that if we cannot change the Harrises and protect society, we will at least not release them back into society to harm it again.

Under the penological theory of containment or preventative detention, we use the conviction for one crime to predict that the offender will commit another; and we contain the criminal, or separate the criminal from society to protect it. Even if we are philosophically prepared to accept the notion of preventative detention, for a system following the containment theory to be a success, it is logical to assume that the offender will be contained until society is safe when he is released. Unfortunately, the safety factor is simply not an integer of the equation used to determine either the minimum threshold of a sentence, or the ultimate date of an offender's release. We simply cannot now say that society will be as safe when an offender is released as it was before he was contained. Containment alone is only a shot of morphine for a sick and painful society. When the morphine wears off, the disease is still there and the pain is worse.

When the court sentences a person to a term of years in prison, it is making a statement that this is the necessary punishment for his transgression. Its intention is offense-based _punishment_, and really no more. My point, however, is that we should also be able to state something more. We should be able to state that the sentence imposed is sufficient in both its duration and its demands upon the offender to *protect society*. This latter half, unfortunately, has no place in our sentencing calculus. It exists, if at all, only as a coincidental byproduct of the first. The myth of punishment is that society will be safer when the prisoner is released.

Punishment, for those whose behavior is not improved by it, has no utilitarian value except to denounce the offending act and the offender. Punishment performed as a part of a social vendetta against criminals does not work. Although retribution assuages the punisher's need for revenge, it does nothing for the punished. An odious punishment imposed upon a person who has committed a vile act, while cathartic to a victimized society, has short-lived effects. A sentencing system should answer the needs of a society who needs to become safer, and not pander to the immediate passions of society who only wants revenge.

Retribution is an expression of society's anger and a revulsion from the past deed with little regard to the future. Our system will never become enlightened or productive until all sentences reject anger, take a pragmatic view towards the future of the offender, towards change and towards correction. The system can punish, but something productive should follow.

Only treatment aimed at reconstructing citizens by modifying offenders' behavior, a correction-based system, has any enduring functional value. From the point of view of public safety, most sentences we now impose cannot be substantiated philosophically, psychologically, or practically. The theory of "lock 'em up and throw away the key" is a desperate solution based on fear. That would work, drastically, expensively, and inhumanely, if we truly did throw away the key. But if the person sentenced will ever be returned to society, and if safety is truly our outcome, logic dictates that *correction* must be the primary goal. Any other goal defies reason.

I was giving a speech on the evening the Camp Hill, Pennsylvania, prison riot broke out.[2] For two days in October of 1989, a riot raged at the medium-security state prison. The prison, designed to hold 1826 juvenile detainees, housed 2607 adult inmates with sentences ranging from two years to life imprisonment. During the course of the riot, over one hundred persons were injured, three seriously; five people were taken hostage; and nearly one half of the prison's buildings were gutted by fire. Purportedly, the riots started as a result of the prisoners' anger over new rules restricting access to health care and prohibiting relatives from bringing them home-cooked food twice a year.

Of course, everyone listening to me was alarmed, and much of the question and answer period was devoted to the riot. For example, one woman asked; "Judge, how many of these people do you think will get out?" I told her, "98 percent of them." I could hear the gasps all across the room. Then I went on to explain that 98 percent of the people we incarcerate in that prison will be released and on the streets within twenty-four to thirty-six months. I suggested to them that perhaps society should give some thought to what it is that causes these people to become so barbaric and to what the penal system ought to do with them. I further challenged them that if we do not deal with them in prison, we had better make plans for what we will do when they, once again, become our neighbors.

Following the prison riots, I was shocked to hear even sophisticated, educated people express their horror that some who looted, sacked, and burned the prison, and committed assaults upon guards and fellow inmates alike, had indeed escaped. What they failed to sense was these prisoners, or most of them, would been released (later, of course) when their time was served.

If any of us believe prisoners will magically become model citizens when released, we should think again. All the halfway houses of the world cannot undo the damage that is done by incarceration in the contemporary American prison. When one goes to prison, one _does_ change. We must begin a system that changes them for the better, instead of allowing prison to change them for the worse.

When we lock people up for periods of time, what do we really accomplish? Are we making that person any less criminal? Quite the contrary, Ambrose H. Harris is no different from the thousands of other people who are placed in prisons. They become meaner. They become more dangerous. They become more antisocial. They become better schooled criminals.[3] Society is safer only during the period of time the person is behind bars.

The law predetermines to hold responsible and punish any who transgress the law. For most, the punishment is prison. Few question why. Society somehow thinks that we need only to imprison offenders and not rehabilitate those who might be able to reenter society and become productive citizens. Prison may seem a fitting epilogue to the drama of a criminal trial but only if we follow the myth of punishment.

The average American prison is systemically successful only as a temporary human warehouse—a social Band-Aid. Beyond that, unless and until prisons are restructured to correct, they cannot, and will not, provide an incentive for a significant and growing portion of society to abide by the law. We simply give offenders too much credit, or credit them with too much power of analysis if we delude ourselves into thinking that the duration of jail time is any consideration whatsoever. Deterrence by punishment, I am afraid, accounts for little.

Our present philosophy of sentencing fails to make an adequate adjustment for the free will of ordinary, mainstream American culture and the determinism found on the fringes. Our penology is libertarian, maintaining that the only circumstantial equality to which all are entitled is equality of opportunity. It assumes that each of us is in control of our actions, and hence, our destiny. Because we are free to make choices, we may enjoy, or must suffer, the consequences of them. Equality of opportunity, however, is insufficient in our social republic to provide a stable economy, a stable workforce, or a stable political equilibrium. So too, it is an inadequate basis to determine the appropriate treatment of criminals and the socially maladjusted.

Penology is based on a theory that presumes a free will: that each person, regardless of whether a resident of the inner city, a tree-shaded suburb, a small town, or a country farm, is equally free to choose between right and wrong—free to do acts that are legal or illegal, free to abide by the law or disregard it, and free to change. This theory is almost totally inapplicable to sentencing as we approach the twenty-first century.

Persons will change only to the extent they believe they are free to choose another lifestyle. To the extent persons feel they are locked-in socially, or they believe themselves to be frustrated from moving to, or adopting a socially acceptable lifestyle, punishment, or the threat of punishment, will not coerce positive behavioral change. Punishment will modify behavior to the extent a persons perceive themselves free to change. If persons see themselves as able to choose among competing lifestyles, punishment can be a deterrent to culturally aberrant behavior. The more offenders' acts are perceived as determined by forces external and exclusive of their will, the less effective punishment will be and the more critical a correction-based sentencing (CBS) structure becomes.

Isn't it time we recognize the hard reality that our system is not correcting a significant number of criminal offenders? Not preventing crimes? Not deterring criminals? Not assuring anyone's safety? The answer is self-evident. But why do we not recognize so significant a governmental misstep as this one-dimensioned punitive system? I suppose that the answer, although simple, is not easy. Think of these questions: If your doctor followed eighteenth-century theory and if your hospital followed nineteenth-century practices, would you not seek change? If your educational system had a 60 percent to 70 percent failure rate, would you not require that something else be done? Again, the answer is self-evident. Nevertheless, the American penitentiary system has advanced little in the 200 years since it was conceived. Some American prisons have an 80 percent failure rate, but our penological system stumbles around in darkness clinging to antiquated and ineffective notions. The American prison is like a cathedral to a false god. Our response is to build more of them.

Few in our legislatures seem to know how to cure the socially destructive malaise of crime. One thing, however, is sure—we cannot begin to cure until we discover causes. Until now little effort has been made in the institutional sense to research and discover the causes of crime, which are, I am sure, as legion as viruses. But I am equally sure that if the behavioral sciences had the resources and applied them with a vigor equal to the physical and medical sciences, breakthroughs would begin. Behavior *can* be studied scientifically. Antisocial behavior *can* be modified.

> ➤ In 1986, 9% of state prisoners were incarcerated for drug offenses. In 1995, the figure was 23%.
>
> ➤ In 1985, 34% of federal prisoners were incarcerated for drug offenses. By 1995, the figure had nearly doubled to 60%. Clearly, we are losing the war on drugs.

Traditionally a crime was committed for one of two reasons: greed or passion. But now we must contend with another reason for crime. It has arisen in the last two decades from a lesser statistic to the point where it now predominates. Indeed, it has been described as the number one health problem in the country. It is a third reason that has come to dominate all other reasons—need. In *The Politics*, Aristotle described another type of need-driven criminal. He is the one who steals out of necessity—to eat. Today, however, there are few crimes in the United States motivated by the need to eat. We, nevertheless, have a close analog in drugs. Drugs also create crimes driven by need. Not the need of an empty belly, but the need born of an addiction.

America is slowly concluding that, in the penological sense, drugs may be little different from food. More and more people are becoming convinced that we will never control the crime that feeds the appetite, we must do something about the appetite. We can, as some propose, begin by labeling addiction a health problem and placing drugs under the control of the medical profession. Or we can, without appearing to sanction drug use, engage in massive measures to cure the habits and fully incapacitate drug dealers and manufacturers. One thing is sure, treatment as a goal is no longer an option: we must seek a cure for the habit, or contain the transgressor. We must question everything, focus on safety, seek solutions and accept the answers.

In seeking solutions, all offenders should be treated like dreaded diseases, and examined just as closely to see what caused them to err. We must *discover* why one commits crimes before we can set about in any deliberate fashion to develop appropriate remedies. Getting "tough" on crime sounds good, but standing alone as it does now, it is an empty slogan that does not work. I have nothing against tough remedies. I do not make a plea of mercy for the criminal, but for society. Let us be practical. Toughness by itself is not enough. It is time we also got *smart* on crime. We must study the motives that produced the offending behavior, with an eye towards the future and prevention, not towards the past and punishment. As Thomas Fuller said centuries ago, "To punish and not prevent is to labor at the pump and leave open the leak."

Do not misunderstand me, I am sure no one but the most pathological of persons wants to be punished. There are those, however, who feel no sense of moral guilt, remorse, shame, or compassion, who can, nonetheless, feel fear. So any punishment has corrective value for some persons. But it is made painfully obvious by the recidivism rates in our prisons that punishment, as now administered by the American penal system, is not enough. Beyond punishment, we must discover what inside this individual makes him behaviorally tick so that we can design a system that will effect change. We must recognize that we simply cannot punish a person away from committing a crime to supply himself with that which he must have (or feels he must have) to live. We cannot control crime if it is motivated by a perceived necessity, whether to fill the stomach of the starving, or the bloodstream of the addict willing to die for a "hit." Drugs have given the theory of determinism new life.

Whatever the causes of crime are, I believe that to confront them we should move towards a system of correction that is organized along the same lines as our triage system for treating the wartime wounded. I believe we must segregate our thinking, our treatment, and our sentencing into at least three discrete groups: the benign for whom nothing need be done, the truly dangerous for whom nothing can be done, and those for whom the expenditure of some effort may effect change. The first group should never be contaminated by a prison experience. The second group must be contained in prison. The third group is the challenge. They must be corrected before they are released. Nothing else makes sense.

As Michel Foucault states, "Even the shallowest emotions and the weakest intellects can meet and master punishment; few can confront change."[4] Rehabilitation, perhaps we should dust this concept off and try it again. I am not talking about the "goody-goody" rehabilitation of the fifties and sixties. I do not bleed for the criminal. I bleed for the society that must reassimilate him after he has served his time. What I propose is real, sincere, no nonsense, severe if necessary, attempts to say to this person in a way he cannot ignore: "You are all screwed up and we are going to change your mind. You must convince us you are capable of living in society, or you will stay in prison until you do." The sentenced individual must realize that he has to change in such a way that society remains safe with him, and know that otherwise he will not be reencultured at all. The key to behavioral change lies with the individual—

whether we are treating alcoholism, drug addiction, or antisocial behavior.

Recently, while watching a Hollywood awards ceremony, I was struck that nearly all who appeared on television were wearing a red ribbon signifying their concern for finding a cure for AIDS. The response of this country to the AIDS epidemic has been a blossom of red ribbons, a great public awareness, public fear, and consequently, increasing interest in and dollars for a cure. I take no issue with that, AIDS is a killer disease. Yet, in my years as a judge, there has been little collective interest in doing something to discover the causes and cures for the greatest, the costliest, and the most potentially deadly social evil of all time—crime. Society, too, is sick of being frightened by crime, and it begs for a cure. But all it has been given is a placebo.

We are seriously considering the prospect of spending billions *correcting* the best health care system in the world. The system that cures the sick and encourages systematic and ongoing research. But in terms of costs and rewards, our health care cost is "peanuts" compared to our failed penal theories and systems, and the concomitant social dangers we thereby create. Our penal methods have simply become too expensive to continue in their present form, and our streets have simply become more dangerous because of an antiquated system based on myths. I am afraid that our penology (punishment) is a theory that thrives politically but is a failure in the cultural crucible.

Immanuel Kant states, "Man's innate right to liberty consists in the right to be free from violence . . . . "[5] Kant further stated that we not only have the right to live under a political order but todemand that others join us in it. Kant believed this to be a necessary condition of the rule of law. So do I. JeanRousseau contended that all persons'legal rights are derived from the single concept of social order, which he called a "sacred right."[6] So do I. John Locke presumed that public safety was the consideration given the public in the contractual relationship among the citizens and between the citizens and their government.[7] So do I. I am deeply concerned, however, because government, by failing to meeting its obligation to protect society, is not fulfilling this contract with society.

Immanuel Kant, 1724–1804, was a giant in the history of philosophy. He thought that the mind is not shaped by the world of experience. Rather, he thought that the world of experience is shaped by the patterns of thought in the mind. He felt that moral law cannot be justified by reason and must be obeyed for its own sake. His ethical theory rests on the concept of an individual's duty to obey, and not on any fear of punishment or hope for reward. His categorical imperative is that a person should "act in such a way that it is possible that for one to will that the maxim of one's actions should become universal law."

No social system can survive long unless its members have some hope that their government will protect them. Unless our government can protect us, the value of that which it offers us is eroded in direct proportion to our insecurity, perceived or actual, and the value will depreciate until the numbers of those who have lost faith reach such a percentage that self-help is perceived by the public to be a viable response to

John Jacques Rousseau, 1712–1778, was an enlightenment philosopher and social critic, who exerted profound influence on political thought. He emphasized the primacy of the individual and individual liberty. His major political treatise is *The Social Contract.* He felt that the individual found happiness and fulfillment only in the social situation, and that politics and morality could never be severed. He felt that the state (a creation of the general will) was created to preserve individual freedom, and that individual freedom was given up only in proportion to the state's power to preserve the individual's freedom.

crime. That would be wrong. If the system breaks down, what we have then is antithetical to our culture and our society: anarchy and lawlessness.

John Locke, 1632–1704, was an English philosopher and political theorist. He is best known as an advocate of civil and individual liberties. He argued that government is based upon the consent of the governed, and exists to preserve the natural rights, such as life, liberty, and happiness, of its citizens. He rejected Hobbs' pessimistic view of mankind. He contended instead that the enjoyment of these rights leads to the common good. He believed that when government fails to protect its citizen's rights, they have the right to rebel.

The caning of Michael Fay became a national topic of discussion. But for all the sometimes heated discussions, for all the ink spread about the country before the caning, America grew strangely silent after Singaporean officials executed the sentence. Perhaps, after the sentence was actually executed, the public's cry for blood, and its desire for revenge, left it feeling a bit guilty for having pointlessly advocated a cruel act. Most of us know how we feel, but few of us know why. Indeed, among the news briefs, the magazine articles and the editorials, none confront the reason why we *do* punish. Why *do* we have such an urge to inflict pain? The painful truth is that the same society that urges vengeful punishment upon others exposes its own desire for violence. Vengeance needs a victim. Michael Fay was as good as any.

Philosopher Jacob Needleman says, "There is a 'modern scientist' in all of us who demands ordinary logic, sensory verification, and everyday common sense. When confronted with ideas that seem to go beyond these contemporary canons of belief, this part of our minds, this *modern scientist* in us, usually turns away from them, or it alters them in order to make them acceptable." To this *modern scientist* I appeal. Our fund of options is diminishing rapidly. Falsity has many shapes: lies, concealment, denial, legend, and myth. They all end in one substance, a deflection from the truth, a deception. It is my firm belief that what deceives must be exposed. If a belief is harmful, it must be excised. If we seek truth, historians, scientists, and philosophers alike, we will probably offend to progress, because we chip at treasured icons, tread upon accepted truths, and, often, make the established credo or ethos look foolish. But myths, even as treasured a myth as punishment, must be examined, regardless of what, or who, is offended by the results. We must seek, and follow, truth.

The government made a deal with its citizens to make the laws and to enforce them in such a way as to protect society. The deal is going sour. Punishment is not making us safer. The cancer of violence which we feed by punishment and permit to fester in our prisons, is becoming thoroughly metastasized in society. The myth of punishment is becoming evident to any who think even casually about its results. And the myth is dangerous because the urge to punish, although emotionally gratifying to some of us, at least for the instant, is turning aside the rational desire, and the real need, to do something constructive. American penology follows the tenets of a moribund philosophy and is neither prepared, nor preparing, for the twenty-first century. It is time that more be done. The Ambrose Harrises of this land must be corrected, or they must not be released.

Salus populi suprema lex esto.

ENDNOTES

1. Fyodor Dostoyevsky, *The Brothers Karamozov*, Penguin Edition.

2. "Pennsylvania Prison Riot Ends," *St. Louis Post-Dispatch*, Oct. 28, 1989, at 8A; Laurie Goodstein, "Search for Answers Follows Prison Riot; Changes in Rules, Crowding Cited in Violence at Camp Hill, Pa.," *Wash. Post*, Oct. 29, 1989, at A8.

3. For a discussion of the effects of incarceration on the prisoner, see, e.g., Jeff Potts, "American Penal Institutions and Two Alternative Proposals for Punishment" 34 S. *Tex. L.J.* 443 (1993).

4. Michel Foucault, *Discipline and Punish: The Birth of the Prison* (Alan Sheridan trans., Vintage Books, 1979).

5. Immanuel Kant, *The Metaphysical Elements of Justice* xix (John Ladd trans., E. Bobbs Merrill, 1965) (1797).

6. Jean J. Rouseau, *The Social Contract* (Great Books ed., 1952) (1762).

7. John Locke, *Concerning Civil Government* (Great Books ed., 1952) (1690).

ESSAY 2

The Philosophy of Sentencing: Why Punish?

I. On Philosophy

> "The primary object of the legislature
> should be to prevent crimes, and not to chastise
> criminals; that object cannot be attained by
> mere terror of punishment."[1]
>
> *Coleman Phillipson*

There is a genealogy for each philosophical theory. And to test the legitimacy of the theory thoroughly, we must trace this genealogy to its origin. This principle is never more true than in testing the philosophy of sentencing. For if there is no legitimate basis for the sentences we impose, or if the bases are no longer valid, then our sentences are no longer legitimate. Although all of this may seem quite complicated, the test is really quite simple—at each generation of our philosophy, we must ask what are we trying to achieve, what works, and is it fair? In the philosophy of sentencing, however, Americans are caught in a parallax between the facile myth of punishment, to which our penology clings, and the reality of life, from which our penology retreats. Society views penology through a warped glass and is so accustomed to, and so thoroughly comfortable with, the distorted image thus produced that it may not recognize either *truth* or *the truth*[2] about the efficacy of sentencing offenders. Nor if recognizing the truth, be prepared to accept it.

"The thrill of punishment—the agony of defeat," could perhaps be a description of the attitude that pervades the system. I watched in professional embarrassment as a prosecuting attorney, who failed to get a conviction in the trial of several Branch Davidians, choked up emotionally before the TV cameras because he had actually lost the case. The game for all too many lawyers is not a search for truth, not to determine guilt or innocence, not to decide upon a need for correction, not to assure the safety of society, not even to exact a measure of revenge upon the offender. The trial is simply a matter of winning or losing, each side often self-righteously believing that it deserves to win; more often, each side simply wanting not to lose. Truth may not even be a high priority of the judge who presides, whose goal is often simply to see that the procedure due the parties is followed, and that the ritual is adhered to, without regard for the result.

The reality is that imprisonment, the central method of criminal punishment, has neither provided sufficient pain to dissuade offenders from their anticultural behavior, nor to assuage the public's desire for revenge. Indeed, the notion of inflicting a *just* measure of *pain* is a paradox. It has created a dilemma in a penal system that is rendered insensitive to both the individual offender's needs in correction and the public's need for a socially acceptable form of deterrent toward those who have offended cultural rules. Our preoccupations with causing pain to the offender and keeping the pain within constitutional limits create an unnecessary philosophical tension, which have left us drifting wide of the target. If we were to concentrate on correction and then imprisonment and pain combined with all other penal measures could become positive instruments for behavioral change.

No penologist would seriously suggest that any single theory can account for the myriad motivations either of the offender to commit, or of the penal system to control, crime. The new science of genetics may provide us with some answers to nagging questions about the physical etiology or embryology of some crime. Penologists, professors, politicians, along with others point to tougher penalties, improved economic conditions, and a host of other factors they contend will control crime. Each may be partly right, at least with respect to some offenders. But until we apply scientific methods and study crime, its genesis, and its cures, we will not truly know. Cultural, educational, physical, religious, familial, and economic agents, all may have an influence upon individuals in setting their lifes paths. And the fact is that some individuals simply will succumb to the temptation to violate the law. Discovering the genesis of crime will involve more than addressing a single issue or seeking a single answer. Until we begin to think about the problem of crime and its causes as the result of many factors, and our responses to crime as having many vectors, we are in no condition to improve and move forward.

Eventually punishment must yield to scientific inquiry and respond to social and cultural realities. Society must be prepared to discard the distorted glass through which we are viewing criminal sentencing and accept the results of real inquiry, no matter how comfortable the current distortion has become. But wherever the inquiry may lead, and whatever the answers it may provide, the difficult question is how to communicate the answers to society so that they can be assimilated harmoniously: first, into personal beliefs and cultural responses; secondly, into politically palatable reactions; and third, into scientifically and psychologically sound penological practices. An individual is always reluctant to release his grasp on what's known and to press into unexplored regions for new answers, but to progress we must. Let us turn first to the philosophy of punishment and its role in sentencing.

We cannot adequately consider the philosophy of sentencing without starting with the normative philosophies of the three greatest penal reformers of all time—Cesare Beccaria, Jeremy Bentham, and Sir Samuel Romilly. These three sages of the eighteenth century, who wrote at their professional and personal peril, changed the way the western Christian-dominated world perceived its criminal offenders. They, however, exerted their influence years ago, and much in our culture, and indeed in the world, has changed. Unfortunately, too little in American philosophy has been altered since then to accommodate these changes.

Before the middle of the eighteenth century, penologists paid no systematic attention to the cultural role of punishment, apart from scattered references in the writings of the earlier philosophers and theologians.[3] For the early philosophers, the purpose of punishment was primarily to teach the offender to become a good person (the moral lesson) and secondarily to teach him to become a good citizen (the penal lesson). Philosophers neither questioned the efficacy of punishment, nor explored alternatives. They viewed punishment as having a "positive moral purpose and not a negative preventive one."[4] The penal purpose of punishment, however, was "a minor consideration for philosophical thought."[5] The larger questions "regard[ed] law, authority and morality."[6]

> Cesare Beccaria was born on March 15, 1738, of an aristocratic family in Milan, Italy. In 1760 he initiated a program of reforms and formed a society known as the "Academy of Fists." It was as a member of this radical society that he took up the pen in 1764 on behalf of penal reform. Because Beccaria feared prosecution for his ideas, *On Crimes and Punishments* was originally published anonymously. In Paris and Austria, however, the truth became known, and although he was ridiculed in Italy, he later became a legend abroad.

Cesare Beccaria was the first philosopher to voice a need for change. He introduced the idea that a criminal sentence should not be imposed upon an offender merely to inflict pain.[7] Before Beccaria made his contribution to the criminal law, philosophers considered pain a necessity because the early criminological and penological approach was that law was to be about the work of punishing sinners in the name of God. God punished the sinner by painful means. The early philosophers further viewed criminal law simply as man doing the work of God, and they felt that the law, too, should inflict pain. Inasmuch as the Biblical concept of hell was eternal banishment to a lake of fire, early punishments reflecting that concept were unbelievably cruel. Torture was a fact of criminological life and was even defended by the clerics.[8] Some considered blood atonement (spilling blood for blood spilled) necessary to redeem the soul of the offender through rehabilitation-by-death.[9] Prison itself was often the equivalent of a sentence of death—slowly, by starvation, disease, or inmate-inflicted injuries. Jails were such indescribably despicable places that even visitors sickened and died. Many offenders preferred the risk of death during escape to victimization by the diseases and cutthroats of prison.[10]

Beccaria proposed the novel idea that the purpose of punishment should be to prevent the offender, and deter others, from committing similar offenses. Hence, by the Beccarian model, any punishment beyond that which is necessary to accomplish these goals was tyranny and, hence, unjust. The liberal, libertarian ideas of John Locke, with its emphasis on rights and how best to protect them, were foundations of American thought and, until Beccaria, virtually unchallenged in the colonies. Beccaria built upon the Lockean concept of free and equal persons who developed and executed laws by delegating a limited amount of their power to representatives "through their consent and within a limited sphere of human activity."[11]

Jeremy Bentham, too, recoiled from the inhumanity of prison. He agreed with Becarria about the legitimate basis for criminal sentencing. In contrast to Beccaria, however, he further believed that after confinement an offender ought not be restored to society without retraining him for habitation in free society. In other words, no release without first *rehabilitating* the offender. Bentham introduced the idea of replacing jails and other cruel punishments with the *penitentiary*.[12] He conceived the penitentiary as a place where an individual would do penance for his offenses, contemplate his shortcomings and, within this confinement, be reeducated for social and civilized life. Bentham called his model penitentiary a *Panopticon*.[13]

Jeremy Bentham, 1748-1832, was an English philosopher and social theorist. He is known as the father of *utilitarianism*. He believed that the aim of the government should be to achieve the greatest happiness for the greatest number. He believed that behavior was the result of the balance between the pleasure and the pain that any act and its consequences would produce. When he died he was decapitated, embalmed and his head replaced with a wax replica. He is still preserved in that condition, and can be seen at University College, London.

Sir Samuel Romilly, 1757-1818, was an English statesman and jurist. Although a paragon of the English bar, he is best known as a law reformer. He consistently urged that the crimes code, which he believed to be cruel and illogical, be totally revised. He was opposed to England's capital punishment laws and urged more equitable and humane treatment of offenders. His greatest work is *Observations on the Criminal Law of England As It Relates to Capital Punishment.*

Sir Samuel Romilly was also opposed to unusually cruel punishment, which he believed inevitably produced an increased level of cruelty in the offender's thinking and behavior. He stated, "[i]t is not by the destruction of tenderness, it is not by exciting revenge, that we can hope to generate virtuous conduct in those who are confided to our care."[14] Romilly envisioned criminal sentences as having a three-fold dimension; first, to punish the offender; second, to incapacitate the offender for whatever period of time was necessary to protect society; and third, to apply whatever means necessary to reform the offender if he was ever to be released to society. As a

Romillian, I fully endorse all three conclusions. I, however, would invert their order. I think correction and reform is the most important goal of sentences. Most offenders in our society, after all, will be released.

Romilly contended that a swift and certain, but mild, sentence is a far greater deterrent to an offender than is a delayed but more severe sentence. He agreed with both Beccaria and Bentham that the most essential element of a social response to crime was not the severity of the punishment, but the swiftness and certainty of its application. That is to say, the sooner after committing an infraction a person is caught, the less severe the rebuke or punishment need be to reinforce the lesson that "You cannot get by with misbehavior." Indeed, _no penologist has successfully countered this conclusion._[15] It is axiomatic that only a foolish offender would steal that which it is _certain_ he cannot keep. And it is only the deranged offender, or one who no longer cares for his own well being, who will place himself in certain, immediate, and absolute jeopardy.

Society's reaction to crime does not reflect much of the thinking of these three philosophers. Society reacts to crime as it does because it feels inequitably treated by those who do not obey the rules and threaten our safety and security. Unfortunately, society now acts on that feeling irrationally and in such a way that the advantage it hopes to gain is far outweighed by the high costs in the time, effort, money, and damage that its reaction does to the American culture. Society's current reaction is a bit like the impatient driver who is carelessly or deliberately cut off by second driver in traffic. The other second driver's action will not impede the first one significantly, for one more car at the turn before us matters little. But nonetheless, many individuals will react angrily and express their anger in such a way as to risk damage to their own reputation, emotional equilibrium, or even safety by a reprisal from the other driver, just for the momentary gratification of some emotional release. The situation is analogous in criminology and penology where we must likewise neither be swept by some immediate emotion, nor simply react without reason, to a deplorable offense. _Reason_, however, by we who either influence or make the laws, must prevail over the public's understandable desire for revenge.

This concern for reason was also foremost in the minds of Beccaria, Bentham, and Romilly, who espoused a simple theme— *public safety*. It is likewise foremost in my mind. The goals or ends of sentencing *must* be redefined in terms of cultural security or safety. We cannot do so realistically or rationally unless we abandon all preconceptions and dysfunctional penal methods, and instead, simply and directly seek to do what is necessary for a safe and peaceful environment in which American culture can flourish. One who wants only to crack rocks views everything in terms of its potential use as a hammer. The one who only wants "tough" sentences views sentences in terms of their potential to inflict pain and punishment. By reading the commentary on new crime laws, you realize that few legislatures consider whether society will be more or less secure as a result of the prescribed treatment of criminals. The discussion is all about new and tougher punishment and about longer prison terms.

The legitimacy of the law depends not upon the might of the state that empowers and executes it. Rather, it emanates from the people's notion that law will protect their natural, material, and positive rights. Further, it emanates from society's collective belief that the government formed by delegating authority to elected legislators to act as its agents will safeguard the rights that society retains. Under this Lockean philosophy, free and equal persons can be subordinated only by their consent, and subjugated only to the extent necessary, in the context of penology, to assure their and their culture's safety. This limited grant circumscribes the authority of government. Hence, a government of legislators who simply react to the popularity polls can draw no enduring comfort from following the immediate fickle passions of society. In a republic, legislators are delegates of the people. They are delegated not to follow the popularity polls or to do as their electors or lobbyists importune them to do. They are not empowered to do what they want to do. Our lawmakers are delegated to do what, we their electors, would do, had we the same facts as the legislators. They are empowered to do what is best for us and for our future and not what is popular or convenient at the present.

Beccaria's penology, like Locke's, is based upon the principle that each person will cede only that portion of his liberty necessary to assure the rest of it. Beccaria's state was premised upon individual freedom. He too believed that humans' basic evil nature renders the enjoyment of this liberty in doubt. Because *uncertain liberty* is a contradiction, he believed that individuals would cede a part of it to their society and its government to secure guaranteed or certain liberties. Thus a civilization, so described and circumscribed, is thereby formed. The portion of liberty ceded by this mutual contract is the limited power of the government—that amount necessary to secure the *safety* of citizens to enjoy their other retained rights. This is ostensibly the goal of and that which legitimizes all laws. The government's authority to impose punishment is, therefore, circumscribed to the minimum degree necessary to fulfill this grant of authority. Beccaria believed that unless law's rationale is grounded in solidly-supported philosophical reasoning, lawmakers, and indeed the criminal justice system, will ultimately suffer reproach for their failure and for abdicating their mandate to do what is genuinely required to assure that *retained liberty*.

Offenders are likewise part of this liberty equation—this contract. They too, as fellow citizens, have likewise ceded to the sovereign the power to govern. They too are required to do their part in the mutual pact of safety, security, and happiness that is our civilization, our culture. Culture demands participation and, without any apology, has the right to demand that all citizens, even offenders, participate and be held accountable for their transgressions and failures. People must either be a part of this culture, or they must be prepared to be excised from it unless, and until, they can participate in, and contribute to, it. If we ask on behalf of offenders, victims, and other citizens punishment fulfills the government's contract with the people, we will begin to see the quality of the penological *product* at the other end of the criminal justice delivery system. We will realize the kinds of citizens who are leaving our jails and prisons when their time is served. Let us become pragmatists, and as pragmatists, "Let us do what is necessary to enforce the contract. But, let us do no harm, and inflict no greater pain than is necessary."

The function of sentencing should not be to degrade, humiliate, or oppress the offender. Self-esteem, so necessary for emotional health, is destroyed by degradation. Obstinacy, so counterproductive to rehabilitation, is simply hardened by oppression.

And enemies, so harmful to social relations, are created by humiliation. The function of a sentence must simply be to make the offender realize that he cannot break the laws of his culture with impunity and to prevent him and others from doing so again.[16] Unfortunately, we do not look at sentencing through the prism of pragmatism. Even though the governmental mandate or delegation is philosophically circumscribed, if anyone were to ask sentencers, judges, and legislators *why* they imposed a particular sentence, I believe I can say with absolute confidence that few in any branch of government would offer philosophical support for *why* a sentence was imposed.

The late management guru, Dr. W. Edwards Deming, stated that the basic question to ask in any organizational study is its purpose—why are you doing what you are doing?[17] Yet, in the criminal justice delivery system, I suspect that those persons who would be asked this question would answer that they act out of a sense of duty. The legislature writes laws desired by the voters; the judge imposes the sentence desired or required by the legislature and the prison executed the sentence imposed by the judge. But, in all the discussions of sentences, the presentence reports, the sentencing hearings, and the prison reports, no one seems concerned *why* a sentence is given. Hence, the duty is more to expedience, or attention to that which is perceived to be demanded by popular acclaim, not to true social need. The sentence is *doing time for doing crime*. It is *pain given for pain received*.

Notions of balance, or attaining some proportionality between the sentences imposed upon offenders and the crimes they committed, actually began when penologists sought a theory to counteract overly-cruel and vengeful sentences. The principle that I call *valence*, (hence, equi-valence, or balance) in punishment theory, probably comes from Aristotle, the first analog-formalist, who stated in his *Nicomachean Ethics* as follows:

> When one man has inflicted and another received a wound, or when one man has killed and the other has been killed, the doing and the suffering are unequally divided; by inflicting a loss on the offender, the judge tries to take away his gain and restore the equilibrium.

Hesiod had earlier written, "If he suffers what he committed, then justice will be straight." Thus, the *form* of the sentence was *analogous* to the crime that the offender committed.

Theoreticians believed by imposing retributive punishments, proportionate to the crime, the sentence would quench the public's thirst for vengeance. One of the earliest examples of proportional imprisonment was the Norwegian Parliamentary invention of prison durational equivalents for, and to replace, branding, mutilation, and the various accepted forms of criminal punishment then in use. Imposing a sentence of ten years in prison, instead of cutting off a hand, or life imprisonment instead of the death sentence, are examples of these types of equivalents.[18] Proportionality or equivalence, however, has not grown more sophisticated with the passage of time. Legislators rely on emotion and popularity polls, not scientific analysis or even trial and error, to determine sentence duration. The valence of crime upon which our politicians still rely for balance is the public's emotional reaction to crime, and its desire for revenge. If judges were free to sentence offenders to a short period of punitive imprisonment, followed by a regimen of work, education, and therapy that requires behavioral improvement for release, we would begin to see progress. If we study the regimen to see what works, upon whom, and when, we could begin to predict just what sentences are most likely to be effective.

A sentencing judge, or for that matter a legislator, generally cannot accurately predict whether one duration is better than another, or whether the sentence imposed will work, because data on what works and what does not have been neither collected nor scientifically studied. I have been a judge since 1981 and have imposed and reviewed thousands of sentences. If you asked me how successful my criminal sentences have been, I would have to state that I don't know. And, I would have to ask in return, "Successful at what?" I suspect that if you were to ask prison wardens the same question, you would get the same answer. Furthermore, if you were to ask legislators, prosecuting attorneys, police (indeed, almost anyone connected to the criminal justice delivery system the same question) you would also get the same answer. If the system were held at all accountable to the people for the success of criminal sentencing in preventing crime or assuring safety, we would all be in deep trouble!

America's penology is positivist. According to the legal positivist, those who make the law decide what is just and what is unjust. To the positivist, penology is what it is, it does what it does, because the law says so. It need not be *just* in a theoretical sense, because justice is what the positivist law says it is. Because the law is so determined, it follows that analyzing as sentence theoretically as either just or unjust is not possible. As a result many sentences, examined for their corrective or humanitarian quality, are an abuse of the power ceded to the legislators because they exceed what is required to correct, and hence, they exceed the power ceded to government to enforce laws. In my view, any punishment that exceeds the limits of necessity is, indeed, an abuse of the power citizens ceded to their government, and is a violation of the social contract.

Sentencing, to be within the contract and embodied in its proscriptions that have become our criminal law, should be viewed as simply a consequence of the offender's guilt. The penologists and offender alike must look at the sentence as a *consequence* of an antisocial act that violates a law and that which is deemed penologically necessary to denounce the act and correct the offender. It is like cancer treatment. The therapeutic response to cancer is a consequence of being infected with certain agents of the disease. The physician does not look at a cancerous patient and make a decision based solely on what is *just* for this person. The tumor is there and if it must be resected, the decision is made on the basis of medical necessity. The patient is ill and needs therapeutic treatment. So it is with offenders. So it is with sentences. We should not look just at the offender and impose a sentence based solely upon what is *just* for the offender. We must treat sentences simply as the consequences of the fact that a person has committed a crime and has a resectable evil. The sentence should be a consequence to be performed by the criminal justice delivery system in whatever measure, and by whatever means, is determined penologically necessary and constitutionally permissible to assure the safety of our culture. We must do whatever is necessary to excise the evil, or otherwise to correct the behavior, and to ready offenders for reintroduction into society. That must be the philosophy of sentencing. Anything more, or less, is unjust.

II. Why Punish?

> *Criminal punishment by government, although universally recognized as a necessity in limited areas of conduct, is an exercise of one of government's most awesome and dangerous powers . . . To this end, at least in part, written laws came into being, marking the boundaries of conduct for which public agents could thereafter impose punishments upon people.*[19]
>
> Justice Hugo Black

Why *do we* punish? The ugly truth is that we punish social offenders because it makes us feel good. Americans try to rationalize punishment by various means. But when the penological smoke clears, punishment is psychologically for the punisher. Neither American penology nor the American public seems to recognize this. But it is true! Society likes to punish, and the rationale for doing so is really quite simple. In the final analysis, we punish because it makes us feel good to get even with the offender.

I think it is important that we do more than get even and more than punish. I think we should correct. To do that we will need to understand more about behavior and to understand why we punish. We will need to examine the theories we rely upon to determine and justify criminal sentences. We will need to look anew at the reasons we offer to rationalize or justify a sentence. This means developing an understanding of the issues surrounding the death penalty, of contemporary notions of criminal responsibility, of the validity of mental defenses against prosecution, of how drugs affect crime control, of whether there are physical or biological causes for violent crime, and of what changes are necessary to make progress.

American penology seems unable to escape the notion of sin and the desire to punish those whom it believe have sinned. The early American approach to sentencing closely followed our puritanical roots. Americans believed, as stated in the Bible, that "all have sinned, and come short of the glory of God."[20] The prevailing belief that mortals were basically depraved, unworthy human beings, who, having sinned, must now face the judgment, influenced American penology. Americans were prepared to administer punishment and, ostensibly, to accept it. Rehabilitation was not a consideration for the Puritan. Pain was the Biblical response to sin. Pain was what you could expect as the *wages* of our sin. I am afraid it still is, but should not be.

We must detach ourselves from the theological notion of sin. The intrinsic morality or the Scriptural definition of an action may be of concern to the theologian. But when the action is defined by government as a crime, it becomes a social phenomenon and obedience becomes the concern of the criminal justice delivery system. There may be a celestial forum for the punishment of sinners; the follies of criminal offenders, however, must be dealt with below. Our systemic response to crime has little to do with God's punishment for sin; only a remedy for crime, and in that light, punishment may not always be defensible. What we do to offenders must have a legitimate reason and a defensible moral and philosophical base.

Punishing criminals is justified, in part, as an expression of society's outrage that one of its members has transgressed the established cultural rules. By punishment we also seek to maintain the rules by showing members of our civilization that society will not accept violations. Punishment is society's way of denouncing the act and the actor for the transgression. By punishing one who has thus erred, a culture vindicates all who have successfully obeyed the same rules—this is the principal of *denunciation*. Punishment, and the hope that it will ostracize the offender from polite society, provides an element of social cohesion between the remaining and obedient members of culture.

Punishment, however, can be a psychological tranquilizer for society, masking the real malaise. As a tranquilizer, punishment causes us to ignore warning signals of deep-seated problems, which, if untreated or not addressed are sure to appear later. Along that vein, the tranquilizer may become a poison. As the United States Supreme Court stated in the case quoted in the epigraph, and in a statement which all-too-many penologists, judges, and academicians alike have failed to challenge, the law and the trial are to separate out whom to *punish*.

I disagree fundamentally with that concept. It thoughtlessly foreordains the consequences of conviction without considering whether punishment is needed at all. My theory is that trials should separate out who needs behavioral modification or remedial treatment, which may or may not indicate punishment. I fear that by focusing so intently upon punishment, we have lost sight of our need to discover the "why" component. I submit that to find out "why," we must answer the initial questions: What is punishment, should we punish, to what degree, and whom?

III. What Is Punishment?

> *People no longer have to rely upon common sense for traveling. The common sense way is to walk, or to ride an animal. Science has discovered better ways by the use of uncommon sense. The common sense time to go to bed is when it gets dark; the uncommon sense of artificial illumination has changed all that. Crime problems have been dealt with too long with only the aid of common sense. Catch criminals and lock them up; if they hit you, hit them back. This is common sense, but is does not work.*[21]
>
> *Karl Menninger*

Punishment for those who violate social rules or norms and who engage in socially unacceptable behavior is present in some form in all but the most passive of societies. It is not difficult to imagine that the first questions any culture answers after it establishes its first rules are how shall we enforce them, and, what shall we do with the transgressor? Historically, the initial response mandated an atonement by the offender and restitution to the victim. If the crime was sufficiently serious, or if the offender repeated, he may be declared an outlaw and banished.

> The earliest criminal code of laws was promulgated by Hammurabi, King of Babylon, whose rule extended over the whole of Mesopotamia from the mouth of the Tigris and Euphrates to the Mediterranean coast, in 2285–2242 B.C.E. The code provides detailed behavioral proscriptions and penalties for violating them. It is believed that these laws and sentences reflect ancient Hebrew traditions.
>
> See, *The Oldest Code of Laws in the World,* Trans. C.H.W. Johns, M.A., Edinburgh, (1905).

Most cultures felt a need to react to crime as a means to vindicate their own self-denial. They had, after all, foregone the pleasures or profits that could be derived from doing whatever they wished to do. Because they had obeyed the rules, they imposed some sanctions, usually punishment, upon those who did not. Some philosophers define punishment, in the penological sense in which we are discussing it, as infliction of pain to instill and enforce culturally desirable behavior. Other philosophers contend that punishment is pain the offender brings upon himself by performing a prohibited action, and which is deserved in proportion to the moral gravity of his offense.

The death penalty, of course, is punishment. But is it always? Socrates was sentenced to death. Yet, he not only died willingly, he voluntarily drank the death potion saying, "Anytus and Meletus may put me to death, but it is beyond their power to punish me." Mikal Gilmore, in his book *Shot Through The Heart,* said that his brother, Gary Gilmore, wanted to die, had attempted suicide several times, and at the time of his execution, the state of Utah had become Gary's willing but unwitting servant. Epictetus may come closer to defining criminal punishment when he says that whatever is done against one's will is punishment and that where a man goes willingly, there is no punishment. There is no chastisement, no punishment, from an action, if one willingly accepts it. Edmund Burke believed that man's normal state is indifference. To him, punishment is anything wherein one is moved from that indifferent state along a continuum towards pain or discomfort. Nils Christie, the internationally known Norwegian criminologist/penologist, states that any way you describe punishment, it involves in some measure the infliction of pain. Jeremy Bentham states that all punishment, whatever it is, is mischief in itself and is to be considered simply as evil done for evil. Dr. Karl Menninger noted, "The idea of punishment as the law interprets, it seems to be that inasmuch as a man has offended society, society must officially offend him."

The term *punishment* is confusing when we are discussing sentencing. Punishment is used interchangeably for a *sentence*, whether it is intended actually to punish the offender, to rehabilitate, to contain, or merely to embarrass him. All penal sentences are, without further examination, then considered to be punishment. Of course, they are not. For example, a fine, which is a lawful sentence in most jurisdictions, is hardly punishment for one who can afford to pay it easily. Incarceration is not punishment for one who easily accepts it or consciously or unconsciously desires it. Gary Gilmore, as I suspect others who have the same pathological personalities have done, expressed his desire to return to prison and to be with his "friends." Prison may also be nothing more that an occasional, socially-acceptable risk for one engaged in some form of criminal enterprise. The fact is that many sentences simply have no sting for those who do not care, or who view them as a temporary inconvenience, or worse, accept them simply a cost of doing "business." For one like Gilmore, even death is not punishment, if he cares nothing for life, or wishes for death. So what, philosophically, is punishment?

Nils Christie, defines, "punishment within the institution of the law [as] the inflicting of pain, intended as pain."

H. L. A. Hart defines punishment in terms of five elements. It must:

1) Involve pain or other consequences normally considered unpleasant

2) Be for an offense against legal rules

3) Be of an actual or supposed offender for his offense

4) Be intentionally administered by persons other than the offender

5) Be imposed and administered by an authority constituted by a legal system against which the offense is committed

Anthony Flew refers to the term punishment as "vague and open-textured." He proposes that its penological definition must contain five elements:

1) It must be an evil (following Hobbes), or an unpleasantness to the recipient (whom he calls a 'victim')

2) For offending a rule

3) Performed upon the offender

4) By a personal instrumentality (that is, not a natural consequence)

5) Pursuant to some special authority conferred by the authority that created the rule violated

What I consider to be punishment, in the context of criminal sentencing, is:

1) The intentional infliction of

2) Some form of inconvenience, disqualification, incapacitation, or pain[22]

3) That has been decided on bythe sovereign who inflicts the punishment

4) To be inflicted by one endowed by the sovereign with the authority to do so

5) For a reason legitimated by society

6) To achieve a justified result, and

7) Upon an offender, against his will, and as a consequence of some infringement or infraction of the law or social code

How do we punish? Christie states that "[s]tates nearly always defend themselves through armour similar to that of their greatest perceived enemies." In America our *armor* is simple: to our offenders we administer probation, impose incarceration, or inflict death. Our fines do not, under most circumstances, penologically qualify as punishment. Fines lack any penological force when, as in most jurisdictions, the amount is tailored to the offender's ability to pay. Ability to withstand punishment is antithetical to notions of punishment. For example, we do not, when determining an appropriate term of imprisonment, examine the subject to determine if he can physically or psychologically withstand the incarceration without adverse consequences. Using a fine as a penal sentence is thus, quite paradoxically, internally designed to minimize its own effectiveness. Consequently, a fine has serious penological flaws. The notion of *ability to pay* is born of an unfortunate ignorance of penological factors that is symptomatic of our system, guided by legislators who are without a notion of *why* we punish.

We have a basic antinomy about the philosophical justifications for punishment. It arises from a confusion that we share about questions of when *can* we punish, with questions of whom *ought* we to punish, how, and to what degree? The first question is usually addressed in American thought by reference to retributive theories, and the answer depends solely upon a finding of guilt. The latter questions are the more complicated to answer, the easiest to elide, and often the ones neither answered nor asked at all. These questions are simply driven out of the sentencing equation by attention to a popular demand for revenge. But I submit that we must both ask and answer them. To do so, however, we will be required to dig deeper into our philosophical arsenal.

In America, we rely upon only four principal penological or philosophical theories as bases for sentencing: *deterrence, rehabilitation, containment*, and *retribution*. Each theory that American jurisprudence currently uses to support punishment indicates that it has made an option for short-term returns at the expense of long-term solutions. The short view is what Dr. Deming refers to as one of the *crippling diseases* of potentially successful systems.[23] Let us look at each of the four theories.

A. *Deterrence*

For what mortal would be righteous if he nothing fears?[24]

Aeschulus

It seems to me intuitive that if a person connects an unpleasant consequence to some form of behavior, that person will be less inclined to engage in that behavior. Moreover, it seems reasonable to assume that the more unpleasant the consequences are of a particular behavior, the greater the likelihood that a person so effected will refrain from that behavior. The linking of unpleasant consequences to proscribed behavior is the essence of the deterrent theory of punishment. Deterrence is the rationale for criminal sentencing with greatest common appeal among academics and theoreticians, and is a traditional justification for punishment.[25] If you were to ask a parent or a judge why a certain punishment was imposed, the likely answer will be "to teach a lesson." Also, when someone seeks to hide the depth of his outrage as the real source of support for severe punishment, *the lesson* allegedly imparted by the punishment becomes the easy answer.

Deterrence is coercion by fear. As popularly used, it means that the threat of punishment, or punishment itself, causes individuals who would commit an offensive act to refrain from doing so.[26] Theorists in law, however, know precious little about its mechanics or *how* deterrence works. They merely assume that deterrence operates because a threat of punishment forces a potential offender to perform a calculation of how that potential punishment balances against the potential pleasures or benefits of a given crime.

Currently, however, there is insufficient evidence from which we can deduce the actual effect that punishing one offender has on either that offender or other potential offenders. Intuitively we know punishment deters, because each of us has governed our behavior by more than *duty*. Hence, the prospect of getting caught and being punished does account for something in behavior. And, empirically we see that individuals become disciplined because they were disciplined. But some individuals are a little slower than others at getting the message and learning from punitive lessons taught to others. Some individuals will learn nothing from lessons taught to others. So, until the effects of punishment are scientifically studied, the deterrent value of punishment as a response to crime is simply speculation.

> "[I]ndeed, empirical studies suggest that shame. . . is already the primary motive that people have to obey the law. Most people refrain from engaging in crime. . . because they've internalized community norms and value the respect of their peers."
>
> Dan M Kahan, "Shaming White Collar Offenders," *Federal Sentencing Reporter*, July/August 1999.

A growing body of social evidence indicates that people respond to legal rules and social norms because they fear that their action will be disapproved of by their social peers, not because they fear punishment. One reason is that each of us generally considers our self to be moral, at least within the parameters of our own cultural vision, and, if our actions lie within the mores of our social structure. That being so, we may behave simply because rules tell us to, and disobedience will create within us a moral dilemma. In actuality, obedience *may* be the result of the denunciatory aspects of detection, conviction, and punishment. Or, obedience may be the result of the social norms that peer, superior, and institutional pressures bring to bear on our behavior. If so, obedience is neither from fear of punishment nor punishment itself, but rather the actor's ethical training and his cultural milieu. Finally, if fear is indeed significant, one must question if it is the fear of punishment making severity or duration of punishment the significant factor in behavior? Or is it the fear of being exposed as a law-breaker, which would make the detection (getting caught) paramount to either the severity or the duration of the sentence? The problem is that we simply do not know. What little we do know from historical practice, however, is that if what we do to one offender has any effect on potential offenders, we should treat it as a fortuitous circumstance of the primary object; correcting the ones we catch.

General deterrence works best in theory and in the academic laboratory. Think for a minute of a couple of extreme illustrations along the continuum of punishment. On one extreme, the illustration has an armed Internal Revenue Service agent who shoots tax evaders on the spot. Another illustration has a traffic patroller authorized to shoot jaywalkers. Few would question that simply from a general fear because others are getting shot, jaywalkers and tax evaders would nearly disappear. But the response is, at what price? Shooting offenders is, of course, unacceptably severe. And so, we impose lesser, culturally acceptable penalties. The result, however, is that the deterrent effect upon one person from another person receiving a summons for jaywalking, or of another person getting jailed for failure to pay his tax, is insufficient to deter everyone, because we still have jaywalkers and income tax evaders. What this illustrates is that as we move along the remedial continuum to the point at which the remedy comes within the parameters of cultural acceptance, its deterrent effect also diminishes proportionately until it disappears for some crimes and for some individuals.

Another difficulty with relying on general deterrence is that a person is deterred by another's punishment only to the extent he identifies with the person being punished. The mind's defensive mechanism that says, "That could never happen to me," is active in most of us. For example, the recreational drug users do not view themselves as *criminals*. Their attitude is that *we* are not like *them*. What happens to *them* simply does not effect *us*. For the offenders of some criminal laws, the difference between *them* and *us*, is that *they* have gotten caught. Most people will not admit it, but that is the reality. There also is little social intercourse between the criminal culture and the social mainstream. The mainstream of our civilization and the citizens of our criminal cultures simply do not identify with each other. Hence, what happens to one means nothing to the other.

General deterrence, as a primary motivator for punishment, also has other serious philosophical drawbacks. For example, in theory it matters little to the general deterrentist that the actual offender is caught and punished. In a practical and a logical sense, (integrity and real justice aside) general deterrence would work just as well if a wholly innocent person were spectacularly arrested, found guilty and punished. General deterrence maintains its logical force even if any one, preferably just a unit of social detritus, so as not to arouse cultural ire, were taken into custody, tried, convicted, and punished. You see, it would not matter to deterrentist theory that the punished person were wholly innocent. All that is necessary is that society, at least the society that you wish to deter from committing crimes, believed him to be guilty and saw him punished. Hence, for the deterrence theorist, it is more important that someone, anyone, be punished quickly, sending the immediate message to all that they must obey, than it is to wait patiently for the truly guilty party to be caught. In this way too, society's values and norms are immediately reinforced. If a sentence is solely to teach others a lesson then once *someone* is punished, it is not too important in the abstract whether it is the actual offender.

An individual is *specifically* deterred when he refrains from doing something to avoid unpleasant consequences that he believes will, or may, befall him.[27] Again, this theory has flaws. First, an individual is specifically deterred from some behavior or lifestyle,

Crime and Punishment Funnel

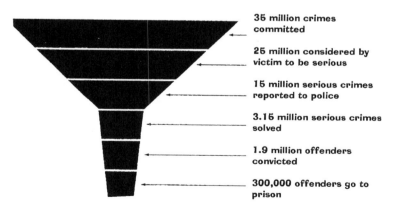

35 million crimes committed

25 million considered by victim to be serious

15 million serious crimes reported to police

3.15 million serious crimes solved

1.9 million offenders convicted

300,000 offenders go to prison

It is obvious that we cannot adequately address crime merely by law enforcement and by increasing our rates of incarceration. With only 5 offenders incarcerated for each 350 crimes, we must work on the top of the funnel. We must prevent crime.

only to the extent that he believes he is free to choose an alternative behavior, or another lifestyle. To the extent that a person feels locked-in socially, or believes himself frustrated from moving to a socially acceptable lifestyle, punishment will not coerce positive behavioral change. The freer a person is to choose among behavioral alternatives, the more effective punishment will be as a deterrent to misbehavior. The more a person's acts are perceived to be determined by forces external, and exclusive of his will, the less effective punishment will be in coercing appropriate behavior. In other words, offenders who do not *believe* that they can change, will *not* change. Committing a crime, even facing the potential of punishment, may be the only perceived option for this individual. As Irwin and Austin stated "For many, particularly young members of the inner-city underclass, the choice is not between conventional and illegal paths to the good life, but between illegal and risky paths or no satisfaction at all."[28]

Specific deterrence becomes even more absurd when you consider that most offenders are not even detected, apprehended, or punished. Out of the 42.7 million crimes committed in the United States in 1994, only 500,000 offenders, or about one percent were sent to prison. As a result, many offenders and many more potential offenders believe, and believe with some justification, that the threat of arrest and punishment may apply to others, but not to them. Other offenders simply discount the future and live totally in the present.[29] For this group "the emotional force of present desire is overwhelming in contrast to the apprehension of future pain."[30] For these *present-dwellers*, the threat of punishment diminishes to nothing, especially for actions motivated by passion or greed to seek an instant gratification.

For many other offenders, however, punishment may be just one of the facts of life or a chance one must take in the daily existence in the anticulture in which he lives. *Doing time* may not even constitute a separation from an offender's society. They socialize with the same persons or personalities, whether they are within prison, or without. It may often be nothing more than a fact of the offender's cultural life, a chance he takes, or perhaps, a cost of doing his illegal business.

Of course, few offenders ever either engage in even casual research, or calculate in any way the potential punishment for the crime they are contemplating. Criminals simply do not consult the law or lawyers before they commit crimes. I doubt that many of them read the newspapers, or at least the section that describes the sentences that others have received and that they might receive if they commit their crimes. Their analysis seldom ventures beyond the likelihood of getting caught. Experience dictates that criminals simply do not become educated by what happens to some stranger. Many offenders will consciously choose to commit crimes and believe, with statistical justification, that they will not get caught. The punishment is for someone else.

Furthermore, interviews with offenders indicate that a significant number of convicted offenders are simply risk-takers, who are ignorant of socially acceptable challenges open to them. As one burglar remarked when asked about his future, "If I could find other work that was as rewarding and exciting, I'd take it." For others, crime is an outlet for their creativity. The game is to steal, to swindle, or simply to beat the system, and many do. These types of offenders also are not deterred by punishment. They prefer the excitement, the risk, the game, and the possibility of getting caught.

The final and most pathological category of offenders are those who commit crimes actually expecting to eventually get caught. Those in this category of offenders do not reflect an irrational optimism, creativity, or even risk-taking. They in fact exhibit a psychosis that is manifested as a need for denunciation and self-punishment. Mikal Gilmore stated that his brother, convicted murderer Gary Gilmore, had attempted suicide several times, and in executing him the state had become his unwitting servant. Gary, who once indicated that he wanted to go back to prison, may have committed the two execution-style murders so that he would be returned to prison and executed.

To the extent that the risk of detection is known to the offender, where his crime is calculated, and where his behavior is not determined by factors external to his will, punishment has a place. Here, however, the pain of punishment administered as a consequence for an offense must exceed the pleasure, profit, or positive results the offender expects to reap from his offense. Deterrence legitimizes punishment in these instances because the potential perpetrators are sophisticated. That is to say, they have calculated their chances of success, and are aware that they committed a crime. Because they thrive on the limited likelihood that they will be caught and punished, there must be a sufficient reality of unpleasant consequences to deter them. In other words, they must be fully aware of the reality that the punishment will be so unpleasant that it countervails the emotional or monetary potential of their crime. In this instance, severe punishment may serve as a real deterrent.

Penologists and philosophers uniformly agree that quick detection is a far greater deterrent than the punishment that follows.[31] As Sir Walter Moberly stated, "The busiest hangman can do little for the protection of society in comparison with an efficient police force."[32] Also, we simply give most offenders too much credit, or credit them with too much analysis, if we delude ourselves into thinking that the *duration* of the prison sentence is any consideration whatsoever when they decide to commit their crimes. Bill Moyers, the noted journalist, interviewed some of the most violent incarcerated youths, and their message was uniform, loud, and clear: "When you're committing crimes, you don't think you [sic] gonna get caught when you're doing it."[33] As one youth, who had been incarcerated for the totally gratuitous murder of a complete stranger, stated: "I was doing little crimes, I never got caught. And then it just progressed [to murder]."[34] When he was asked why, he stated: "I was in a real bad mood that day. And someone was in the wrong place at the wrong time."[35] It is my observation from two decades of experience that many crimes have more of an emotive than intellective genesis. Deterrence by punishment, specific or general, I am afraid, accounts for little in these cases.

Deterrence theory thrives mainly because its nearest competitors, correction and accountability, are dead or dying in our penology. As it stands, the criminal counterculture operates within, but is nearly autonomous from, both our culture and conventional government. It is apparently neither influenced by our democratic social form nor ruled by conventional laws. To the contrary, the counterculture operates under an anarchical social form whose primary goal is to avoid social contact with the elements of conventional society. Offenders, who are part of that counterculture, know from what goes on around them that they face little chance of detection and conviction.

The justice system simply lacks moral authority, force, or credibility for a significant and growing portion of our society. As one gang member, who was incarcerated for a murder in a drive-by shooting, states, "It just seemed fun. [Y]ou live in it for the excitement . . . that fear gives you."[36] Deterrence thrives upon fear. But unfortunately, many criminals are afraid of neither detection nor punishment.

We must divert the function of sentencing from the desire to do something *to* the offender, and instead, combine the social control we have over the sentenced individual with the goal of creating self-control. The goals of all sentences should be to require that the offender transform his behavior so that it conforms to our socially selected cultural norms, and to require that the offender exhibit a culturally accepted level of self-control before he is permitted to reenter society. Bentham was right when he said that we must correct or contain, because, I submit, nothing else will work.

B. *Rehabilitation*

[R]ehabilitation is no longer a goal of sentencing under the [Federal Sentencing] guidelines.[37]

U.S. Supreme Court

Rehabilitation in our current penal system is too often a false hope. The system itself rehabilitates very few. Criminal sentences are no longer even designed to do so.[38] The system probably does more to discourage rehabilitation than it does to encourage it. Indeed, were social scientists to devise a system specifically to destroy cultural skills, social desire, to corrupt morals, as well as to provide criminal instruction, they would have to think very carefully to develop a better institution for doing so than the average American prison. If an offender changes for the better in prison, it is not because of it. It is because a dedicated corps of prison personnel, in spite of the rest of the system, facilitated change. And if individuals come out of prison better than they went in, it is because they looked down deep inside, found something they did not like, and decided to change it. Bentham's panopticon may have been appropriate in his day.[39] Today, however, something more than isolated contemplation is needed to bring offenders face to face with the reality of their character and behavior; and that is not happening, at least not by design, in prison.

C. *Containment*

Following containment theory, the conviction for one crime is used to predict that the offender will commit others. Then, to protect society from the offender's potential transgressions he is sentenced for what it is believed he will do in the future, by *containing* him in prison. This is also a philosophically problematic rationale for sentencing for two principal reasons. First, a containment sentence is based upon a blind prediction of future behavior, based solely on actions of the past. Consequently, in offense-based sentencing, regardless of how contrite the offender is, how insignificant his potential for recidivating, or how real his potential for rehabilitation, he gets contained for his past conduct. Second, it supports incarceration for something a person has not done, and may never do. American penology accepts containment as an exception to the rule that we do not punish people for future crimes, nor do we use detention to prevent people from committing crimes. By this principle we find it acceptable to say that when an offender is convicted of a crime, he forfeits any presumption of future innocence, at least for the duration of the containment sentence. Hence, the offender is being punished for something he did not do.

Statistically containment works, but only because while the offender is contained he simply cannot commit other crimes. The question of whether he would otherwise do so is not addressed. Of course, increased levels of incarceration may have a positive correlation to reduced levels of crime, because some of those who are among our two-million incarcerates, could, if not incarcerated, continue to commit crimes. Hence, containment has some short-range validity. That, however, is not the end of the story for several reasons. First, because the majority of persons in prison will get out, and we have not addressed the negative impact upon our communities that the number of prison "graduates" may have as their numbers grow in relation to the law-abiding persons in society.

Second, if we honestly intend to correct and segregate our successes from our failures, only those who deserve continued containment, or who are determined to be unsafe, would be contained. In an intellectually honest system, the corrected would be freed knowing that if *they* fail, *they* have shown that they are not corrected, that they are perhaps not correctable, and the doom of prison awaits them with a diminished possibility of release. This, of course, is not now happening. Instead, Americans foot the bill for unnecessary containment by incapacitating those who may well be corrected, those who need no correction, or those who can be corrected more economically without incarceration.

Finally, the corrected or correctable are being contained among the most predatory persons in our culture, and are thereby contaminated and not improved by the experience. Even if we were philosophically prepared to accept the notion of preventative detention, for the containment theory to be a success, the offender would be contained only for the length of time sufficient to assure that society will be safe when he is released. I think it is simply unjust to imprison a person for any time beyond that which is necessary to correct, or otherwise to teach him a lesson. Unfortunately, the safety and correction factors are simply not integers of the equation used to determine either the minimum threshold duration of a sentence or the ultimate date of release. We simply cannot now say that society will be as safe when an offender is released as it was before that person was contained.

In 1991 the Brookings Institution released a study that concluded that containment was economically successful.[40] To support this conclusion, the study's authors quantified the number of crimes a released criminal would potentially commit before rearrest and what these crimes would cost society, then they compared this number with the cost of keeping the criminal incarcerated.[41] The author estimated that the theoretical prototypical career offender commits between 187 and 287 crimes per year, which, at a cost per crime of $2300, costs society in excess of $400,000 per year. Following this reasoning, it costs society 25 million dollars per year to incarcerate 1000 felons, but it would cost 430 million dollars per year *not* to jail them.

Nevertheless, all that this study shows us is that prisons, as containers of individuals, are economically successful, only *if* we can also assume that the same theoretical offenders who are contained are the ones who would have otherwise committed the 187 to 287 crimes per year. But they do not show that our system of penology is a success because we still cannot rely upon containment to determine the need for a prison sentence for any specific individual, for the duration of any specific incarceration, or for whether prison has succeeded at containing or correcting the offenders who need it. To carry this logic to its conclusion, it would have to be argued that for specific crimes, the justice system should simply incarcerate the perpetrator after his first offense, and keep him incarcerated. That would be absurd. Current short-range statistics aside, in the long term, history may not tell a success story.

The Brookings' conclusion, standing alone, is never a penological justification in a sentence for a first offense; is of only slight use in a second; and, is only of significance when, with other factors, it points to a continuing, career course of criminal conduct. Even then, however, a containment justification is not philosophically justifiable unless we can determine how long the offender must be contained to protect society. Without such an accurate decision as to duration, the containment-based sentence is no more than a shot in the dark.

When we can identify with some acceptable degree of specificity the offenders who place society at risk when released, studies such as Brookings' can be good evidence against our present system. Indeed, they would support a system in which an offender who has been convicted of a crime is given an indeterminate sentence, whose term of incapacitation is consistent with the public safety, and whose release date is determined wholly by his progress and correction. Unless we know who to contain and who to release, in the final analysis, containing an offender does nothing more than postpone his predations. Unless the contained are corrected, we are only be delaying their crimes for the period they are actually in prison. Containment is only an opiate for a sick and painful society. When it wears off, the disease of crime is still there, and the pain it causes is worse.

D. *Retribution*

The Criminal Law stands to the passion of revenge in much the same relation as marriage to the sexual appetite.[42]

Sir James Fitzjames Stephen

In the philosophy of punishment, a sentence linked solely to what one has done is retribution. Etymologically, the "re" in a word points to the past.[43] Retribution, in criminal law, is "based strictly on the fact that every crime demands payment in the form of punishment."[44] In penology, it is the result of an avenging society's reaction to a crime. As one commentator stated, "Revenge is what the avenger wreaks; retribution is simply what happens to the wrongdoer."[45] American sentences are revenge-retributivist, pure and simple. For two centuries we have followed the theories of Locke, Hume, Kant, Hegel and others, and base our response to crime upon a desire for revenge. We recycle the concept, and euphemistically call it retribution. Some penologists labor greatly to distinguish "revenge," as being personal reprisal and outside the law, from "retribution," as being the law's appropriate and somehow proportionate response. They fail. Retribution comes from the same place in the heart as revenge. We have discovered, although we have not admitted, that justice is not a Kantian or Hegelian balance sheet, it has human emotion. Nonetheless, retributivist theory follows the myth that there is some social valence that can be attached to a crime to come up with a degree of retaliation that is equivalent.

A majority of the public believes that because a person has violated the law, the violation itself legitimates the punishment because the offender *deserves* to suffer for having transgressed social order. It is the most simplistic form of reaction, the payback. I take significant issue with this. Retribution may be the sole moral justification for punishment in current sentencing policy. It does not, however, comport with contemporary humanitarian views of justice. The role of retribution, or "just deserts," I submit is legitimate solely to set an outer limit of punishment, and not to provide its *raison d'etre*. Moreover, moral justification for punishment evades the real issue which is whether the punishment makes society really any *safer*. A "get tough" retributivist sentencing system does not necessarily correct an individual. Conversely, it may harden him and render him even more cruel.

No one may discount the hope for future benefit of even cruel, painful punishment because there is some corrective value for a person who is coerced into proper behavior just by knowing he will be paid back if he misbehaves. Nonetheless, if an offender is punished beyond his just deserts, the sentence merely becomes a part of the spiral of violence, as recrimination between our laws and the rebellious escalates. Coercion, experience proves , *changes* no one. It merely *alters* behavior, and only for the time an individual fears the consequences. The recidivist rates of our system's products, the released offenders, graphically indicate that to control by coerced behavioral change is inadequate. We do not have the resources to continue the coercion, and without constant pressure or real change, behavior simply tends to revert to what it was pre-punishment. It is not enough that a system of punishment is considered by contemporary penologists to be moral, or that the pain it inflicts is just. The system must be sufficiently effective to accomplish that which legitimates law—public safety. Penal science must discover how to influence real change in our offenders, and our system must resolve to execute it.

Nietzsche stated that "[f]or that man be freed from the bonds of revenge: that is the bridge to my highest hope."[46] Clearly Nietzsche's hopes are not realized by our current sentencing system. Only truly corrective measures can produce any enduring change. Beccaria stated this centuries ago.[47] We have failed, however, to stand upon the shoulders of our philosophical forefathers such as Beccaria, Bentham, Romilly, and others, and from there, to look ahead for newer and more effective responses. As a result, penological thought has progressed little and the current system is fair to no one. It neither appears to be nor is and tragically few any longer even care. But care we must!

Justice requires not only that an offender receive all his rights, substantively and procedurally, and not only that a sentence be free from cruel and unusual aspects, but also that society itself be dealt with justly. The citizenry has, in reality, turned over to the government the right it has to protect itself. In the interest of society, the citizenry has, in a practical sense, ceded to the government its right to shoot back, and in the actual sense, the right to shoot first. But in doing so, society is entitled to expect the treatment given those convicted of crimes will not merely punish them, but will also correct them so that when released, they have not only served time but are corrected to such an extent that society will be safe when they are reintroduced. This is not now happening and will not happen if all we do is "get even." Penology must be redesigned so that society comes out ahead.

Retribution has other philosophical problems, too. First, a vengeful sentence structure represents a cultural revulsion from crime and offensive behavior generally and not *just* this crime in particular. So in a sense, retributive theory offers a justification for us to punish one for what others have done. Also, in theory, retribution cares little about the offender's specific victim, unless the specific victim draws some sympathy. Take the example of when one drug dealer or one thug kills another. It is a serious breach of the moral and legal rules to be sure, but does the culture really care? Is polite society, or culture, really injured? Actually, when one evil person kills another, society in a practical sense achieves a net gain. Hence, a retributive sentence vindicates the collective attitudes of society towards the crime, not necessarily the victim, whom society may be better off without.

Second, like general deterrence, in both a practical and theoretical sense, it matters little for retribution that the actual offender is punished, only that someone whom the public thinks offended its rules is punished. For example, if we set aside other rationales for punishment, society needs only to *believe* that we have indeed "zapped" the guilty person (he need only qualify as a scapegoat) and society will feel vindicated because it feels it has gotten revenge. Again, like general deterrence, retribution would function just fine if a non-productive cultural drop-out were quickly arrested, speedily tried, and severely punished without regard for whether he is the offender or not. The victim would feel vindicated. The crime would be appropriately denounced on behalf of the law-abiding citizenry. Society would have the satisfaction of revenge. Culture would be rid of one of its dropouts. Outside of the system, only the punished person and truly guilty party may know of the scam. And, society will have received its measure of retributory satisfaction.

If a sentence is not functional, however, no one knows it better than the sentenced offender. Society can deal in generalities and tolerate imperfections in the law. The punished offenders are not deceived by a sentence without an underlying reality that has no rational basis, or by a sentence imposed in excess of need. It is the fervent desire of our system that the innocent person always go unpunished, else he becomes a victim of it. I submit that excessive punishment is no different, and to the extent of the excess of punishment over a legitimate need for it, the law and the system become instruments of oppression. The offender becomes a second victim of the system, and as a victim, one for whom we must care as diligently as we do for the wholly innocent. Even in the engagement policies of war, the limitations on unnecessary "physical suffering" suffering must be observed.[48] If an instrumentality of war performs beyond that which is necessary, it constitutes "unnecessary suffering" and is condemned.[49]

If people think that excessive punishment is not evil, they need only talk to a few prisoners to discover how sharply they resent any wanton additions to a punishment, which by itself they will often accept as just. As Keen stated, "Listen to what the enemy says about you and you will learn the truth you have repressed."[50] The public's demand for safety must be satisfied, and the public must know that its safety is the bedrock principle of each sentence. It is, nonetheless, of equal importance that the sentenced offender also know that justice has been done. The criminal justice delivery system must constantly endeavor to both commit and release offenders in a reasonable state of mind, free of any legitimate hatred for the system that punished him, and without the unnecessary venom we generate by excessive imprisonment, or for that matter, vile prison conditions. And that endeavor is not even addressed when all we base our system upon is revenge.

There is no emotion so futile as regret. And, the verdicts of history may mean nothing when a practice is examined in the glare of contemporary experience. What worked yesterday may not work today. What works today may not work tomorrow. We must mistrust both our current convictions and conclusions. We must look ahead and prepare for the future. The social catharsis of revenge, retribution, what is in law called the *lex talionis,* does not rationalize the anger, the bitterness, and the recriminations we perpetuate by retributive sentences. Punishment performed as a part of a social vendetta against criminals has not worked because although retribution assuages the punisher's need for revenge, it has done little for the punished, and the recidivist rates show this. The public has said that the sinner must suffer. But an odious punishment imposed upon a person who has committed a vile act, although it may be cathartic to a victimized society, has short-lived effects. A sentencing system must address real needs and not pander to the immediate emotions of society, and that is all retribution does.

Retribution only provides a fertile bed for the malignant growth of hatred. It lives wholly in the past. It has no future. It is an expression of society's anger and a revulsion from the past in spite of the future. Plato thought that to measure punishment by reference wholly to what an offender had done was like "lashing a rock." He believed that looking back, unless it was to determine an appropriate remedy to correct, was irrational. He said that "he who desires to inflict rational punishment does not punish for the sake of a past wrong which cannot be undone . . . He punishes for the sake of prevention."[51] Plato was right. I suggest that the system can really neither call itself enlightened, nor consider itself productive, unless all criminal sentences take a view towards the future, towards change, towards correction, towards public safety.

We must have realistic *corrective* CBS sentences, for without them, we will merely continue to isolate criminals and create a larger outlaw class. Both practically and philosophically, retribution suffers serious deficiencies. We must eliminate it as a sole support for sentencing. Our sentences must have more to stand on. We simply cannot determine the most appropriate remedy by which to protect society, as long as either our stated and officially accepted goal is to inflict retaliation. We know that:

> [T]he human thirst for vengeance, the human instincts of hate and fear, need no encouragement from the law. So long as they exist, we must of course take them into account, but we need not reinforce them and give them dignity by legal endorsement.[52]

Noted criminologist Professor James Fox decries the American fascination with what he calls *the three R's*:   retribution, revenge, and retaliation. So do I. He then adds a fourth *R:* reelection—as an unfortunate reality that results from of our legislatures' use of the first three to appear tough on crime.[53] The offender may not deserve a full measure of dignity. But we cannot compromise *our* dignity by sacrificing it on the altar of penological expediency. We have too much at stake. Society is ours. We created our culture for each other. There is an American civilization. It is us, all of us. If the offender by his actions has declared he does not care for it, he must be excised and contained until he convincingly demonstrates his willingness to rejoin our civilization and be a participating citizen. We who have a commitment to our culture and our civilization, and we who must rely upon it, must succor and nurture it. Carrying out a sentence of revenge does neither. Instead our sentences *must* contain until corrected.

ENDNOTES

1. Coleman Phillipson, _Three Criminal Law Reformers: Beccaria, Bentham, Romilly_ 298 (1970) (quoting Richard Price, _Observations On Civil Liberty and the Justice and Policy of the War With America_ 4 (1776)).

2. "Truth" involves metaphysics; "the truth" involves morality; and, there is a difference. _See_ Richard K. Sherwin, _Law, Violence, and Illiberal Belief,_ 78 Geo. L.J. 1785, 1787-88 (1990); Lisamichelle Davis, Note, _Epistemological Foundations and Meta-Hermeneutic Methods: The Search for a Theoretical Justification of the Coercive Force of Legal Interpretation,_ 68 _B.U.L. Rev._ 733, 739 (1988).

3. _See_ John E. Witte, Jr. and Thomas C. Arthur, _The Three Uses of the Law: A Protestant Source of the Purposes of Criminal Punishment?,_ 10 J. L. & Religion 433, 439-44 (1993).

4. Devine, _supra_ note 9, at 8; _see_ Witte and Arthur, supra note 8, at 438.

5. Devine, _supra_ note 9, at 8.

6. _Id._

7. Matthew A. Pauley, _The Jurisprudence of Crime and Punishment from Plato to Hegel,_ 39 _Am. J. Jris._ 97, 115-20 (1994).

8. Richard M. Fraher, _The Theoretical Justification for the New Criminal Law of the High Middle Ages: "Rei Publicae Interest, Ne Crimina Remaneant Impunita,"_ 1984 _U. Ill. L. Rev._ 577, 582-83; Nagel, _supra_ note 7, at 888.

9. _See_ Jeffrey C. Tuomala, _The Value of Punishment: A Response to Judge Richard L. Nygaard,_ 5 _Regent U. L. Rev._ 13, 20-22 (1995). Brigham Young commented on blood atonement and stated the following: "There are transgressors who, if they knew themselves, and the only condition upon which they can obtain forgiveness, would beg of their brethren to shed their blood, that the smoke thereof might ascend to God as an offering to appease the wrath that is kindled against them, and that the law might have its course."

10. Michael Madow, _Forbidden Spectacle: Executions, the Public and the Press in Nineteenth Century New York,_ 43 _U. Buff. L. Rev._ 461, 493 (1995).

11. Beccaria, _supra_ note 13, at 43; James Heath, _Eighteenth Century Penal Theory_ 131 (1963) (citing Beccaria, § 9 (1764)).

12. _Id._ see Madow, _supra_ note 18, at 492-93. _See generally_ John G. DiPiano, Note, _Private Prisons: Can They Work? Panopticon in the Twenty-First_

Century, 21 *New Eng. J. On Crim. & Civ. Confinement* 171 (1995) (discussing private prisons and Bentham's "panopticon" concept).

13. *Jeremy Bentham*, "Panopticon Papers," in *A Bentham Reader* 194, 196-97 (Mary Peter Mack ed., 1969); DiPiano, *supra* note 25, at 178-79.

14. Phillipson, *supra* note 1, at 274.

15. See Anita Ramasastry, *The Parameters, Progressions, and Paradoxes of Baron Bramuell*, 38 *Am. J. Legal Hist.* 322, 348 (1994).

16. Charles W. Thomas, *Corrections In America: Problems of the Past and the Present* 36-52 (1987); Pauley, *supra* note 14, at 98-100.

17. W. Edwards Deming, *Out of the Crisis* 156 (1982).

18. Nils Christie, *Limits To Pain* 9 (1981).

19. *Id.*

20. *Romans* 3:23.

21. *The Crime of Punishment*, Viking (1966), p.

22. We have substituted the removal of something desired (freedom) for the infliction of positive or corporal suffering. Walker should not be understood to suggest pain in that sense.

23. Deming, *supra* note 42, at 98-100.

24. Aeschylus, *The Eumenides,* in *Aeschylus I Oresteia* 160 (Richmond Lattimore trans., 1953).

25. Paul B. Weston and Kenneth M. Wells, *The Administration of Justice* 269 (3d ed. 1977).

26. Black's Law Dictionary defines a deterrent as "[a]nything which impedes or has a tendency to prevent." *Black's Law Dictionary* 450 (6th ed. 1990).

27. Thomas, *supra* note 41, at 36, 42-34.

28. John Irwin and James Austin, *It's About Time: America's Imprisonment Binge.*

29. Margery Fry, *Arms of The Law* 83 (1951). Fry refers to this group as "present-dwellers."

30. *Id.*

31. See, *e.g.*, Phillipson, *supra* note 1, at 61.

32. Sir Walter Moberly, *The Ethics of Punishment* 55 (1968).

33. *Bill Moyer's Journal: What Can We Do About Violence?* (PBS television broadcast, Jan. 9, 1995).

34. *Id.*

35. *Id.*

36. *Id.*

37. *United States v. Dunnigan*, 507 U.S. 87, 98 (1993).

38. Francis A. Allen, *The Decline of the Rehabilitative Ideal: Penal Policy and Social Purpose* 10 (1981).

39. *See supra* notes 24-28 and accompanying text.

40. John J. DiIulio, Jr. and Anne M. Piehl, *Does Prison Pay?: The Stormy National Debate over the Cost-Effectiveness of Imprisonment, Brookings Review*, Fall 1991, at 28, 34.

41. *Id.* at 28 (citing Edwin Zedlewski, *Making Confinement Decisions*, in *National Institute of Justice: Research in Brief* 4 (1987)).

42. Sir James Fitzjames Stephen, *A General View of the Criminal Law of England* 99 (ed ed. 1890).

43. *Oxford Latin Dictionary* 1578 (1988).

44. *Black's Law Dictionary* 1317 (6th ed. 1990).

45. Samuel R. Gross, *The Romance of Revenge*, 38 L. *Quadrangle Notes* 44, 49 (1995).

46. Friedrich Nietzsche, "Of the Tarantulas", in *Thus Spoke Zarathustra* 123 (R.J. Hollingdale trans., 1969).

47. Beccaria, *supra* note 13, at 49, 53.

48. *See* International Committee of the Red Cross, *Status and Treatment of Protected Persons*, in *Commentary IV Geneva Convention: Relative To The Protection Of Civilian Persons In Time Of War* 199-231 (Jean S. Pictet ed., 1958).

49. *Id.*

50. Sam Keen, *Faces of the Enemy: Reflections of the Hostile Imagination* 95 (1986).

51. Plato, *Protagoras* 22 (324b) (Benjamin Jowett and Matin Ostwald trans., Library of Liberal Arts, 1956)

52. Henry Weihofen, *The Urge To Punish* 143 (1956).

53. Fox, *supra* note 104, at 5; Howlet, *supra* note 104, at 12A; Mallia and Flynn, *supra* note 104, at 7; Stone, *supra* note 104, at 3A; Urschel, *supra* note 104, at 8A.

ESSAY 3

Freewill, Determinism, Genetics, and Punishment

"I am a part of all that I have met."[1]
Alfred Lord Tennyson, *Ulysses*

pproximately forty years ago, Francis Crick and James Watson deciphered the DNA molecule's struc-ture and forever changed the way human beings will look at themselves, each other, and how we will generally look at humanity. The discovery of how DNA replicates itself has given humankind a new prism through which to see the spectrum of its *self*. As a consequence, we will never be the same again.

> Genes are the chemical messengers of heredity. They are constructed of DNA (deoxyribonucleic acid) molecules, and carry instructions for synthesizing the protein that the body needs to function. DNA is composed of different combinations of molecules called nucleic acids, the sequence of which provides instrucitons for assimilating amino acids, the basic structral units of proteins. Genes determine our appearance, and every life process from the digestion of foods to defenses to disease. Genes also have some effect on behavior.

Indeed, today it is a rare newspaper or magazine that contains nothing about the human genome. Genetics is both big news and big business. Molecular biology is eclipsing many other fields of science. In so doing, however, genetics holds forth the possibility of overwhelming us socially, legally, and ethically. It is already apparent that the moral, ethical, and legal implications of genetic code discoveries test the boundaries of our laws' limitations. And, we in the social sciences must stop and consider what we will do in this new biologically sophisticated world. If our traditional codes and laws will not control, comfort, and protect our values, and if they cannot guide us through the "third wave,"[2] we must evolve a new moral response to meet the challenges that this new science of genetics represents to the values and rights we wish to preserve. But, to do so, we have not much time, and, the challenges are enormous.

Nonetheless, in the face of these stimulating challenges to existing social codes, I confess to a rather limited professional interest in the Human Genome Project specifically, and genetic research generally. I recognize, of course, the smorgasbord of moral, ethical, and legal issues that genetics research is creating. These issues, in turn, will provide philosophers, ethicists, and academicians from many fields with an intellectual and profes- sional banquet. As a social scientist and a penal theorist, I do not retreat from a need to sound the tocsin because, if resolved unwisely, these issues will only produce more exceedingly difficult questions for society to answer for years to come. For example:

> ➤ Is a removed gene, or a combination or recombination of genes, human life? If so, what form of human life is it, what are "its" rights, and who shall protect them?

> ➤ Should human life, whether created in a laboratory, cloned, or sustained, be marketed for research?

> ➤ After cells are taken from an individual for research, to what extent should the donor be able to exercise control over those cells? To what extent may science use the cells? What regulation or oversight is necessary to protect both the research scientist and the donor?

> ➤ Should a physician or other health care professional be liable for failing to perform tests that could have discovered genetically inheritable diseases, such as Tay-Sachs disease, sickle-cell anemia, Huntington's

disease, or beta-thalassanemia? What tests should be required of newborns? What may (or must) be done with the genetic information from those tests? How can privacy be assured for the socially sensitive genetic information derived from such tests?

➤ Once an individual is discovered to be genetically at risk for a disease, are relatives who are also at risk entitled to this information?

➤ If every cell after the first split following conception contains all the genetic information needed to identify the person, what are the implications?

➤ If persons with a certain genetic makeup seldom live beyond a certain age, should a prospective life insurer be entitled to discover that fact about an individual? Should laws prohibit discrimination in insurance coverage based on genetic information?

➤ If an individual carries a gene that predisposes that person to a disease, should a prospective health insurance carrier be entitled to that information? And, if so, what should the carrier then be entitled to do with it?

➤ Should new or altered life forms be patentable? If so, in what manner and to what extent?

➤ How will behavioral genetic data change our notions concerning the criminal justice system? Will information about predispositions to antisocial behavior that leads to crime compel us to reconceptualize our theories of criminology and penology?

I am delighted that discoveries in biomedicine may prolong our lives. I, for one, have so much left to do. I am also pleased that gene therapy may some day give my life a better quality, whatever its tenure, because I love life. As a penologist, and that having been said, my deep, but quite narrow, academic interest is in criminology, behavior, and in sentencing criminal law offenders. Indeed, my not-so-modest criminological and penological agenda is to transform completely the criminal justice delivery system. As a result, and as we enter the twenty-first century, I look to research from all the allied sciences, including genetic research, with a measure of hope, mingled with some anxiety. My hope is that this research might provide another variable in the total equation by which social scientists may determine the causes of, and practical remedies for violent criminal behavior. This narrow interest, however, plunges me into the most ethically challenging field of genetics, human behavior.

Even though science convincingly demonstrates that genes produce traits that compose the individual, my intuition as one outside the physical sciences is that no "magic bullet," no lone violence gene, exists by which we can manipulate and, thereby, control all violent crime.[3] Because genetic expressions depend upon the entire individual human ecology in which genes exist, I am not so naive as to think that gene therapy alone will stop crime.[4] I say "individual" human ecology because I am certain that no race, nationality, or ethnic group is "pure" enough, or physically isolated enough, to contain seeds of specific behavioral traits that the balance of the population does not. Only the rankest of racists would likely choose to espouse such nonsense. Stanford University geneticists Luca Cavalli-Sforza, Paolo Menozzi, and Alberti Piazza conclude that once the genes for skin pigmentation and physical stature are dealt with, "the differences between and among individuals . . . render[s] the concept of 'race' virtually meaningless."[5]

Moreover, I also find it preposterous that any statistician would consider skin pigmentation for example, as creating a genetically-based, statistically definable population for behavioral studies. Professor C. Ray Jeffery posits that the "so-called *black population* of the United States is so genetically mixed that conclusions based on group data cannot be applied to individual cases."[6] Professor Jeffery maintains that "(t)he concept of 'black' is a social and not biological concept."[7] Who, for example, is "black"? How "black" must one be to be included in the group? 100 percent African-American ancestry? 50 percent? 10 percent? I am delighted that many folks find their ethnic origins to be a source of pride and identity. So do I. I am proud that my ancestors were Norwegian. I doubt, nonetheless, that the slight difference between one who has greater skin pigmentation, or whose skin is freckled like mine, or whose hair is red, blond, straight, or nappy or, for that matter, who is tall, short, fat, or thin, means anything in isolation. Indeed, I am willing to speculate that discoveries in the field of biomedicine and genetics will place race-based populations for behavioral statistics into the category of junk statistics, placing social and other environmental factors into causal prominence.

Each individual's genetic menu is different, regardless of one's racial or ethnic ancestry. Genetic research is not premised on social class or racial matter, but can only examine the individual's genetic makeup. Dr. Gregory Carey, a behavioral geneticist at the University of Colorado, believes that:

> (G)enes do not fate behavior, they do not determine our behavior or make us act in a certain way. . . . They have a probabilistic effect that makes us more likely to act one way or another, but that action is always done in conjunction with the environment.

I recognize, nonetheless, that certain diseases are now identified with specific ethnic populations. For example, sickle-cell anemia is found with greater frequency among African-Americans and Tay-Sachs disease among Ashkenazi Jews. Hence, we cannot completely discount the possibility that such ethno-specific identifications someday may be made with respect to other genes as well, or that some genetic behavioral trait, may be found with greater frequency in some ethnic statistical groupings than in others.

It seems equally apparent that we cannot look myopically to social and environmental models for all the answers. Biology accounts for something. As individuals, we share gene sequences in common with other individuals that may predispose us to certain behavioral traits when coupled with other environmental, physical, and social factors. "I think we are going to have an explosion of understanding," says David Valle, of the Howard Hughes Medical Institute at the Johns Hopkins University. "For example, the causes of mental disorders certainly include environmental factors, but biological psychiatrists believe the genes are whispering an important message, if only it can be heard."[8]

If genes are whispering message to us, we must listen. Indeed, if any factor or factors are whispering or shouting to us, we must listen. What we learn about one individual offender may help us in therapeutically *treating* other offenders who share the same genetic characteristics and other determiners, rather than our current practice of simply *punishing* them. Additionally, isolating the genetic factors from the environmental factors may help us in our quest for a rational sentencing scheme and may help in developing therapeutic and preventive techniques. We may be able to determine whom to punish and how, and whom to treat, and what should be our treatment methods. Therefore, criminology and penology must not shy away from whispered answers to its biological questions, from boldly seeking the truth, from testing all hypotheses, and from being honestly attentive to answers. We can, and I think that we must, do something more than punish all offenders. To assist us in doing more, I am hopeful that biomedical science will provide social scientists with some answers, but therein also lies my anxiety.

I feel a political anxiety because we Americans increasingly feel that we are losing control of the forces that govern our lives. Indeed we may be. Thus, the notion that genetic actuators may also have a directional role in the quality and duration of our lives is disturbing. This fear requires that we reach a new equilibrium between ourselves, each other, and our environs. This will be difficult.

I feel a socio-legal anxiety as well. As science provides answers, legal philosophers, ethicists, and sociologists must struggle mightily with the moral, legal, and social implications of the answers, and question the best uses of, and responses to, the answers. At the same time, if the answers threaten or test current moral and social standards, social science must strive to maintain, and if necessary rebuild human dignity and respect for each other, and struggle to protect the new minorities that genetic science could create. This may be difficult. Moreover, the answers that genetic study identifies must find their way quickly into the fabric of our civil and criminal protections. We have no choice. But, such timely integration may prove to be especially challenging, because change is difficult even with scientific fact to support it. We do not easily give up our grasp on the known present, to embrace the uncertain future, especially in law.

Development in science is nearly the antipole of development in law and the legal system. In science, a proposition is stated as law only after scientists observe a phenomenon, hypothesize about it, test it, and, rule out alternative hypotheses with repeated observation and testing. In addition, the proposition must be generally accepted by the scientific community and substantiated by colleagues and critics who are able to replicate the original studies. In contrast, within the legal system, and more specifically the criminal justice delivery system, the law posits and defines the norm, and hence, the deviations. Hypotheses need not be accurate, only popular. Indeed, under the case law method, a decision reached by a court in one case is law and likely to control many others until determined by the court, a reviewing court, or the legislature to be wrong. There is little science, and scientific method is virtually unknown, in the development of the common law.

Common law is jurisprudentially bound by precedent, which extends behind us like a giant sea anchor on the end of an ever-lengthening line. Statutory law is changeable only by legislatures who seemingly sail with the winds of popular opinion. As a consequence, in many areas, the rigidity of law thus politically established, places it in great conflict with science, which itself yields constantly to new discoveries. This conflict is most marked in the unreality of American criminal law, which must presume that individuals have a totally free will. This presumption depends for its legitimacy upon the fiction that we all *choose* to do what we do. Indeed, Americans are so preoccupied with punishment that we pay almost no attention to, and consequently receive little guidance from, either the social or physical sciences, which may have divergent views about free will, determinism and the factors that influence human behavior. We seem to shun any evidence that might help us explore the genesis of crime for fear that the evidence will indicate that our historical bases for criminal sentencing and our penal modes themselves have fundamental shortcomings. It is difficult to admit mistakes. Even worse, elected officials fear being perceived as *soft* on crime. As a result, American criminal law and jurisprudence rely upon an unscientific, underdeveloped theory of personal responsibility and blameworthiness.

Ostensibly, we want to avoid inflicting punishment upon a fellow citizen unless he is truly responsible for his acts. For example, we do not want to execute or punish the mentally impaired or the mentally immature. Our focus on individual responsibility has nothing to do with whether the accused actually

performed the illegal act or is dangerous; indeed, both may be true. We simply draw the line at killing or punishing an individual who draws sympathy from us for being a child or having a mental deficiency, and so we say he lacks the requisite degree of *legal responsibility* for his acts. However, criminal law degrades this reality and creates a myth of punishment by crudely drawing the line so as to include nearly the entire population of offenders within the *responsible* category, regardless of why one committed the crime or what may actually be necessary to prevent a reoccurrence. I disagree and opine that to gauge moral accountability accurately, the law must presume that each person possesses *some* level of responsibility and accountability for his actions. Then, it should methodically explore what I refer to as the full "ecology" of the crime and the offender. There is a reason, or more likely reasons, why some people obey the law and some do not. Criminal law and penology must question why this is so and honestly seek answers to penological problems because the penal myths society currently relies on are clearly failing us.

None of us can escape the fact that our lives, in significant measure, have been shaped by antecedent causes such as other people, external events, developmental milieu, and, as we are discovering, our genes. Unfortunately, we are not, as Immanuel Kant contended, free and rational sovereigns in the "kingdom of ends."[9] Indeed, few philosophers continue to believe that. Behavioral science now acknowledges that a mind-boggling array of factors and agents may influence an individual's behavior, including prenatal, perinatal, and neonatal effects; fetal derangements; parents' marital status; siblings and one's station among them; home environment; the neighborhood in which one was raised; church; school; nutrition; injuries; health; and economic and cultural status. This list of agents also grows commensurately with the time we spend thinking about it. Indeed, behavioral influences are legion. Moreover, the discoveries in the exploding science of behavioral genetics point, with ever-increasing frequency, towards including inheritable or genetic factors in the equation for an offender's behavior and in the causes of crime. New knowledge of the human gene may soon be used to develop clinical tests to determine if some individuals have genetic characteristics that predispose them to violent behavior towards others. Human behavior may be influenced, shaped, or even determined by antecedent events and factors outside the will—or it may not. *This* is the eternal debate over free will and determinism with recent modifications based on scientific discoveries about our physical, environmental, and mental makeup. This is Spinoza's determinism in genetic clothing.

Baruch Spinoza, 1632–1677, was a Dutch metaphysician and an early advocate of intellectual freedom. He was one of the most significant philosophers of the European *Rationalism.* Spinoza defined God as the only true cause, and stated that human liberation and perfection is found ultimately in referring all affections to God. As a philosophical pantheist, he was appreciated neither by the Christians nor the Jews, and was expelled from his synagogue in Amsterdam. To maintain his intellectual independence he rejected offers from universities as compromising patronages, and instead ground lenses to support himself. He died of tuberculosis.

Determinism, one of the oldest philosophies, teaches that all human events proceed from other eventual causes, and that whatever happens to us is connected in some fashion to other, past and future, events. In an early expression of the doctrine, Spinoza asserted that "all things are determined by the necessity of divine nature for existing and working in a certain way."[10] Spinoza's "God's will" variety of determinism contended that nothing happens without being caused by God and that everything happens as it was caused. Many others joined Spinoza, modifying his theories somewhat, but nonetheless holding to the belief that we are somehow under God's minute control. Still others, Rene Descartes and Immanuel Kant among them, rejected this view in favor of a belief that we each are in control of our futures and must fully account for our actions both to God and to our cultures.

Gottfried Wilhelm von Leibniz was born in 1646 in Leipzig. He studied law, philosophy, and mathematics and he received his doctorate of law at the age of 20. He served as a court councilor and librarian at Hanover until his death in 1716. Leibniz was one of the leaders of German thought in the 17th century. He believed that the essential characteristics of the bodies in the universe were forces. He broke substance into an infinite number of units of force, which he called "monads." Leibniz's universe was not mechanical—it was dynamic and alive, with each monad in harmony with the others. By means of his theory, Leibniz felt that he had reconciled contemporary science with the moral values of his day.

I, however, prefer Leibniz's more liberating approach. For Leibniz, free will did not mean totally unimpeded volition or the true power of choice. Instead, he believed that the will is hobbled, varying with the individual, to behave in accordance with one's internal nature and original purpose. He contended that our individual volition is limited by the parameters of the determiners at work in our lives. We each have freedom just sufficient to make adjustments within what we were otherwise semi-destined to become.[11] Leibniz attempted to forge a compromise, to reconcile the deterministic view of man's nature with the notion of a free will. Although I am not so sure that he succeeded, perhaps with the assistance of modern genetic science, he might have.

I believe that each of us has a capacity for free choice. I believe we have a free will, but that it is limited to a degree that depends upon each person's genetic, physical, mental, and emotional makeup, the sum of all life experiences, and the environment and circumstances in which the will is being exercised. I believe that none of us has a wholly unfettered free will. At the same time, I believe that no one's actions are totally determined by either God or nature. This view, however, places me at odds with contemporary trial procedure, which aims simply to determine if the accused is guilty, and contemporary penal philosophy, which aims simply to punish the guilty, regardless of why he did what he did.

The determinist says simply that what will be will be, because each person's behavior is shaped entirely by non-willed events, or by God. On the other hand, the indeterminist believes there is room for some autonomy because all events are a consequence of an exercise of free will.[12] Today, however, few philosophers are comfortable at either polar extreme. Nonetheless, few will deny that a person's present status is at least in some part the consequence of his environs, of the past actions either of himself or of others, of the decisions made both by himself and others, and of the genes he inherited. Consequently, most theorists believe that a persons's future state will result, at least in some part, from non-willed external and physical determiners.

Today, the real philosophical debate is not about absolute, bipolar choices, but countless shades in between. Instead of debating nature or nurture, or *whether* "free will" or "determinism" control, contemporary philosophers debate the *extent* to which "free will" *and* "determinism" shape each person's destiny. Free will and determinism are now considered just the opposite ends of the street on which each of us live. In other words, we each occupy an elastic and perhaps a transient position somewhere along a free will-determinist avenue. Each of us occupies a different position depending upon all the agents, vectors, and factors, symbiotically and antagonistically, at work in our lives. Psychologically and physically each of us dwells in a life-state in which no one is wholly free, nor is anyone's fate wholly determined. We are equals in at least one respect, the theoretical freedom to make our own decisions. We are unequal in at least one respect—practically, each of us has a different psychological and physical inheritance, and environmental and external forces impinge upon our free will in different degrees, providing each of us with a different context and situation in which to exercise our wills. Thus, theoretically or conditionally, we are equals—circumstantially, we are not.

However, although we philosophically recognize the degrees to which a person's will is both free and determined by many factors, the philosophical basis of American penology is still Cartesian and Kantian. As a result, our penology experiences grave difficulties with any degree of determinism, whether environmental or biological. Like Descartes, Americans believe that "since my will is free, since antecedent causes do not necessitate my actions, I am responsible for my actions."[13] Similarly, we are content with Kant's morality, which also rejected any notions of determinism as incompatible with the full accountability of all persons. In the Kantian and Cartesian models of punishment, because all persons were morally autonomous, always free to act or refrain from acting, they could be punished for transgressing a rule without that punishment violating any humanitarian notions of justice, because as free moral agents we deserve to be punished if we err. Both Descartes and Kant believed that a just God could only punish humans for committing a sin if they were morally free to refrain from sinning. Accordingly, the law, as God's mortal agent, was empowered only to do the same thing. That is, penology assumes that punishment is just because man, possessing a free will, is the author of his acts, and can thereby be held responsible for them and face punishment for his bad acts.

As a consequence, the dominant theory, or philosophical basis of sentencing, retribution by punishment, requires that, with limited exceptions, we reject any notion of determinism. In fact, we adhere to a view of free will that presumes that each individual has an equal moral obligation and capability that makes all individuals equally responsible and equally accountable for their actions. These presumptions enable us to justify moral and penal condemnation of the offending individual. Thus, our penology is based upon the fundamental premise that each person, regardless of situation and context (whether a resident of the inner city, a tree-shaded suburb, or a family farm), is equally free to choose between right and wrong, free to do acts that are legal or illegal, free to abide by the law or disregard it, and hence, free to change. Aside from the myth of *responsibility* that we continue to embrace, the law largely ignores why someone becomes an offender and presumes that, no matter how enmeshed in the criminal society he is, he can choose somehow to escape his society, break bonds with his past and present, and "go straight." The law assumes that this reversal can be achieved with no compulsion except punishment for exposed error, without institutionalized, positive incentives and assistance, and without reward for obedience. This theory, however, is almost totally antithetical to any form of realistic, scientifi-cally-based sentencing because all too few of us are in fact like the Kantian, "equally free and rational sovereigns in the kingdom of ends." Even though some of people appear to operate within the established parameters of this mythical, legal responsibility, and some, others simply have been unable to substitute rational choices for their immediate impulses.

> I use the term *ecology* to refer to all the factors that impinge upon or have an effect on our behavior. Thus, in order truly to understand crime and the criminal offender, I believe that we must consider and analyze any and all the factors that contribute to, or for that matter, prevent crime and criminal behavior—the full "ecology" of crime.

Although social scientists no longer seriously contend that human behavior is unaffected by non-willed factors, American penology, in its preoccupation with justifying our punitive re-sponse to crime, chooses to ignore both the antecedent and immediate factors leading to crime and the whole ecology of the criminal offense and the offender. Penologically, Americans are libertarian and are comfortable to maintain that the only circum-stantial equality to which all offenders are entitled is the equality of opportunity, that each person has an equal opportunity to obey the law and must bear the consequences for failing to do so. Equality of opportunity in our social republic, however, is insufficient to provide a stable economy, a stable work force, and a stable political equilibrium. As a result, we employ a whole panoply of equalizing statutes. Equality of opportunity is, I submit, a similarly inadequate basis to determine the appropriate treatment for criminals. Indeed, equality of opportunity itself may be a myth, for most of us realize that "the legal roads to approved social goals are still far from equally open to all."[14] The biological, environmental, and psycho-logical equipment of all humans is unique, and their behavioral expressions of this uniqueness are likewise different. Nonetheless, we deem all offenders to be the same and, concerned only with what they have done, not with what may be needed to prevent a reoccurrence, we punish them.

Punishment, however, has the potential to modify an offender's behavior only to the extent of the lesser of his actual capacity to change, and, the extent of his perceived freedom to change. The fact is that the freer people are, or the freer they perceive themselves to be, the more effective punishment will be as a deterrent to them. The more that a person's acts are determined, or perceived to be determined, by forces external and/or exclusive of the individual's will, the less effective punishment or coercion will be. Moreover, if an offender perceives his acts to be determined by forces other than his will, any sentencing scheme other than a correction-based, remedial sentencing structure based upon reasons why an act was performed is useless to effect change.

Time changes our environs. Time changes us. And to keep abreast of the changes of time, we must change our philosophy. As the Tofflers point out, changing the structure of society also changes its peoples' character: "Behavior is not a matter of conscious decision as to whether or not to follow the social pattern, but one of wanting to act as they have to act."[15] As American society changes, as Americans change, penology must likewise adapt.

Must some persons act in counter cultural ways, commit antisocial acts, and thereby become offenders? If so, should society not desire to root out the negative compelling factors and penology think of something besides punishment to correct them? If not, should not the sentencing practice identify those offenders who are free to choose and deal with them accordingly, perhaps by a measure of punishment? Let us recognize that some citizens are not free to choose at all, and others are free in varying degrees only. Then, in response to their bad acts, sentences should encompass a combined response that includes, in addition to punishment, therapeutic methods of treatment. Better yet, the criminal justice delivery system should encourage proactive elimination of the reasons for the crime whatever they may be, thereby preventing offenses.

Unfortunately, however, our jurisprudence does not recognize the benefit of a response calibrated to the criminal, and fails to differentiate in its standards between culpability, (where determinism is properly rejected) and corrections, (where I suggest determinism must be explored as a legitimate source of an offender's actions and a basis for determining an appropriate remedy). If we wish merely to punish without regard for either the fairness or the pragmatic results of our measures, Kant and Descartes offer as good a theoretical foundation as any other philosopher. I do not want to give the impression that I believe I can look down my philosophical nose at such great thinkers as Kant and Descartes. It is just that American penology embraced their philosophy long ago, and has failed to keep up with changing mores, emerging and evolving ideas, the changing context of the social situation, and the results of scientific research. American penology did not advance to the next generation of thinkers, or the next, but instead it stood still. I submit that we cannot, as either Descartes or Kant would have us do, simply separate the intelligible world from the world of sense, or the mind from the body. The bodily ship may indeed be inseparable from its emotional or intellectual pilot. If the system wishes to correct behavior to the best of its ability, it must discover the true reasons why that person misbehaves, and then respond to those reasons. Whether a factor is an excuse for an action is a question for the culpability portion of a trial. Whether a factor is a reason for an action is a question for sentencing, for tailoring a remedy, and for preventive intervention and correction. If we wish to correct bad behavior, we can no longer rely on Kant and Descartes and the notion of an absolute free will. We need a new Leibniz armed, however, with the discoveries of contemporary science.

American philosopher Jacob Needleman states that American culture has "generally tended to solve its problems without experiencing its questions" and that we are unprepared for the "shock of genuine questioning."[16] I quite agree. Although it is perhaps easier to live by closely guarded and historically nurtured prejudices, we can no longer do so. Science teaches us (Needleman says Socratic philosophy teaches us[17]), to penetrate behind the world of appearances for cause and effect and to understand and accept, not merely to manipulate, the answers we find. Human actions are probably about as predictable as any other natural event. But to make our best attempt at predicting human behavior, we must pay close attention to external actuators, to cultural milieu, to character, and to genetics. The free will with which each of us is supposed to be endowed must be modified by our twenty-first century understanding of determinism, and how it is changing our concept of the free will with which we are each presumptively endowed. Then we can challenge Kant's reign over American penology, and develop a new theory by which we can reconcile the free will/determinism dilemma.

First, we might ask how the newest notions of, and discoveries about, the human genome will affect our new penological theory. Given that there are external and non-willed actuators, do some predispose us to fall prey to our tempters? As we look for actuators, will we find help in our genes? Are we about to discover new answers to nagging questions about the freedom of the will? The twenty-first century may indeed offer a new therapeutic ray of hope. We are coming to the realization that the physical and psychological equipment we inherited through our genes may play a role in some behavior. Some of us may be better equipped physically and mentally than others to resist certain behavioral temptations. Leibniz believed that individuals "behave in accordance with their original purpose which they received from the beginning through God's creation."[18] If God's human creation includes genes which predispose individuals to certain behaviors or which make some of us more susceptible to environmental and sensory stimuli, perhaps a Neo-Leibnizian theory is now appropriate for our penology.

Tangentially, we have recognized such a Neo-Leibnizian theory for generations. Perhaps intuitively as well. Who among us has not been displayed by a proud (or despairing) relative as having received some trait from one side of the family tree or the other? Neither myth nor lore is scientific in origin. Nonetheless, it usually has a measure of empirical data for support. Genetic influence on animal behavior is beyond dispute.[19] There is empirical evidence of the influence that genetic factors have on human behavior from the study of separated monozygotic (identical) twins.[20] Case studies have also shown that criminal behavior in parents will increase the likelihood that their offspring will commit offenses.[21] P.A. Brennan, S.A. Mednick, and J. Volavka concluded that this "relationship is due, in part, to genetic transmission of criminogenic characteristics."[22] Travis Hirschi similarly suggests that, at least in part, crime may be a family affair. He posits that the "criminal records of parents and siblings are among the best predictors of one's own trouble with the law."[23] Nonetheless, I do not believe that we can accurately draw much from this data because the populations and cohorts used shared both genes and environment. Thus, more study is necessary to definitively ascribe the traits to the family environment, the family genes, or some combination thereof. Although scientists will become better able to isolate genetic from environmental factors, the incorporation of helpful scientific data into the law will not come easily.

The historical interrelationship between genetics and the law, as a combination or synthesis of socio-legal controls with science, has been almost universally negative. Until now, the genetic data we have used, or more accurately misused, has not helped criminology and penology advance convincingly. Moreover, for the first part of the twentieth century, human behavioral genetics was reviled, ridiculed, and sometimes feared. Even today, choosing to believe that all behavior has solely a willed etiology and an environmental embryology, many people condemn any suggestion that genes can help explain behavior. Others understandably fear that an emphasis upon the discoveries in biomedical science might detract from efforts to seek whole ecological explanations for crime and full explanations of cultural problems. I do not. Even if genetic research concludes that genes have nothing at all to do with criminal behavior, this conclusion is helpful to the penologist and the criminologist because we can then confidently emphasize that only environmental, instrumental, and social factors should be considered in crime prevention and treatment.[24]

Perhaps others cannot help but feel that they have heard it all before and fear that genetics will again be used as a basis for invidious discrimination.[25] Quite frankly, I wrestle with some of the same concerns. As we enter the twenty-first century, researchers are increasingly turning to genetic information to help us understand the complexities of human behavior.[26] Even if this scientific research is wholly objective (I am willing to grant that it is or will be), if we were to ignore the social and cultural variations among us, the discoveries could play into the hands of those who merely want to reinforce their racial and social stereotypes. The result would be a giant step backwards for mankind. It is natural to fear that knowledge of human genetics may be misused for base and venal purposes, because it has been, and it likely *will* be if we are not vigilant. I submit, however, that ignorance can also be used for illegitimate purposes and, I firmly believe, with more culturally destructive results.

Genetics and gene research will not just go away because some of us do not like the concept, or fear what its discoveries might tell us about our biological heritage. We *will* have to cope with, and *must* decide how we will use, the results of genetic research to better mankind. Genetics, gene research, and its discoveries are here to stay whether we like the idea or not. Yet, many questions remain unanswered. What are we going to do to prevent illegitimate uses of these discoveries? How are we going to protect persons who are *marked* by genetic research, either as possessors of a gene that indicates a predisposition to an illness or to violence? There is a point in the embryology of a proposition beyond which it can no longer be ignored or deterred and must be explored to its conclusion. This is what I call the *breakpoint* of an idea, theory, or proposition. We must question not what will be discovered, for we are beyond that breakpoint, but what will we do with the discoveries once they are made. The genetic genie is out of the bottle, and it will not go back.

Penologists must decide what happens now that science can ascribe to genetics a role in behavior. Furthermore, we must decide what *should* happen if it can ascribe to genetics a role in violent criminal behavior. Brennan and Mednick would probably phrase the last as a question, "What should happen now that science *can* ascribe such a role to genetics?" They contend that their survey of twin-studies "has demonstrated that genetic factors can and do influence certain types of criminal behavior, and recidivistic criminal behavior in particular." They conclude that "biological factors must be added to the list of causes of crime."[27] I am not willing to go quite that far. It appears to me that the more that physical science learns about genes, the more that social science must correlate behavior with environmental factors to determine *cause*. Nonetheless, how American penology should handle such information is where it gets scary. This is where searching for answers becomes a weighty moral and professional obligation. We all must prepare ourselves for the real shock of where this questioning leads, for the answers will undoubtedly lead to new fundamental scientific, social, civil, and criminal laws. Our way of life is destined to change. The challenge to the social sciences is morally and ethically to guide that change.

Fortunately, the lessons of history and the failures of quasi-social science provide some guidance. The new penologist does not look for a quick fix in *utopia,* but seeks long-term solutions from *dystopia.* We look with cautious optimism toward biomedicine, not for the solution, but for some help. Behavioral genetics may have once been held to a lower scientific standard, perhaps because of the sheer number of genes, generalized ignorance, and the seemingly unlimited possibilities presented to us by human behavior, but this is no longer true. Behavioral genetics is held to stringent scientific standards and cannot be easily dismissed. Advances in genetics and biochemistry have given behavioral researchers new scientific tools in their search for clues to human behavior. Although the genetic answers may remain on the horizon for now, within view but out of reach, geneticists, biologists, and criminologists are beginning to believe that genetic science can help shed some light on the perplexing enigma of violent criminal behavior, and provide penologists with a ray of hope for therapeutic remedies, where now only prison and punishment exist. I welcome that ray of hope, for I view therapeutic justice as the most probable avenue for penal improvement.

Human behavioral genetics has been considered by some geneticists to be the unwanted child of biomedical genetics research, which primarily seeks to discover the genetic components of, and therapies for, diseases. Genetics as a behavioral tool is difficult for many geneticists to accept, and is downplayed by others. Geneticists understandably fear being identified with the old eugenicists who prostituted the science for their own biased agendas. Nonetheless, behavioral genetics has inherited, and will continue to inherit, at least the residue from biomedical research. This fallout from medical research, combined with behavioral researchers' use of sophisticated quantitative methods, has given the field new respectability. Now, some scientists believe that important discoveries about the human genome, including the identification of genes that may predispose towards violent behavior, are not far off. So, criminologists and penologists must determine what we going to do with these discoveries. They must decide whether it will use the science or allow it to use them. If genetic discoveries are used wisely, fairly, and humanely, not to *determine* social policy, but to help *inform* sentencing decisions about reasons why one acts as one does, I predict that behavioral genetics will one day achieve a measure of acceptance in penal theory. The positive impact of all this information, both biological and environmental, upon crime prevention could be enormous, if we are cautious and jealously guard our human dignity from compromise by those who just look for the quick fix and who are not concerned with protecting our fellow citizens from misuse.

The Human Genome Project may well be the most significant organized research endeavor in the history of medicine. I believe that, not only in the physical sciences, but in philosophy, sociology, and theology, as well, the shock waves from the discoveries in biomedicine will be the greatest since those felt from the theories and conjectures of Charles Darwin. So I am not surprised that the controversy that will surely continue to surround this science is of commensurate dimensions. Thus, we in penology must ensure that the *social aspects* and the racism of Social Darwinism are excised from (and indeed, as I earlier explained, I believe it will be refuted by) this science.[28] The Human Genome Project's goal is not only to map human genes, but to learn their relationship to approximately four thousand diseases. If the project's research enables scientists to map and translate the one hundred thousand-plus genes that contain the extensive, but individual-specific, blueprints by which each human being is built, it will have a profound impact on our understanding of diseases, and how to treat or prevent them. The legacy of the project may enable future biomedical research to provide us with detailed data about human DNA. The project and its companion, neuroscience, will increasingly occupy the attention of biomedical research and will revolutionize the practice of medicine far into the next century. Dr. Edward Pierce, of Gannon University, calls this the "Last Frontier" of science. He predicts that, because of genetics discoveries, the practice of medicine will increasingly occupy itself with presymptom therapy for diseases and that genetic medicines and therapies will evolve the profession

of medicine, with increasing velocity, towards therapeutic prevention, with disease treatment decreasing commensurately.[29]

The project may be an important behavioral research endeavor as well. There is little doubt that the discoveries from this
project will produce an increased awareness and understanding of
the role that genetics and the inheritability of certain human traits
plays in human behavior. For example, it seems clear that certain
traits associated with violence are influenced by genes.[30] The
National Institutes of Health (NIH) has built a database relating
deficiencies in neurotransmitters such as serotonin, a chemical in
the brain that facilitates transmission between neurons, to aggression and suicide. Now the NIH is working on a project to identify
genes that control the manufacture of serotonin and to study how
they are related to factors that may predispose people toward
aggressive behavior.[31] Behavioral genetics is here to stay.

Nonetheless, human behavioral genetics is in its infancy.
Behavioral genetics remains ambiguous and controversial, and
may still be a distance from formulating a scientifically sure,
biological component to use in equations through which we might
discover the reasons for violent criminal behavior. Certainly, there
are likely to be only a few antisocial human traits that are one
hundred percent heritable. Regardless, by identifying the biological reasons for why some of us do what we do, and for why we
become of what we are, and by pointing towards social and
environmental factors where biological reasons do not exist,
science does empower criminologists to isolate the role that genes
play in behavior and, with greater accuracy, to search out the actual
reasons why individuals act as they do. If we adopt an interdisciplinary approach, science permits penologists to be optimistic that
new therapeutic help is not only on the visible horizon, but is
attainable. As Dr. C. Ray Jeffery says:

> (T)oday the neural sciences are totally chang-
> ing our view of human behavior, as well as the
> treatment and prevention possibilities which are
> available from neurology, neuropsychiatry, brain
> chemistry, and neuropharmacology. That is why an
> interdisciplinary [approach] to [the] study of] vio-
> lence is so badly needed.[32]

Our genes cannot, however, be viewed as providing a myth-like, social scapegoat for deep-seated cultural problems. Complex social problems will require complex, and probably largely social, answers. Whatever may be the role of genes in human behavior, I am sure that environmental feedback is a significant ecological overlay to the biological components of the will. Regardless of the genetic subtleties we each have been given, what our social world reverberates to each of us may well be the strongest determining signal in predicting how any of us will respond to either a perceived peril or a potentially gratifying opportunity.

Similarly, a person's genetic inheritance cannot be expected to provide an excuse for what that person does. Decisions about criminal sentences and remedies for crime should not be conflated with determinations of culpability and guilt. There may be no *excuse* in law for what a person does, even if there is a *reason*. It is that *reason* that sentencing science must focus upon, without regard for what it might discover about offenders and ourselves. It is that *reason* we must respond to in our penology, regardless of what comfortable myths of punishment we must cast aside in the process, or else we will not progress at all. To find that *reason*, penology must enlist the support of and accept assistance from the entire field of allied sciences.

Although many have tried, we in criminology and penology have not yet discovered how we can, with any accuracy, distinguish the voluntary act from the compelled or compulsive act. Leibniz was right, however: penology must recognize that both our fund of options and our ability to exercise them is limited. I am sure Leibniz would not suggest that the law excuse offending behavior as the product of theological, biological, or uncontrollable determiners. Nor, indeed, would I. I press for graduated levels of moral and legal accountability upon all offenders, commensurate with the sum of all factors impinging upon their behavior. With equal emphasis, however, I think that a neo-Leibnizian would conclude that punishment should not be considered the reason for the trial and, therefore, must not be considered the entire penal answer. As our Supreme Court said "Criminal punishment by government, although universally recognized as a necessity in limited areas of conduct, is an exercise of one of government's most awesome and dangerous powers."[33] Some of that danger could be avoided if *safety*, not mere *punishment*, were to become our criminal justice delivery system's product. Now as we enter the twenty-first century, there is little choice but to view all the evidence and use all the sciences, both physical and social, to *prevent* crime and either to transform offenders into responsible citizens with a commitment to our culture's rule of law, or else to contain them separated from our culture.

I doubt that genetics will ever become *the* answer to behavioral questions and must not be given such prominence. Indeed, "geneticists do not argue for a direct causal link between a given gene or genes and behavior, including criminal behavior."[34] Even if genes influence either passive or aggressive tendencies, whether, and how, those character traits are expressed in overt behavior surely depends to a significant degree upon the actor's social and physical environment. Yet, despite the role of the environment, genes remain one of the factors we must examine for possible answers to the questions raised in the study of human character.

As I explained above, people's character, including their tendency toward (or resolve) in avoiding violence or other forms of antisocial behavior, is unquestionably molded by varying combinations of education, environment, training, experience, chance, genetics, and a host of other variables. This ecology of the crime and the offender remains to be fully explored. In penology, however, we can no longer cling to the irrational notion that all individuals are equally free and equally able to resist the temptation to disobey. Few of us fully understand why we act as we do, especially when it comes to making highly charged, emotional, or spur-of-the-moment decisions. Most human decisions simply are not made in a deliberate, Cartesian fashion. Our environment, subliminal and genetic influences, and the sum of life's vicissitudes may well be the real determiners at work in a number of antisocial and criminal acts. The exact role that each factor plays must be isolated and studied for what it can contribute to our understanding of humanity and the proper role of legally sanctioned punishment.

The early decades of the twentieth century have been called "the decades of the physicist." Some of the brightest minds and greatest scientists were studying physics, and the discoveries they made were new and exciting to the world.[35] One particular discovery from those decades changed the world forever—atomic fission. Physics and atomic science, unfortunately, were leagues ahead of any moral inquiry into the implications of their discoveries. We are still haunted by the specter of Armageddon which that lapse almost created. We must not make the same mistake again. The Human Genome Project will be educating scientists, professionals, and the general public as it progresses. James D. Watson, Director of the project, asked that five percent of its budget be dedicated to study the ethical, legal, and sociological impact of the project's genetic discoveries.[36] Penology is a portion of that study. All of science, whether social or physical science, must be held to account for itself morally. Our culture must learn how to use science wisely and morally and to harness its power. Thus, we must all be on guard because the period between the diagnostic and the therapeutic discoveries will leave a window of opportunity for the unscrupulous, which will cause trouble for the individual and for the science unless we anticipate both the misuses and the uses of new discoveries.

Our scientists have theories as varied as the sciences themselves. Among behavioral scientists, there are tangled threads of diverse and conflicting theories that have yet to be woven into a recognizable pattern. Some theories focus on genes, some on the brain, some on nutrition, some on pollution and toxins, and some on social and environmental factors. All such theories have some form of scientific data upon which to base their claims for legitimacy. Data in one area alone, however, is not enough. The goal, after all, should not be just to amass scientific data about a problem. Sentencing theory and practice cannot rely solely upon answers from the physical sciences as panaceas to complex social problems it must address. Crime is all about behavior, and behavior is all about humans. Our goal, as contemporary penologists, criminologists, and legal philosophers, is the full integration of all disciplines to focus upon real wisdom and understanding of human weaknesses and strengths.

Some states have already begun to collect DNA samples of convicted offenders for later uses. Other states are now developing DNA databases of their convicted offenders by requiring that they submit to DNA testing, raising a host of other legal and constitutional concerns. In addition to using this information as tracking data, it may also be the beginnings of a database to explore commonalities among crimes and offenders. Hence, although it may assist penologists to develop the whole ecology of crimes and offenders and help scientists identify areas ripe for genetic research, the legal ethicist must continue to ask what human cost this will impose. We must rule science and not be ruled by it. In the final analysis, all we have in civilized culture is our humanness, and we must foster that which feeds it.

The treatments for cancer, the vaccines for polio, and the cures for a myriad of diseases that once plagued us did not just appear. They came about because some of the best and brightest scientists, professionally and socially motivated and properly funded, applied themselves to the task. Unless America makes an identical or greater commitment to discovering the causes and cures of violent behavior, substance abuse, and other offensive, antisocial acts, crime will continue its negative impact on American culture and will continue to bleed our economy. The costs of crime are enormous. In addition to the billions it takes to house America's prisoners, the billions more to detect, arrest, and try offenders, the cost of goods stolen, and the other hidden costs of crime, there is an entire *crimin-economy* that sells Americans billions of dollars worth of devices to prevent crimes or protect property. In addition to the police forces paid for by our taxes, most businesses and industries have private security forces to augment the public forces. Of course, we pay for these additional security efforts in the increased cost of goods sold. Crime is a big and costly business and the businesses supported by crime are also too costly.

The behavioral component of all studies and research projects performed in all the sciences must be allied and arrayed in pursuit of the causes of and cures for crime. I suppose there is a temptation in every scientist to treat other sciences as mere suffixes to their own. The discoveries of contemporary science in all fields, however, show the fallacy of this benign (or sometimes malicious) ignorance. The integration of all disciplines is fundamental to understand the complex enigma that is human behavior. Americans can no longer afford either the human or the material cost of any ignorance about the reasons for, that is to say, the full ecology of, crime.

Arnold Toynbee, a great historian, says that the history of a civilization is always a story of challenge and response. An examination of the myths and religions a civilization developed and drew strength from also reveals a story of how it responded spiritually and morally to its current crises of life and the challenges by which it felt threatened. Our civilization now faces a great challenge because genetic research is on the very cusp of progress that may influence our civilization in an almost chain-reaction fashion. This is a defining challenge and, in the history of our civilization, will mark a historical demand for an appropriate moral and legal response. We cannot stem progress. We cannot frustrate change. We must use them. Legal philosophers, ethicists, and legal academicians must have a specific vision of what our civilization ought to be and do, have a professional obligation in the face of the challenge posed by genetic research to engage in "real questioning" of its results. Yes, we must challenge genetics ethically. But I emphatically add that we must also determine if it can help us to live longer, to live healthier, and perhaps to live more peacefully with each other. The tragedy of American philosophy is that historically we have paid insufficient attention to it. As a result, we are bound to be intimidated by the great chasm between the ideal of what we want to be and the reality of what we really are. We in penology can, however, rise to that challenge. Indeed, we must respond positively and affirmatively to the challenge.

Plato was right when he stated that our philosophers must become *kings* or, alternatively, our *kings* must become philosophers.[37] Of course, America has no kings as such. But the challenge is clear. We do have leaders: religious, cultural, scientific, and governmental. We, the leaders, must be the philosophers, must develop the wisdom to use discoveries wisely, and must foster the proper moral response to protect the values these discoveries threaten. That would be Plato's admonition and is the solemn challenge of leadership. Science must remain culture's faithful servant, not its technocratic sovereign. Unguarded reliance upon science invites injustice.[38] The cold hand of science cannot balm the aching soul, cure a moral malaise, correct social inequality, staunch the bloody flow of personal hatred, nor correct the criminal offender. For that, we need each other, each caring for the other.

It would be pleasant to believe that Kant and Descartes were right that you and I are fully in control of our rational choices and that thought, reason, and a free will are what make us human.[39]

However comforting these beliefs are, they defy what we at the close of the twentieth century now know about human nature and some of what we are discovering about human genetics. Penology must recognize this because it is both morally indefensible and penologically unproductive simply to punish those whose actions are determined, at least to the degree their actions are truly determined. It is equally immoral and penologically indefensible to fail to demand a full accounting from those whose actions are not determined. Our new understanding reminds us that the only long-term remedies for crime are prevention, diagnosis, and treatment. Alexis de Tocqueville said that Americans are Cartesians, but have never read Descartes.[40] De Tocqueville was right. Perhaps if we read Descartes, we would challenge his thinking on free will and adopt a theory closer to Leibniz's.

I am not a biological determinist, nor am I an environmental, social, or theological determinist. Both genetics and human behavior are far too complex and interconnected with the environment in which each is expressed. So, I suppose I am a Neo-Leibnizian. I suggest that human free will is really just maneuvering room within the parameters created by the facts and factors of life. I believe that American penology must recognize this and carefully study mankind's entire nature, including his intellectual, sensory/environmental, and biological nature. Whether a creation of God, of nature, or of both, the human genome contains answers to questions about our existence as yet unasked. But the questions will be asked and the answers are forthcoming. Our challenge and our task is to be ready to respond to them.

ENDNOTES

1. Alfred Lord Tennyson, *Ulysses*, in Alexander W. Allison, et al, *The Norton Anthology of Poetry* 704 (Norton 3d ed 1983).

2. Alvin Toffler, *The Third Wave* 381-459 (William Morrow 1980) (discussing mankind's "psychological breakdown" in the wake of technological changes and social upheaval and concluding that the responsibility for reconstruction lies within each of us as human beings).

3. Dr. David Comings, a medical geneticist at the City of Hope Medical Center in Duarte, California, shares this opinion. He states, "My feeling is there is certainly no 'gene' for criminal behavior. There are (only) genes that predispose people to an increased frequency of impulsive-compulsive behaviors and that put them at greater risk of being involved in criminal behavior." Natalie Angier, *Disputed Meeting to Ask if Crime Has Genetic Roots, N.Y. Times* C1, C6 (Sept 19, 1995) (quoting Dr. David Comings). See also, generally, Chi Chi Sileo, *Violent Offenders Get High on Crime, Insight* 12 (May 2, 1994) (reporting that criminal behavior is not purely a result of genetic makeup).

4. Dr. Evan S. Balaban of the Neurosciences Institute in San Diego notes, "I have a strong opinion that biology doesn't have anything to contribute to public policy discussions about crime in society." Angier, *N.Y. Times* at C6 (cited in note 5) (quoting Dr. Evan S. Balaban). See also Sileo, *Insight* at 12 (cited in note 5). See also Adrian Raine, *The Psychopathology of Crime: Criminal Behavior as a Clinical Disorder* 47-49 (Academic Press 1993). But see H.G. Brunner, et al, *Abnormal Behavior Associated with a Point Mutation in the Structural Gene for Monoamine Oxidase A*, 262 *Science* 578 (1993); Virginia Morell, *Evidence Found for a Possible 'Aggression Gene,'* 260 *Science* 1722 (1993); P.A. Brennan and S.A. Mednick, *Genetic perspectives on crime*, 1993 *Acta Psychiatr Scand* 19 (Supplementum 370); Arturas Petronis and James L. Kennedy, *Unstable Genes—Unstable Mind?*, 152 *Am. J. Psych.* 164 (Feb. 1995).

5. Jerome G. Miller, *Race*, "Applied Science and Public Policy: The Case of the Criminaloid," excerpted from Jerome G. Miller, *Search & Destroy: African-American Males in the Criminal Justice System* (Cambridge 1996).

6. C. Ray Jeffery, *Genetics, Crime and the Cancelled Conference*, 18 *The Criminologist* 1, 6-8 (Jan-Feb 1993).

7. C. Ray Jeffery, *The Genetics and Crime Conference Revisited* 2 (1995) (unpublished manuscript on file with the author).

8. Harold M. Schmeck, Jr., "The Future of Genetic Research", in *Blazing a Genetic Trail: Families and Scientists Join in Seeking the Flawed Genes That Cause Disease* 50, 51 (Howard Hughes Medical Institute 1991). See also Diana H. Fishbein, *Prospects for the Application of Genetic Findings to Crime and Violence Prevention*, 15 *Politics & Life Sci* 91, 91-93 (Mar 1996).

9. Immanuel Kant, *Groundwork of the Metaphysic of Morals* 100 (Harper Torchbook 1964) (H.J. Paton, trans).

10. Samuel Enoch Stumpf, *Socrates to Sartre: A History of Philosophy* 259 (McGraw-Hill 2d ed 1966) (quoting Spinoza).

11. *Id.* at 258.

12. At the furthest philosophical extreme is the doctrine that chance totally rules destiny and that life is just a roll of the dice.

13. T.Z. Lavine, *From Socrates to Sartre: The Philosophic Quest* 125 (Bantam 1984).

14. Wootton, *Crime and Criminal Law* at 24 (cited in note 21).

15. Toffler, *The Third Wave* at 397 (cited in note 2) (quoting Erich Fromm).

16. Jacob Needleman, *The Heart of Philosophy* 6-7 (Knopf 1982).

17. *Id.* at 22-26.

18. Stumpf, *Socrates to Sartre* at 268 (cited in note 17).

19. See Tabitha M. Powledge, *The Genetic Fabric of Human Behavior*, 43 *BioScience* 362 (June 1993); Melissa Hendricks, *The Mice That Roared, Johns Hopkins Mag.* 42, 42-46 (Feb 1996).

20. See Tabitha M. Powledge, *The Inheritance of Behavior In Twins*, 43 *BioScience* 420 (July 1993). For another sampling of twin-criminality studies, see Brennan and Mednick, 1993 *Acta Psychiatr Scand* at 19-26 (cited in note 6).

21. See generally James Q. Wilson and Joan Petersilia, eds, *Crime: Twenty-eight Leading Experts Look at the Most Pressing Problem of Our Time* (ICS Press 1995).

22. Patricia A. Brennan, Sarnoff A. Mednick, and Jan Volavka, "Biomedical Factors in Crime," in James Q. Wilson and Joan Petersilia, eds, *Id.*

23. Travis Hirschi, "The Family," in James Q. Wilson and Joan Petersilia, eds, *Id.* 121.

24. I See also Tabitha M. Powledge, *Genetics and the Control of Crime*, 46 *BioScience* 7 (Jan 1996).

25. See generally, for example, Dorothy Nelkin and M. Susan Lindee, "Genes Made Me Do It: The Appeal of Biological Explanations," 15 *Politics & Life* Sci 95 (Mar 1996); Robert L. Bonn and Alexander B. Smith, "The Case Against Using Biological Indicators in Judicial Decision Making", 7 *Crim Just Ethics* 3 (1988); Dr. James Bowman, "The Road to Eugenics," 3 *U Chi L Sch Roundtable* 491(1996).

26. See Paul R. Billings, Jonathan Beckwith, and Joseph S. Alper, "The Genetic Analysis of Human Behavior: A New Era?," 35 *Soc Sci Med* 227 (1992).

27. Brennan and Mednick, 1993 *Acta Psychiatr Scand* at 25 (cited in note 6).

28. See Charles Darwin, *On the Origin of Species by Means of Natural Selection.* (Atheneum 2d ed 1972). See also Will Durant, *The Story of Philosophy: The Lives and Opinions of the Greater Philosophers* 267-68 (Simon and Schuster 1961).

29. Dr. Edward Pierce, Unpublished Letter to Author (on file with author).

30. See, for example, Raine, *Psychopathology of Crime* at 47-79 (cited in note 6); Gregory Carey and Irving I. Gottesman, *Genetics and Antisocial Behavior: Substance versus Sound Bytes,* 15 *Politics & Life Sci* 88, 88-90 (Mar 1996); Morell, 260 Science at 1722-23 (cited in note 6).

31. Jane Ellen Stevens, "The Biology of Violence", 44 *BioScience* 291, 293 (May 1994). A recent Associated Press wire story had preliminary results of other experiments in which mice lacking a single gene needed to manufacture another neurotransmitter, nitric oxide, became uncontrollably aggressive. *Aggression Gene Probed in Mice*, Assoc. Press (Nov 22, 1995). See also Hendricks, *Johns Hopkins Mag* at 42-46 (cited in note 31).

32. C. Ray Jeffery, Unpublished Letter to the Author (Nov 22, 1995) (on file with the author).

33. *Ginzburg v. US*, 383 US 463, 477 (1966) (emphasis added).

34. Jeffery, *Genetics and Crime Revisited* at 1 (cited in note 8).

35. For an excellent work on the scientific, political, and cultural milieu of this period and its discoveries, see Richard Rhodes, *The Making of the Atomic Bomb* (Simon and Schuster, 1986).

36. See, for example, Laurie Garrett, "The Dots are Almost Connected. . . Then What?," *L.A. Times* 22 (Mar 3, 1996); Gordon Dillow, "Toward a More Perfect Human?", *Orange Cty Register* E1 (July 2, 1995).

37. Plato, *The Republic,* Book V, 203 (Modern Library, 1982) (B. Jowett, trans).

38. See generally Jacob Needleman, *Sin and Scientism: An Interview with Jacob Needleman* (Robert Briggs 1985).

39. See generally Rene Descartes, *The Passions of the Soul*, in John Cottingham, Robert Stoothoff and Dugald Murdoch, eds and trans, *The Philosophical Writings of Descartes*, Vol I (Cambridge 1985).

40. Alexis de Tocqueville, *Democracy in America,* 429-33 (Anchor, 1969) (J.P. Mayer, trans).

ESSAY 4

Is Prison an Appropriate Response to Crime?

A pack of hounds, and a number of men, dogs, and horses will spend hours in hunting a fox, which, when caught, is abandoned to the dogs without an observation. The criminal, when fairly run down, is sentenced by the judge, and turned over to another set of authorities utterly unconnected with and unrelated to him, as if the law had nothing whatever to do with a man after asserting its right to punish him.[1]

James Fitzjames Stephen

Before I became a judge in 1981, I took no issue with the role of the American prison in our criminal justice delivery system. Indeed, I gave little thought to it. I assumed, as many others do, that whatever happened to criminals as a result of their crimes mattered little to polite society. It was the offender's own fault that they were imprisoned. *They* simply did not matter to *us*. I was wrong! It did not take me long to realize that simply imprisoning offenders for a specified period of incarceration, the duration of which was almost arbitrary, was an insufficient penal response to crime. Something else, something more, had to be done. It *is* their own fault (at least to a significant extent) that they are in prison, and I firmly believe that each of us must account for our own behavior and face a stern response if it contravenes the law. Moreover, I also believe that punishment must be an important component of correction, whether of our children or our fellow citizens. Further, I believe that prison, in some form, must continue to play a role in our response to crime.

That being said, I have concluded after thousands of criminal sentences, that the current system is a failure. As a primary response, in many cases a solitary response, to crime, the contemporary American prison[2] will simply be inadequate to meet the challenges of crime in the twenty-first century.

Where did the modern concept of *prison* originate? Why does prison even exist in its current form? Is prison adequate to meet the current and future needs of our criminal justice delivery system? If prison is failing us, why? Finally, what is necessary, and what can we do, to repair our criminal justice delivery system? In this essay I will explore these questions and a few more.

First, some history. A little over two hundred years ago, two significant events happened in America. Both were reforms, both took place at approximately the same time, both occurred in Philadelphia, both constituted drastic changes in their respective professions, and, both built upon profound new ideas that evolved during the first half of the eighteenth century.

The first occurred when a prominent Philadelphia physician, Dr. Thomas Bond, became concerned about the suffering of the city's physically and mentally ill citizens. The mentally ill were left to wander the streets; the physically ill, to die in their homes. Dr. Bond took his case to another public-spirited Philadelphian, Benjamin Franklin, who convinced the Colonial legislature to establish the first hospital in what was soon to become the United States. Medical science was so primitive then that the Pennsylvania hospital, and the others that followed soon thereafter, were often little more than institutions in which to die. It was, however, a new concept, a new beginning, and an event upon which the medical profession could build.

The second event, contemporaneous with Dr. Bond's initiative, was the result of efforts by Philadelphia Quakers, who established the Walnut Street Prison. The prison was a new concept: a penitentiary. It was a place where the offender was isolated to enhance inner reflection and did penance for offending society's rules. It was also a reformatory, whose overall scheme was a concentrated effort to reform the offender and effect positive behavioral change. The prison was designed to be more than a static human warehouse of society's miscreants. Like the hospital, the purpose of the prison was to treat its occupants.

The Philadelphia model of prison came into being in response to punishments, which were then outrageously cruel. Eighteenth century jails throughout the world were primarily for pretrial detainees, the towers and dungeons reserved for important offenders or those convicts whom the kings or courts wanted to keep alive. When convicted of a crime, the ordinary offender was usually punished by humiliation, banishment, torture, mutilation, or death. Punishment was usually a spectacle, following the axiom that a sentence executed in secret lost much of its value. Flogging, branding, mutilation, hanging, beheading, dunking, quartering, tearing flesh from one's body with red hot pinchers, dismembering, and burning at the stake were all punitive methods employed throughout the seventeenth and into the eighteenth centuries.

The savagery of law and the severity of punishment, however, are less the product of citizens' brutality than of their ignorance of, or indifference to, the offender's suffering, coupled with a sense of frustration created by a government that fails to protect them. Hence, when a government's punishment becomes too savage and indiscriminate for the public's level of compassion, it rebels. The spectacle of the offender's suffering caused the witnessing public to *transfer* their mercy from the criminal's absent victim, to the criminal himself who was now suffering before their eyes. Torturers and executioners were booed, and some incurred wrath, and even violence, from the spectators. A myth of punishment was exposed. At least when they viewed the punishment firsthand, the public did not hate enough to do hateful things, even to criminals. It is not surprising then, in light of the public attention that had been drawn to the public execution of punishment, that it was not governmental intervention, but rather public outrage that ultimately led to the reforms throughout the world that resulted in the development of prisons such as Walnut Street.

Albert Camus wrote a brilliant essay called "Reflection on the Guillotine" about the execution of a man who had committed a particularly shocking homicide and robbery of a farmer and his entire family. The crime, the criminal, and his capture were widely publicized, and it was generally agreed that even decapitation was too mild a punishment. Camus' father was so particularly incensed that, for the first time, he wanted to witness the execution. When he returned home, he refused to speak of it and became physically ill. Camus wrote,

> [H]e had just discovered the reality concealed beneath the great formulas that ordinarily serve to mask it. Instead of thinking of the murdered children, he could recall only the trembling body he had seen thrown on a board to have its head chopped off.[3]

A myth of punishment was exposed, and it sickened him.

Punishment had gotten out of hand and change was necessary. Among the European philosophers who led the reform was Cesare de Beccaria. To him, the prison had become a necessary and humanitarian alternative to abuse, torture, and capital punishment. Earlier punishments required few public resources. The convict, if he survived the predations within prison by fellow inmates, the isolation, flogging, torture, banishment, or mutilation, was released. In contrast, correction required control for extended periods. The concept of extended enclosure was born. Prisons were now necessary. To the European philosophers, prison would provide a place to divert some convicts, away from the contemporary forms of penalty.

Beccaria also introduced the idea of analogical sentencing: that each crime had a criminal valence, or value, to which criminologists could assign an equal (equi-valent) prison term. As Michel Foucault added, "[t]o find the suitable punishment for a crime is to find the disadvantage whose idea is such that it robs forever the idea of a crime of any attraction."[4] Beccaria sought to make the penalty conform so closely to the nature of the crime that when one thought of a crime, the consequences of committing it were indelibly fused together with the act itself and would be immediately considered.

Francois Vermeil further developed this notion and called for penalties that were formed out of the content of the crime.[5] Accordingly, those who abuse liberty will be deprived of their own. Those who abuse the law will be deprived of the benefits of citizenship—including civil rights. Those guilty of usury must pay fines. Those who steal will suffer confiscation of their own property. Finally, those who kill will die.

Le Peletier de Saint-Fargeau, also an analog-formalist (one who believed that the penalty must be an analogy of, or formed by, the crime) added:

> Exact relations are required between the nature of the offence and the nature of the punishment; he who has used violence in his crime must be subjected to physical pain; he who has been lazy must be sentenced to hard labour; he who has acted despicably will be subjected to infamy.[6]

Although these ideas never fully caught on, they were considered by the Quakers in establishing Walnut Street Prison, and they formed a basis for the Quakers' penal reforms.

Two hundred years ago at Walnut Street Prison, behavioral correction was a condition of release, and this condition was made known to the prisoner. When a new prisoner arrived, prison administrators received the crime report, detailing the circumstances surrounding the crime, a summary of the examinations of the defendant, observations about his behavior, and suggestions for correction. Guards observed and noted the prisoner's conduct daily.

At Walnut Street Prison, prisoners were segregated more according to their dispositions than their crimes. Walnut Street housed essentially four categories of offenders. The first, those who were dangerous even in prison, were held in solitary confinement. Repeat offenders, whose potential for rehabilitation was in doubt, but who were not sufficiently dangerous to warrant solitary confinement, were in the second category. The third category comprised those who were deemed not to be habitual offenders. The fourth category consisted of the totally benign. The categories

were not static. As one improved, one could *graduate* to the next
level. Common to each category, however, was the requirement
that the offender convince his jailers he was suitable for advance-
ment *before* advancing to the next category and suitable for
reintroduction to society *before* he was released from prison.[7]

Labor formed a fundamental component of the Walnut Street
Prison's primary purpose which was treatment. Work was compulsory and labor demands kept the prisoners constantly occupied.
Labor was a means of inculcating both the ethos of the market
economy and the morals of daily social life. The prison was
partially financed by the work of the prisoners, who were rewarded
according to their productivity. The Philadelphia Model viewed
prison quite forthrightly as "a machine for altering minds."[8]

The common feature of Walnut Street, and the other new
penitentiaries patterned after it, was their primary goal of correction. Prisons were not, nor were they designed to be, warehouses
for human refuse. Prisons primarily attempted to save the individual, if possible, and contain him if necessary. Preventing crimes
was declared to be "the sole end of punishment."[9] These new
prisons treated mind, body, and soul. Outside inspectors, who
were the first parole boards, interviewed prisoners and helped
decide the correctional method to be employed. They evaluated the
inmates' progress and made recommendations about release dates.

To the Quakers, God mattered. During his study of America,
Alexis de Tocqueville was struck by our ability to blend success-
fully what he called the "spirit of religion and the spirit of liberty."
He said:

> Liberty regards religion as its companion in all
> its battles and its triumphs, as the cradle of its infancy
> and the divine source of its claims. It considers
> religion as the safeguard of morality, and morality as
> the best security of law and the surest pledge of the
> duration of freedom.[10]

Correction under the Walnut Street concept included a strong
sense of, and attention to, the spiritual side of the person, and the
need to develop and nurture it to induce positive behavioral

change. Bible study and prayer were encouraged, and ministers were invited into the prisons.[11] Finally, much like the research hospitals and cancer centers of today, early prison administrators and inspectors viewed their prisons as laboratories to learn about people and to experiment with methods of behavioral correction.

The difference between what has happened in the intervening time in the prisons and what has happened in hospitals that began so auspiciously two centuries ago, is remarkable. In hospitals the change has been dramatic. The hospital of today would hardly be recognized by an eighteenth century doctor. The surgeon has progressed from lancing boils to open-heart surgery and organ transplants. Autopsies are performed on their failures to discover precisely why the patient died. Clinicians within the hospitals have begun to accept and apply the discoveries of their colleagues in the several sciences. Doctors undertake research in the hospitals, and discoveries quickly find their way into patient care and treatment.

Treatment for the mentally ill, and psychology generally, was also crude in the eighteenth century. Indeed, it was not until the nineteenth century that insanity was even considered a mental disease, and not the work of demons. In the intervening two hundred years, we have begun to understand human beings as having dynamic combinations of behaviors. Discoveries in psychotherapy, psychopharmacology, and neurophysiology have combined to treat disorders and mental illnesses and to correct behavioral misfunctions and dysfunctions. Continuing etiological discoveries have brought psychology from the shadows of medical science to a separate discipline capable of treating, caring for, and curing the mentally ill, and correcting disordered human behavior.

Research has shaped the hospital into an institution for cures, rather than a mere repository for the sick. Hospitals and asylums, far from being places the physically ill go to die, or in which the mentally ill deteriorate, have become institutions from which we expect medical and psychological miracles—and often get them. Since Thomas Bond developed the hospital, medical science, and psychology have surged forward together. By studying the dying, medical science learned how to help us to live. By studying the diseased, medical science learned how to keep us healthy. By studying the offenders penology can likewise learn how to keep us safe and how to make people obey.

Curiously, Jeremy Bentham's concept of the *Panopticon* has returned. Bentham's Panopticon had the cells arranged in tiers amphitheater-like, so that a guard seated at a central desk could observe the prisoners through their cell windows. The new prototypical prisons in Pennsylvania have pods, or blocks that, like petals on a flower, branch out from a central electronic and visual monitoring station, whose operators can observe the prisoners and see all the cell doors.

But, what about prison? What happened to the Philadelphia concept? Progress stopped, and for some reason, reversed itself. Why and where did this happen? The nineteenth century became the "Time of the Great Incarcerations," when the mentally ill were concentrated in asylums, the children were concentrated in schools, the workers were concentrated in factories, and the criminals were concentrated in prisons.[12] The American prison is what the Tofflers call a "second wave" institution, operating only to respond to the needs of a manufacturing-type culture. It is highly structured, fully synchronized, and utilizes mass containment as an end in itself, rather than as an opportunity to perform individual correction. Prison responds only to the needs of our waning manufacturing, second-wave culture. Progress is leading America, willing or not, into the information age and into a vastly different cultural landscape of ideas. Our penology and our prisons systems must change to prepare for it.

The early American prisons were models for the world. Alexis de Tocqueville's trip to America in 1831, in which he gathered the data to write his epic work *Democracy in America*, was sponsored by the French government to study and report on prisons in the United States. Indeed, Tocqueville's report was the source of prison reform in France. The Quakers must be praised for developing the renowned institution of the American prison two hundred years ago.[13] *We* must be blamed for failing since then to improve on the idea, for failing even to sustain the Quaker's idea, and then carry it forward. Instead of progressing from the Quakers' idea, American penology corrupted the best elements of it and embraced its worst. The deficient performance of our criminal justice delivery system (notably, our legislation) stems from the fact that it has failed to advance beyond fulfilling the visceral demands of society. The public is largely ignorant of what goes on in prison, and viewing prison in the abstract, sees prison conditions, no matter how horrible, as the pain that an offender must suffer in retribution for his transgression. Some prisoners view it all too often as just a condition to be endured at worst, or defeated at best. Neither the public's nor the offender's view is acceptable.

The "pain" of incarceration is theoretically supposed to be sufficient first, to punish and teach the offender a lesson, and second, to reinforce the social fabric and the rules that civilize us. This is what it is supposed to do, but does not. The pain to the offender is often neither sufficient punishment to prevent the offender's return to crime, nor to reinforce the morals of the law-abiding public. Statistics show quite the opposite. Recidivism in some prisons, running over 80 percent, is testimony to the fact that prison prepares its graduates for crime, while failing to impress upon them that they should not return.[14] Nor has the imprisonment of millions of offenders civilized us. The opposite may well be true. What we do to offenders is in reality a significant indicium of the soul of our culture. America's penology is out of step with the rest of the civilized world. Importantly, it is also out of step with dominant themes in American history. The de-socializing and solely punitive experience of prison may be creating more harm than it ameliorates. Prisons may be a necessary evil; they need not, however, be unnecessarily evil.

Prison as a penalty in and of itself, instead of as a means of correction, is a creature of evolution, not design. The penality of detention is more like a malignant growth on a legitimately conceived penitentiary system. We have mistakenly abandoned that which formed the basis for the prison (correction) in favor of a perverted form of banishment. It is time to return to the path of progress. Prison reform is not new. Prison is *intended* to be reform. The temptation to punish is great, however, and because punishment seems, at least in the short run, simpler to conceive and easier to execute than reform, it has lured us from the somewhat more complex correctional task we began 200 years ago. Justice James Fitzjames Stephen called the human-warehouse form of jail ". . . one of the stupidest penalties that ever was devised."[15] I quite agree. The human warehouse is not what the prison was designed to be. It is not what prison should be. Correction must again become the theoretical centerpiece of sentencing law, the practical goal of sentences, and the program of prisons.

> "Prisons have become our nation's substitute for effective public policies on crime, drugs, mental illness, housing, poverty and unemployment of the hardest to employ. In a reasonable culture we would not say we had won the war against disease just because we had moved a lot of sick people from their homes to hospital wards. And in a reasonable culture we would not say we have won the war on crime just because we have moved a lot of criminals from the community into prison cells."
>
> Source: *To Establish Justice, To Insure Domestic Tranquility: A Thirty Year Update of the National Commission on the Causes and Prevention of Violence.* The Milton Eisenhower Foundation, Washington D.C. 1999.

A number of years ago the National Advisory Commission on Criminal Justice Standards and Goals recommended that prison be considered a last resort for correctional problems. It said prisons had failed to reduce crime, were not deterring, provided only a temporary protection for society, and, although they did change the offender, it was usually for the worse. The Commission concluded that "the prison . . . has persisted, partly because a civilized nation could neither turn back to the barbarism of an earlier time nor find a satisfactory alternative."[16] Caught between a failed past and an unknown future, we did nothing.

"Toughness" may not even matter. Twenty-five years ago a group of Stanford University psychologists assembled a group of normal college students and divided them into guards and inmates in a mock "prison" set up in the basement of one of the university buildings, in what has become known at the "Stanford Prison Experiment." The results were shocking. Otherwise normal students were quickly transformed into psychologically traumatized and emotionally broken "prisoners." The mock "guards" too, although many were avowed pacifists, readily internalized their randomly assigned role. From gentle and caring men, they became sadistic and harassing captors, who devised sadistic and degrading ways to treat their mock prisoners. Although the experiment was to last for two weeks, they had to abort it after less than a week, illustrating the power of situations and their context.

Source: "The Past and Future of U.S. Prison Policy," *American Psychologist,* July 1998, p. 708.

Until now, we have successfully swept the problems of prison under the social carpet and left them hidden from the public. We legal professionals have deluded the public by our silence (or worse, our ignorance) into thinking that punishment and a base desire for revenge will somehow stop crime. Politicians have done worse and routinely capitalize on "toughness" by proposing long-term imprisonment as a panacea for crime control. Unfortunately, it is not. We can no longer ignore the problem of a correction system that does not correct and a justice delivery system that is not just. The lumps under the social carpet are too large to ignore.

Our system of punishment does not work, is unjust, and is respected by few: not by the citizen, not by the victim, and, significantly, not by the offender. For some offenders it does not punish, for most it does not deter, and for certain it does not rehabilitate. Even the stigma of prison means nothing to many, when many or most of their peers have "done time," and they are part of the criminiculture itself. Prison, for all too many, may only present a temporary, otherwise tolerable, condition of life. For these offenders, the American prison is neither punitive enough nor rehabilitative enough to effect positive change. It does quite the opposite. For these people, the culture of prison teaches new antisocial skills, or reinforces their own anticultural values, and their own violent code of honor. In this strange penal alchemy, the contemporary prison is a perverse crucible that burns off all but the dross.

For other offenders for whom there is yet hope of redemption, however, prison is only despair. There is no progress built into either the sentence or the system. Real self-help or improvement is systemically frustrated at worst, and rendered difficult at best. There is no up and out, only down and in until one believes there is nothing to lose. Sometimes even life is no longer worth the seemingly never-ending wait for the offenders who have received sentences that are excessive. For these offenders, the American prison has destroyed hope. I submit that an excessive sentence is unjust to the offender to the extent that it goes beyond its necessity or function. We must face the fact that when a law or a system perpetuates an injustice upon any individual, whether that person is the victim or the offender, that *law* and that *system* have become instruments of oppression, not justice. That individual, and all who are aware of the injustice, will lose faith in the law and the system. I cannot say it better that De Tocqueville, who wisely said, "[j]ustice is the end of government. It is the end of civil society."[17] I wholeheartedly agree. A fundamental tenet of my beliefs is that vengeful sentences are inhumane, unjust, economically wasteful, and socially destructive. Prison, or its alternative, must be instead, functional and pragmatic, and its purpose must be to contain the dangerous offenders and to correct the rest. This will produce a just result for both society and victim, and a just consequence for the offender.

Prisoners are now easily forgotten because most of us prefer to forget unpleasantness. Someone has been victimized, someone hurt—but, the newscast is over! The scene has ended. The offender is swept off to prison and the social catharsis is complete. That, however, is not the end of the drama. For the nearly two million in prison, it is just beginning, and their role goes on day after day.

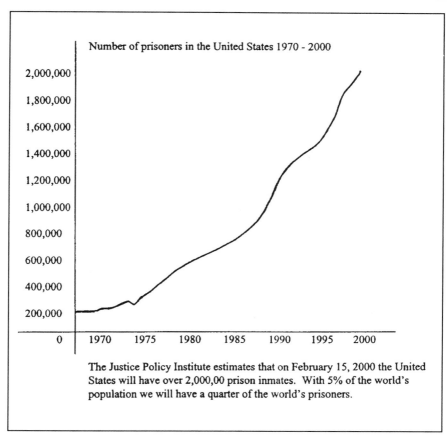

Number of prisoners in the United States 1970 - 2000

The Justice Policy Institute estimates that on February 15, 2000 the United States will have over 2,000,00 prison inmates. With 5% of the world's population we will have a quarter of the world's prisoners.

It is becoming increasingly more difficult to sweep two million convicts and millions more ex-convicts under the carpet. In 1995, prisons and jails housed approximately 1.5 million offenders. In addition, nearly 4.9 million persons were under some form of sentence supervision, such as probation or parole.[18] It is getting more difficult to hide the failures of a system that creates more criminals and perpetuates more crime than it corrects. At the beginning of the twenty first century, all too many prisons are an international embarrassment. Worse, they are punitive, correctional, economic, physical, psychological, and humanitarian failures.

America simply can no longer afford the twentieth-century concept of prison, where it can cost well in excess of $100,000 to house one prisoner for one year. With two million persons incarcerated at any one time, the cost is staggering. Moreover, current per-prisoner costs cannot be used to project accurately the future cost of incarcerating offenders. Although it may cost as little as $7,500 per prisoner in some jails, these costs reflect the much lower construction costs of decades ago when many jails and prisons were built. It takes little foresight to see that the costs of new prisons will far exceed the costs of established prisons and drive the per-prisoner costs up dramatically. For example, the new federal penitentiary in Florence, Colorado (known as the Alcatraz of the Rockies) opened in 1994 at a cost of $60 million, or $123,751 per bed (as cells are euphemistically called).[19] An education at America's best universities costs substantially less. I do not mean to imply that mere education of offenders is an acceptable alternative to imprisonment. Nevertheless, what I do state with confidence is that if we can educate the minds of nonincarcerated Americans for less than this price, we can afford to employ the efforts of the finest educators, psychologists, and social scientists to induce change in the minds of offenders, turning them away from the culture of crime, and towards productive life. Furthermore, with the purposeful application of necessary resources, Americans can expect success.

Although the direct costs of our system are staggering, even more astounding are the indirect costs. Americans spend billions of dollars on a secondary front for products and services to protect themselves from those whom our government has failed to correct or contain.[20] Most corporations employ their own police or security forces. Retail stores have their own security or anti-theft patrols. Americans buy home security services to protect their homes, car alarms and such devices as the "Club" to prevent car-jacking, and untotaled millions of dollars for handguns to protect their persons from predation, intrusion, and harm. Moreover, we spend unquantifiable sums of money covering the increased cost of merchandise from theft, and to compensate manufacturers and vendors for losses from crime. Crime costs Americans millions of dollars each year. In our courts, prisoner lawsuits alleging claims for various forms of unjust acts account for a substantial percentage of case-filings, all, of course, costing taxpayers millions more dollars. In sum, the secondary or indirect financial and social cost of failing to correct offenders, settling instead for "warehouse-style" prisons is too expensive and too wasteful to allow it to continue. The mission of the prison must be changed—prisons must contain offenders until they are corrected. I take great issue with the old chestnut that the "time must fit the crime." This is a corruption of the notion that is well-nigh axiomatic in behavioral and penal science that the remedy must fit the *degree of guilt*.[21] For the corrected, or those who need no correction, we must release them before prison contaminates them. For the dangerous and predacious, they must be contained.

As our predecessors began to do two hundred years ago, we can and must begin again to treat the offender, not just the crime. Prisons must again become laboratories for social scientists and workshops for behavioral practitioners with their output becoming a safe and productive citizen being returned to society. I recognize that, at least initially, a significant number of prisoners are pathological offenders who cannot be corrected and must simply be abandoned or banished to the system, and therein contained as economically as possible. I am equally certain that there are those who do not need to be imprisoned at all. I am not alone in these beliefs: A national poll taken by the Wirthlin Group in 1991 that found that four out of five Americans favored a nonprison sentence for offenders who are not dangerous.[22]

I firmly believe there are a significant number of cultural offenders now in prison who can be changed. Dr. Gertrude Barber, of Erie, Pennsylvania, who developed the much-copied concept of the "sheltered workshop" for the mentally retarded, bases her universally successful theory on the premise that everyone is capable of some productive endeavor.[23] She determines, and then starts with the talents of each individual, however limited, and builds upon that base. Her clients must participate, and are made to realize that they have value, and, developing self-esteem. We, too, must start with the talents and limitations of each offender; and, if we ever wish to release them, offer a coherent plan to assist them in a truly correctional process. And then, of course, we must require that *they* change before they are even considered for release. The American penological system, both at sentencing and in prison, must begin to offer this option to sentencers and offenders alike. This will require substantial changes in direction, human resources, and attitude.

The Dr. Gertrude A. Barber Center's Mission states that:

"[A]ll individuals are people of God with feelings, emotions, needs, and capabilities unique to these persons and their heritage. In a world where all men differ, individuals should have the opportunity to develop their fullest potential.

It is further believed that all persons can learn, have the right to learn, and must be provided with experiences for growth and development: spiritually, morally aesthetically, socially, physically and educationally.

It is further believed that education is a continuing process from infancy through adulthood.

Following this credo, Dr. Barber has given dignity to many mentally-challenged persons, who otherwise would have been ignored, and socially, educationally, and culturally left behind.

From Michael J. McQuillen, Ph.D., *A Legacy of Love*, Erie, Pa.

It will be worth it. Irwin and Austin, in their classic work on sentencing, stated:

> What may be . . . surprising is that a majority of all persons sent to prison, even the high-rate offenders, aspire to a relatively modest conventional life and hope to prepare for that while serving their prison sentences.[24]

It is axiomatic that a pilot cannot truly learn to fly jets while on the ground. Nor can an offender who is culturally deficient develop culturally acceptable behavior in the septic social system of the average prison. We must provide more than mere care taking to offenders who have proven dramatically that they require more, much more. They may indeed require vast corrective measures. The prison correctional process must rigorously train every offender in at least the basics of what is expected, and the threshold skills that are required, of all citizens in our culture.

I am not sure how many of us have a compassionate view towards offenders.

I am sure that society must create a new model of compassion and helpfulness for those offenders who are candidates for correction and eventual release. We must because it is necessary. We must because most of them will once again become our neighbors.

We cannot create gentle beings by treating people cruelly. We cannot recreate humane natures by treating people inhumanely. We cannot teach respect for others by destroying self-respect. We cannot foster trust in an atmosphere of fear. Do we foster compassion by a system that shows none? We gain nothing by rancor, regardless of why we discipline either child or criminal offender. The fact is that there is little to be gained from imprisonment except enclosure and the opportunity to work on the behavior of the offender. It *is* an opportunity because we have this individual in our grasp as a convicted offender.

Millions more offenders are not caught, so we lack the same opportunity with them. It is painfully obvious that we cannot control crime by simply punishing those whom we catch, convict, and imprison. But at the rate of 500,000 incarcerations a year, we can begin to require that these offenders change, we can direct our efforts to facilitate in the receptive offenders a positive behavioral change. And then, we can turn our efforts and resources toward prevention.

Unfortunately, what little we gain from imprisoning offenders, currently we squander. This must stop. If Austin and Irwin's study is correct that prisoners genuinely hope for a conventional life, it is to our advantage to foster and nurture that hope, and to institute a program for them that *cures*, rather than reinforces, his criminality. If offenders have abandoned conventional life, if they will not assume the responsibilities of our civilization, if they are not willing to accept the vision of what it means to be "American," then the criminal justice delivery system must get them out of culture's hair, and allow its citizens to feel, and be, free. If, however, the offender wishes to change, the system must if necessary, assist him (or at least not deter him) from that endeavor. If the offender is willing to become a citizen and rejoin our culture, he must be encouraged to do so.

Human behavior is intensified in the insular life, and it is not surprising that prisoners, who are among the least socially skilled, the least physically and emotionally healthy, and the most susceptible to influence, *are* influenced by prison and fellow offenders. Prison is a schoolyard of the socially unskilled, which teaches one how to survive and thrive in a violent anti-culture. It is a reverse cultural Darwinism. The prison experience, unless rigidly controlled, becomes a matter of the survival of the most aggressive, the most anti-social, the most predatory, and of the least socially fit. The worst elements in society are the strongest elements in prison, and their behavior is perpetuated in these criminicultural incubators we call prisons and their brand of "education" is spread as these offenders "graduate." As Irwin and Austin warn,

> We should be concerned by the fact that the prison systems are spewing out such damaged human material, most of whom will disappear into our social trash heap, politely labeled the "homeless" or the underclass, or, worse, will violently lash out, perhaps murdering or raping someone, and then be taken back to the dungeon.[25]

All too often the imprisoned offender will emerge from prison, still unskilled, still culturally gauche, still broke, still unemployed, having now learned survival skills in the anti-social world of the criminiculture. Society has had its revenge, has paid for it; and will now quite painfully continue to pay.

In prison we have pooled our social weaknesses and lumped together the erring good with the incorrigibly bad. The sad fact is that when classed with wretched beings, many in the former category find it irresistible not to sympathize with the latter. As a result, the ethically weakest and most pathologically antisocial and uncivil elements are thus propagated, enhanced, and perpetuated in prison. Recall with me, an example from the classic Victor Hugo work, *Les Miserables*, how Jean Valjean changed through his prison experience. It is typical of the experience even today.

> Jean Valjean entered the bagne [prison] sobbing and shuddering: he left it stoically. He entered it in despair: he came out of it gloomy. What had taken place in this soul?[26]

What, I ask, is taking place in the souls of offenders whom we incarcerate today? What are we doing to our fellow man? It is something that I think we should begin thinking about. Without assistance the good do not triumph in prison. Lives deprived of freedom become lives void of direction, void of sense, void of dignity, and void of beauty. This void is unfortunately, but naturally, filled by the prison culture.

> [A] replica of the childhood state; the prisoner is clothed, housed, fed, cared for, told what to do and what not to do, where to go and where to stay. As in childhood, he has a good deal of free time . . . . But prisons are usually pervaded with great hostility. Prisoners are cut off from the possibility of normal sexual outlets; they are constantly threatened by homosexuality; they feel that they have been steamrollered by the police . . . cheated by their own lawyers, misunderstood by the judge, and let down by so- called friends, even by family. Already immature, they tend to regress to still earlier phases of development.[27]

What should ultimately be a building or rebuilding experience leaves our ex-prisoners less able to augment or even to cope with our culture than before their prison exposure. Our current system deters providence and prudence in the incarcerated individuals and rewards violence and indolence. As we enter the twenty-first century, it gets worse.

Prison-related literature over the past fifty years is peppered with articles tending to prove that incarceration has a positive correlation to reduced levels of crime. It may. I suggest, however, that we can take no comfort in raw statistics unless we know why the figures change. Indeed, in some states such a New York, where incarceration rates declined, so did crime rates. Crime rates in other states, such as California, rose along with their incarceration rates. The fact is that we simply do not know why crimes rates increase or decrease. We can only guess. Unless we employ scientific method, isolate all variables, and study all programs and social factors that may bear on what causes crime, all we can do is speculate on what works. Crime rates may drop because we are corralling among our incarcerates those who would continue to commit crimes. This is like a "chemotherapy" approach: if we kill enough cells, we will kill the cancer. Likewise, if we incarcerate enough offenders, we will contain those who would continue to commit crimes. That, however, is not the end of the story, because, the majority of the two million persons now in prison will get out and, then what? The simplistic policy of prison banishment will have an extremely negative impact upon our civilization as the number of prison "graduates" grow in proportion to the number of law-abiding persons in society. Moreover, we are squandering an opportunity to foster positive behavioral change, allowing it to slip through our fingers by doing nothing.

The cancer of violence we permit to fester in our prisons is metastasizing in the neighborhoods of America. The prison's current product, the behaviorally maladjusted, are being reintro-duced into society in sufficient numbers following this anticultural education so that the convicts now tear at the fabric of our culture. American prisons, as a result, are destructive social forces that counter-educate significant numbers of our citizens. The sheer volume of released prisoners is now reaching such a critical mass as to cause social deterioration in some communities and social disintegration in others. Our malfunctioning system and obsolete philosophy are now center-stage and screaming for attention.

I have nothing but praise for most persons who administer our prisons. They are, for the most part, dedicated professionals who take great pride in accomplishing the goals given them. Indeed, among the "thinkers and doers," they are the ones who come closest to doing both, and hence, must be given deference in any movement to reconfigure either the theory or the mechanism of sentencing. The Federal Bureau of Prison defines its mission as protecting society by confining offenders in the controlled environments of prison and community-based facilities that are safe, humane, and appropriately secure, and that provide work and other self-improvement opportunities to assist offenders in becoming law-abiding citizens. In my view, the institution is philosophically far ahead of both our legislatures and our courts, is closest to the real theater of action, and should be heeded. We must correct. Period!

That having been said, I do take great issue with the basic contemporary concept, the goals, and the mission we give to our prisons. The United States Sentencing Guidelines and the federal sentencing policy have abandoned rehabilitation in favor of punishment. Hence, the mission Congress has given the federal prison in fact is simple containment. Regardless of the Federal BOP's mission or intentions, correction will remain a by-product of incarceration until sentencing theory and practice, and the institution have coordinated goals.[28]

Until then our prison system, like a major university with a student body now two million strong, will turn out "graduates" daily. Its alumni are becoming more numerous, and they are all well-educated. Let there be no doubt, everyone who goes to prison changes and, unless we apply positive social efforts, will learn antisocial lessons. Paradoxically, the same American society that condemns anger and violence, lobbies for a policy that throws individuals into institutions where both are a certain result. The American prison contaminates and compromises incarcerated offenders. And the released but unrehabilitated offenders will contaminate us.

Our criminal justice delivery system must begin to inculcate the values and vision common to our culture into any released offender, and to require that they learn at least the threshold and entry-level social skills. The Federal Bureau of Prisons recognizes its role in the rehabilitation process and does provide inmates with self-improvement, literacy, work and vocational training programs. Some state prison programs do also. However, offenders' deficiencies must be specifically identified, remedial programs must become individualized and available for qualified and willing offenders, and the federal facility thus become a model for states to follow. Beyond that, we must contemplate developing the incarcerated offenders into more than obedient citizens.

There is no margin for error, and there is a diminished possibility of success for an individual who merely obeys to avoid unpleasant consequences. It is both counterintuitive, and highly unlikely in a free society, that such a prison product can succeed. Freedom and individual responsibility is a fundamental tenet of our government and culture, and the prison must reflect and teach those values. Our criminal justice delivery system must produce, at a minimum, responsible individuals capable of self control and capable of living successfully in our society. This will take much effort and much thought. The tested programs mean little until studied on a long-term and scientific basis.

For example, I recall when the notion of a "boot camp" was introduced to the system with much fanfare. It developed both popular appeal and correctional merit for some offenders who will eventually be reenculturated. Its flaws soon became evident to me. Boot camp is not new to me. I have been through two of them, both military style, first in the Navy and then for the Los Angeles County Fire Department. Boot camp is not simply a "grunt and sweat" physical experience designed to produce fictional-quality "Rambos." It is a psychologically complex, carefully evolved scheme to precipitate what in mythology is called the "death/ rebirth" experience. That is to say, fundamental change. It enculturates individuals and teaches them how to cooperate with others to accomplish physical and social tasks. It teaches the consequences of anti-cultural behavior. It teaches people how to respond to anti-cultural acts. It teaches them how to obey and how to lead.

By itself, however, the boot camp, or such programs as Scared Straight, may be counterproductive and encourage recidivism if boot camp is treated as an end, rather than as a beginning. It is insufficient, and perhaps meaningless, by itself. As one who has both experienced and analyzed the military-style of boot camp, I have observed that in the military style of boot camp, only a fraction of the initial effort is to "break down" the individual. The balance of the time is spent building the new person into a team member. Moreover, and most importantly, the boot camp psychology is only an initial segment in the death-rebirth experience; the beginning of, and preparation for, further training. In the military boot camp, a teenager dies and a soldier is born. In prison, a criminal must die, and, a responsible citizen must be reborn. To be correctional, the depersonalizing aspects of prison, whether during boot camp or beyond, must at some point in the offender's experience give way to a recognition and development of the individual.

A prisoner can be stripped of all his emotional defenses and resources in a boot camp-like experience, but that is productive only as a means of putting him in the proper position for receiving further instruction. If we give no further goals, instructions, training, and incentives to the new-born citizen, the boot camp experience itself will accomplish little. As an end unto itself, boot camp is little better than a prison. It still perpetuates punishment rather than being just the gambit for a whole program designed to correct and to prepare an offender for reenculturation. Just as the soldier or sailor, who following boot camp becomes part of a system that provides career-track employment and merit-based promotions, so must the corrected offender, following prison, have the potential to thrive upon honest endeavor if we are to have any hope of reclaiming him. Full employment is not just a political goal, it is a social necessity.

Some punishment is necessary. The well-worn expression among prison officials that "offenders are in prison as punishment, not for punishment," is both hackneyed and inaccurate. The primary, positive function of retribution, hence punishment, is to make the victim and society feel vindicated by having the offender "repaid" for what he did. I agree that some short, severe "shock treatment" type of punishment, whether in a "boot camp" or in some other form, may well be necessary for many offenders' correctional experience and for the law-abiding public's perception of the sentence. Our goal, however, first and foremost must be to assure social safety. To reach our goal, the offender must be permitted, encouraged, indeed required, to "earn" his resources and rights back. The offender must be taught to assume his cultural responsibilities and, with institutional help, must have them all firmly in place before he is released.

I also recognize that for many in prison it is too late to do anything to correct their behavior. We must start earlier, much earlier. Programs must be started in our preschools and schools that do more than help children become literate. Criminologists James Q. Wilson and Richard Herrnstein state that, when a child enters school, "he or she becomes part of one of the few state-supervised institutions in our society that attempt to alter, by plan, individual differences in behavior."[29] I suggest that in that milieu we should teach ethics, law, leadership and perhaps many other subjects, to the end that they guide children toward becoming responsible citizens.[30] And in the prison milieu as well, the programs must begin to resemble in their correction mission: what Dr. Phillip Q. Roche called, a "child rearing system for grown-ups."[31] I suggest that we introduce the idea of the prison as a form of "correctional academy" for those who have demonstrated that they can successfully pass from the indoctrination, or boot-camp phase of a sentence, through the punitive stage towards release. Many prisons now offer some vocational training and education. I am pleased that an offender can earn a degree or learn a craft while in prison. But that is not sufficient.

Fox Butterfield's book, *All God's Children: The Bosket Family and the American Tradition of Violence,* presents a chilling look at the legacy of hate, violence, and its roots from pre-revolutionary white rural South to contemporary urban America. He follows four generations of the Bosket family, ending with Willie, (Willie James' son) who has the IQ of a genius, but by adolescence had committed 200 armed robberies and 25 stabbings. When he was 15 he killed two men on the Manhattan subway. He is serving a life sentence in total isolation because he is deadly and dangerous to everyone. He referred to his life sentence as "a license to kill."

Willie James "Butch" Bosket, killer, bank robber, and consummate anti-social, became the first prison inmate in American history to win his Phi Beta Kappa key while earning his Ph.D. in prison. A widely-read intellectual, philosopher, and model prisoner, he was enthusiastically recommended by his teachers and correspondents for parole. Very soon after he was released, however, authorities tried to rearrest him. During a shoot-out with the police he executed his girlfriend by shooting her in the head, and then took his own life. Butch was an educated genius, but a psychopath who could not make it in our culture. As Fox Butterfield states, "He had finally gotten out of prison, but he couldn't get prison out of himself. . . Butch had found freedom the only way he could."[32]

Simple education is not the entire answer. Instead, the penal academies I envision would be designed to develop positive habits, to teach basic life skills, to foster positive group and social skills, and to inculcate American culture and tradition. Foucault refers to this as the need to "[r]eanimate the useful, virtuous interest that has been so weakened by the crime." As I do, he suggests that the prisoner must be taught or retaught the respect for others, for property, for "honour, liberty, life—this the criminal loses when he robs, calumniates, abducts or kills."[33] It is not enough to have craftsmen, or for that matter Ph.D.'s, who are still crooks. Many of our larger prisons have schools to teach inmates, among other things, the "three R's" and several vocational crafts. And, this is fine as far as it goes. Simple education, however, will not inculcate the qualities required for good citizenship. The criminal justice delivery system must also begin to think of sentencing as an opportunity to build character. Prisons must become academies to do so.

Crime itself represents, in a sense, a failure of our social system. I do not suggest that somehow society should accept responsibility or blame for the crimes of others. However, we must recognize the importance of, empower, and extol all social institutions (schools, the Boy Scouts and Girl Scouts of America, YMCAs, churches and synagogues, societies, and fraternal organizations), the Arts (movies, theater, music and literature), and businesses and corporations, indeed any organization that works to form character, develop positive cultural norms, and provide incentives to obey socializing rules and its code of manners. These institutions have become weakened, in part because governmental intervention over the past three decades has usurped their traditional role. The balance of our culture through this period became disrupted, and our collective norms of behavior and control have decayed. Specifically, each time the system arrests, convicts, and sentences an offender, it give very dramatic testimony of how a strengthened governmental enforcement system and a weakened cultural control and prevention system, have failed to protect the citizenry. Recidivism is most specifically a failure of the criminal justice delivery system. It shows that the system had an opportunity to correct, and failed. The prison as an academy, as with all other academies, must be judged, not on the numbers it contains and graduates, but on the social success of its alumni. The prison will be deemed successful only in relation to its success at containing the incorrigible, correcting the redeemable, and thereby playing out its role in assuring the safety of our citizens.

It has become painfully obvious that simply dumping the offender back into society after years of incarceration, will build almost-certain failure into the system. When it releases an individual, unimproved by his prison exposure, often into the environment from whence he came, with limited financial resources, and impaired social skills, it will be a rare person indeed who does not return to what he knows best, the criminiculture and crime, to support himself psychologically, financially, and socially. All we can hope for then is that he will be rearrested, reconvicted, and reincarcerated all at great human and economic cost to our culture. This is foolish and expensive in the extreme. The system must contain offenders, correct them if possible, and if they are released, it must be to some form of productive endeavor with some rational hope for success. We do not want ex-prisoners or criminals to be released. We want productive and law-abiding citizens to be reenculturated.

The release must also be coordinated and gradual. As Bentham urged:

> A convict, after having finished his term of imprisonment, ought not to be restored to society without precautions and without trial. Suddenly to transfer him from a state of surveillance and captivity to unlimited freedom, to abandon him to all the temptations of isolation and want, and to desires pricked on by long privation, is a piece of carelessness and inhumanity which ought at length to attract the attention of legislators.[34]

I fear that parole commissions are being scrapped prematurely. Those that remain have been given an insufficient mission. In addition to boot camp and/or punishment and the academy, I suggest that an offender must also be required to pass successfully through a de-programming from the institution, designed to prepare him for a life of liberty. Before release, an offender must be made to pass a thorough screening process, a second sentencing if you will, during which all factors would be reconsidered by the sentencing court in light of how the prisoner has progressed in his correction. He must convince the court that he is capable of functioning at cultural levels in a free society and is ready for release. And, I submit, this novel "hearing for release" is at least as, and perhaps more, important than, the initial sentencing hearing. The primary purpose of the entire criminal justice delivery system is, ostensibly, the safety of the public. Hence, like the initial sentencing, charged with determining if the offender must be incarcerated, the resentencing release hearings would determine whether he is safe to be reenculturated, or must remain in the institution for containment.

Offenders should also be made to pay for at least a portion of the cost of their confinement. It is another lesson in self-support and responsibility. Offenders must be compelled to pay full restitution to their victims and society. The logic of the limitation imposed by law ("ability to pay") totally escapes me. The offender who has caused damage must be made to rebuild.

When one man has inflicted and another received a wound, or when one man has killed and the other has been killed, the doing and the suffering are unequally divided; by inflicting a loss on the offender, the judge tries to take away his gain and restore the equilibrium.

Aristotle

It is fundamental to the social responsibility we ostensibly require of other citizens. It is part of the healing process between victim and offender. It is absolutely necessary as punishment and for rehabilitation.

Foucault states that, "Work must be the religion of prisons."[35] Nationwide, however and depending upon the prison, only from one to thirty percent of prisoners are actually engaged in some productive form of prison industry. As in the Walnut Street Prison, work and repayment must once again become an integral part of penology.

The prison can no longer be considered a monolithic institution designed to contain our cultural detritus. It must meet the requirements of any successful organization that seeks to produce a product useful to society. It must produce persons who can operate in the American civilization. America can no longer afford either the financial or the social costs of "warehouse-style" prisons. The mission of prison must be changed from simply warehousing humans to correction if possible, and containment if necessary. I am confident that by doing so, change will begin. Given a new mission, the professionals in our prison system will develop new techniques and literally restructure the prison around the process of behavioral correction, rather than criminal warehousing.

Prison must be reconceptualized, not as the end of criminal trials, but as only one element or segment of a total social system designed to prevent or deter crime and recreate citizens. The system must be composed of a series of vectors, cultural agents and agencies, operating together, not only to contain and correct offenders, but to identify problems and potential offenders so as to prevent crime. Correction technology must expand to meet the demands placed on it by a numerically superior force of offenders.

As the Tofflers explain, our culture has transitioned "from brute-force to brain-force."[36] Penology must not lag behind. As the counter-culture surges on, we must be ahead of it. Prisons and corrections technology must get into the information business. Instead of being overwhelmed by the chaotic world of the criminal counter-culture, we must capitalize on its turbulence by creating a new order into which they are swept.

The goals of the criminal justice delivery system must return to those held two hundred years ago. The system must organize itself, developing responsible citizens who, upon release, are capable of leading a legally responsible life-style. We (in law and penology) must resist the temptation to treat research in the other sciences as mere suffixes to ours. The discoveries of contemporary science in all fields show the fallacy of this sometimes deliberate, usually benign ignorance. Integration of all disciplines is fundamental to understand this complex enigma, human behavior. Computers and interactive technology used in conjunction with research in the fields of psychology, medicine, psychopharmacology, sociology, biology, and genetics can lead us from backward and haphazard techniques of control, toward real correction and proactive personal development of the offenders who come under our control.

Every conviction should initiate a longitudinal study of every offender, and the accumulated findings must be used by correction personnel; and, in the event of lapses by the offender, by future sentencers. By accumulating data on crimes, personalities, rehabilitation programs, and methods of correction, a systems approach to sentencing can develop information and flexible knowledge that can be used in computerized, individually tailored correction models and programs. Additionally, the system can thus accelerate our therapeutic and punitive responses to crime to such a velocity as to overwhelm offenders psychologically and intellectually, many of whom are, after all, ignorant, insecure, illiterate, and culturally gauche.

A sentence must be more than a period of prison confinement, followed possibly by a period of parole with varied degrees of supervision. As Alvin and Heidi Toffler point out, in industry "'production' neither begins nor ends in the factory."[37] The process must extend "both upstream and downstream . . . into aftercare or 'support' for the product. . . [and] to provide post-use cleanup. . ."[38] In like fashion, the concept of crime prevention and corrections must be considered on a birth-to-death time line, with prison representing only one contribution. The safe society and the corrected offender is our product, and each segment of our system, whether prevention, detention, or correction must be considered in terms of the value it adds to the finished product.

The treatments for cancer, the vaccines for polio, and the cures for a myriad of diseases that once plagued us did not just appear. They began as dreams and came about because some of the best and brightest scientists, socially motivated and properly funded, dared to follow their vision and applied themselves to the task. Unless America makes an identical or greater commitment to discovering the causes and cures of crime, and implements its discoveries into systemic changes, we will permit crime insidiously to seduce or victimize our citizens and bleed our economy. We can no longer afford either the human or the material cost of failing to contain, or alternately, failing to correct, those who fail to obey our laws.

Now, approximately 2000 years after the life of Hippocrates, medical science is returning to the original Hippocratic concept that patients are sovereign human beings capable of generating dynamic and powerful responses to their own diseases, and not merely passive vessels upon which the physician exerts therapeutic energies and into whom the physician pours medicines. It is also approximately two thousand years after the lives of the two persons whom philosopher Jacob Needleman says most influenced Western philosophical thought and laws, Jesus and Plato.[39] Should not we also return to look at their original premises and lessons—that most individuals have a basic desire to obey rules, and that each person has potential for positive change? Autogenetive responses cannot produce medical cures in all disease or illness, nor social cures in all offenders. Nonetheless, what I believe and state with great confidence is that if we begin to show a measure of faith in the offenders who wish to correct their behavior, and who have been isolated from the incorrigible and indifferent, if we treat all facets of these persons, if we call upon all the allied sciences as potential contributors to treatment, if we place the onus upon the offenders to change, and if we expect change, we will begin to see some.

The concept of the iron-bars and concrete cell prison is not dying, it is dead. It is an obsolete concept. As a correctional facility, that prison has failed. As a human warehouse, it has failed. As a punitive instrument, it has failed. Failure, however, is but a step toward success if we do not give up. Honest error is no vice, if when we err we try something else. Great scientific breakthroughs come only after much trial and error. So even a misstep can be a step in the right direction if we vow not to make it again. It is reported that Thomas Edison conducted over 4,500 experiments that failed before producing the first lead-acid storage battery. Given our current prison population, we could have two million experiments in behavioral control and correction now going on. Let us view our failures with offenders the same as Edison did—we are using a concept that is not working, but can be made to work. If we do, each experiment will bring us closer to solutions.

A significant criticism leveled at "health care" is that it is preoccupied with its historical goal of treatment, and pays too little attention to prevention. The criticism may have some merit. I regret to say, however, that penology has only reached a "leper colony" mentality, and has not even developed to the treatment stage. The whole criminal justice delivery system cries out for change and we must change it. We can no longer react out of ignorance and fear; we must act out of prudence and ration.

Primum non nocere (Above all, do no harm) the Hippocratic aphorism which was enunciated two thousand years ago to guide physicians, is as vital to them now as it was then. I suggest that perhaps the oath is applicable to the field of penology as well. The fact is that the curative properties of the contemporary prison, like any universal antidote, is a myth: it cures few, destroys many, and damages most. It is imperative that we use the opportunity given us while we have offenders under our control to effect positive behavioral change. This is not always, perhaps not often, being done, but it should be. We have a problem to solve and we must solve it. One place we can begin to make changes is to rethink American sentencing and the American prison.

ENDNOTES

1. James Fitzjames Stephen, *The Punishment of Convicts, the Language of the Law: An Anthology of Legal Prose* 63 (Louis Blom-Cooper et al. eds. 1965).

2. I include in the term "prison" the 3,304 local jails, operated by counties and municipalities, which housed over 490,000 prisoners in 1994. *Local Jail Population Doubles*, AP, Apr. 30, 1995.

3. Albert Camus, *Reflections On the Guillotine* 5 (Richard Howard trans., Fridtjof-Karla Publications, 1959).

4. Michel Foucault, *Discipline and Punish: The Birth of The Prison* 104 (Alan Sheridan trans. 1977) (1975).

5. Francois Michel Vermeil, *Essai Sur Les Reformes A Faire Dans Notre Legislation Criminelle* 105 (1781).

6. Foucault, *supra* note 5, at 105 (citing Le Peletier de Saint-Fargeau, *Arch. parl.*, XXVI, June 3, 1791).

7. Foucault, *supra* note 5, at 124.

8. *Id.* at 125.

9. *Id.* at 127 (quoting William Bradford, *An Inquiry How Far The Punishment Of Death Is Necessary In Pennsylvania* 3 (1789) *In American Law: The Formative Years* (Morton J. Horwitz et al. eds., 1972)).

10. Alexis de Tocqueville, *Democracy In America* 45 (Phillips Brandley ed., Vintage Books 1945) (1835)

11. Americans today seem to have made a deliberate attempt to leave God out— perhaps at our peril. *See* Stephen L. Carter, *The Culture of Disbelief: How American Law and Politics Trivialize Religious Devotion* (1993).

12. Alvin and Heidi Toffler, *The Third Wave* 53 (1980).

13. Phillips Bradley, Preface to De Tocqueville, *Democracy In America* at x (1945).

14. Jeffrey Reiman, *The Rich Get Richer and the Poor Get Prison: Ideology, Class, and Criminal Justice* 26 (3d ed. 1990).

15. Stephen, *supra* note 1, at 68.

16. *Dept. of Justice, Corrections Task Force* 343 (1976) (on file with author).

17. De Tocqueville, *supra* note 12, at 269.

18. *See Prison Population at Record Level*, AP, Aug. 9, 1995.

19. Bernard Gavzer, "Life Behind Bars," *Parade*, Aug. 13, 1995, at 4.

20. In 1990, Americans spent $52 billion for private security measures. Paul S. Robinson, "Moral Credibility and Crime", *Atlantic Monthly*, Mar. 1995, at 72.

21. *See* Sir Samuel Romilly's comments in Bernard L. Shientag, *Moulders of Legal Thought* 208 (1943). This, of course, has something to do with the crime; but, much to do with the person's nature, state of mind, and personal deficiencies. *Id.* Proportionality of "time to crime" is only of significance to gauge the extent of popular outrage and the intensity of retribution. *Id.*

22. John Irwin and James Austin, *It's About Time: America's Imprisonment Binge* 61 (1994).

23. Gertrude A. Barber, *Sheltered Employment Work Experience Program* (1975).

24. Irwin and Austin, *supra* note 24, at 143.

25. *Id* note 24, at 111.

26. I Victor Hugo, *Les Miserables* 69 [Lascelles Wraxall and Chas. E. Wilbour trans., Donohue Bros., 1862

28. U.S. Dept. Of Justice, A Judicial Guide To The Bureau Of Prisons 1 (1995).

29. James Q. Wilson and Richard J. Herrnstein, *Crime & Human Nature: The Definitive Study Of The Causes Of Crime* 264 (1985).

30. *See* Ernest L. Boyer, *The Basic School: A Community For Learning* (1995

31. Phillip Roche, "Criminal Responsibility", in Hoch and Zubin, *Psychiatry & Law* 108 (1955) *quoted in* Henry Weihofen, *The Urge To Punish: New Approaches To The Problem Of Mental Irresponsibility For Crime* 27 (1956).

32. *See* Fox Butterfield, *All God's Children: The Bosket Family and the American Tradition of Violence* (1995).

33. Foucault, *supra* note 5, at 107.

34. Coleman Phillipson, *Three Criminal Law Reformers: Beccaria, Bentham, Romilly* 211 (1923).

35. Foucault, *supra* note 5, at 242.

36. Alvin and Heidi Toffler, *War and Antiwar: Survival at the Dawn of the 21st Century* 10-11 (1993).

37. Alvin and Heidi Toffler, *Creating A New Civilization: The Politics of The Third Wave* 60 (1994).

38. *Id.*

39. Jacob Needleman, *The Heart of Philosophy* 27 (1982).

The Death Penalty and Punishment

No man is an island, entire of itself;
Every man is a piece of the continent, a part of the main;
If a clod be washed away by the sea,
Europe is the less, as well as if a promontory were,
As well as if a manor of thy friends or of thine own were;
Any man's death diminishes me,
because I am involved in mankind;
And therefore, never send to know for whom the bell tolls;
It tolls for thee.

John Donne, *Meditation XVII*

We are most at peace with law when it comports precisely with our individual visions of morality. If society condemns as illegal that which we condemn as immoral if society's manifestation of justice coincides with our practical notions of fairness if society imposes only those official sanctions that we in good conscience could personally impose; then the rule of law is easily understood and largely autoenforced. When they who enact laws consciously observe these bounds, laws thus enacted enjoy wide acceptance. Most of us feel a genuine, yet almost subconscious, obligation to obey laws because psychologically we seek equilibrium with norms around us, desire order and logic in our lives, and because we are, after all, elements of the government that enacted the laws. If the legal duty imposed is also perceived to be a moral duty, our sense of obligation acquires the force of an imperative. If the law directly runs contrary to a moral tenet, however, or if the sanction for violators responds only to a passionate demand for revenge, or other morally infirm motivations, the law itself creates a tension between civic duty and moral conviction and will spawn an anxiety that is certain to erupt at cultural fracture points. Nowhere is this tension more evident than in our reaction to legalized killing as in abortion, medically assisted suicide, and the death penalty. No other penal issue is as socially divisive in this last decade of the twentieth century as officially sanctioned death.

Victor Hugo, addressing issues surrounding the death penalty, said it well.

> The scaffold . . . when it stands erect before you, has something about it that hallucinates. We may feel a certain amount of indifference about the punishment of death, not express an opinion . . . so long as we have never seen a guillotine; but when we have come across one the shock is violent, and we must decide either for or against. Some admire it, like De Maistre, others execrate it, like Beccaria. The guillotine is the concretion of the law, it calls itself vindicta; it is not neutral, and does not allow you to remain neutral. The person who perceives it shudders with the most mysterious of shudders. All the social questions raise their notes of interrogation round this cutter. The scaffold is a vision, it is not carpentry work, it is not a machine, it is not a lifeless mechanism made of wood, steel and ropes. It seems to be a species of being possessing a gloomy intuition; you might say that [it] lives, that [it] hears, that the mechanism understands, that the wood, the steel, and the ropes, have a volition. In the frightful reverie into which its presence casts the mind the scaffold appears terrible, and mixed up with what it does. The scaffold is the accomplice of the executioner; it devours, it eats flesh and drinks blood. The scaffold is a species of monster, manufactured by the judge . . . , a spectre that seems to have a sort of horrible life made up of all the death it has produced.[1]

Thirty-eight states now offer the death penalty option. Following passage of the 1994 Federal Crime Bill, the federal government now imposes death as a penalty for more than sixty crimes. Although few Americans express no opinion about official killing, few likewise fully understand its basis or implications penologically, philosophically, or culturally. Is death a penologically legitimate form of sentence? Is the death option culturally productive? Is it socially constructive? Or is it simply a closely guarded and comfortable myth by which a society that increasingly feels victimized by those citizens who fail to follow the rules, attempts to strike back decisively and dramatically? I submit that our death penalty policy is at cross purposes with morality and at odds with reality, and creates a strife that must be reconciled. As with most punishments, the public reacts viscerally and emotionally to the death penalty, and it is either content with the myth of punishment, or afraid to look beyond it.

Punishing criminals is a concept with which each of us must wrestle, and we cannot fully examine the implications of punishment without discussing the death option. The death penalty is the ultimate sanction and brings the philosophy of punishment sharply into focus because of its drastic and irreversible consequences. Philosophers, theologians, psychologists, and sociologists struggle with the propriety of killing criminal offenders as a form of punishment. The dilemma reaches each of us, and in the face of it we must reconcile our innermost moral, cultural, and penological beliefs, all of which are inextricably intertwined. The death penalty is more, however, than just a penological debate, which few enter. It is also more than just a moral issue, which divides most. It is more because it has become the surrogate for society's frustration with our government's failure to protect it and maintain order. Some people may decline to express an opinion about the death option. No one, I submit, is truly neutral about it.

Let me give an example. Perry Carris is dead (not his real name). I doubt, however, that any will mourn him. He was a brutal killer and not one with whom any of us would easily sympathize. Indeed, even among those who did not want him to die, most would readily admit that the world is a better place without him. He and a friend entered the home of his friend's elderly uncle and aunt, then killed and robbed them. They stabbed the uncle 79 times; and they stabbed the aunt, who weighed only 70 pounds, 66 times. Carris and his friend killed them with a bayonet.

From this day forward I shall not tinker with the machinery of death. For more than twenty years I have endeavored, indeed I have struggled. . . to develop procedural and substantive rules that would lend more than the mere appearance of fairness to the death penalty . . .

Rather than to continue to coddle the Court's delusion that the desired level of fairness has been achieved and the need for regulation eviscerated, I feel morally and intellectually obligated simply to concede that the death penalty experiment has failed. It is virtually self-evident to me now that no combination of procedural rules or substantive regulations ever can save the death penalty from its inherent constitutionally deficiencies. The basic question, does the system accurately and consistently determine which defendants "deserve to die?" cannot be answered in the affirmative.

The problem is that the inevitability of factual, legal and moral error gives us a system that we know must wrongly kill some defendants, a system that fails to deliver the fair, consistent, and reliable sentences of death required by the Constitution.

Justice Harry Blackmun's dissenting opinion in *Callins v. Collins,* February 22, 1994.

But, you see, Carris didn't just die, we killed him. One night recently, officers of the prison where he spent his final hours injected him with a lethal combination of chemicals, and quietly he met eternity. And there are many more who are, in like fashion, scheduled to die. Carris's act was deliberate and fully planned. So was ours. Carris's act displayed a cruel disregard for life. What about ours? The first killing was clearly immoral, criminal, and unjustified. But how about the second? It was legal. Was it moral and justified? These issues are, at their core, elements of our culture's complex myth of punishment.

Many who refer to themselves morally as "pro-life," quick to condemn abortion because it kills an innocent being, just as quickly accept the death penalty, ostensibly because it kills a guilty being. Innocent or guilty, however, by whose standard? Each act is the killing of a human being. The first is one whom we say knows no sin. The second is one whose sins can be forgiven. Is there a difference? Or more basically, is the notion of *sin* even a relevant penological consideration? Should attitudes and beliefs about the offender's *sin* even be a part of the equation?

This is not a paradox just for those who wrestle with notions of morality or sin. We must *all* face it. The philosophers most instrumental in developing our penology held a fundamental view that God would punish us for sinning because we were free moral agents. Their philosophy reflected a belief that the law was simply God's mortal agent, and as such, empowered to do as it determined that God would do. I disagree.

Regardless of how pure or divinely inspired we think our motivation is, society cannot mend the damage of one violent act by practicing another. There must be a rational, pragmatically supportable purpose for death as punishment if we are to use it. It must not be offered merely because it is demanded by the public as a visceral, morally indignant reaction to crime. Beccaria states "[T]he laws [that] punish with death commit homicide reflectively and formally."[2] If Beccaria's statement is true, are we prepared to view killing criminals as official homicide? In our republic, we are the government and the laws are a reflection of what *we* are. Hence, Americans each must reconcile these ambivalent attitudes about death by abortion, suicide and as punishment. Can we? Perhaps the *sin* to be considered in penology is not the offender's, but ours. Let us see.

First, it is important to know why we punish and why we killed Carris and hundreds like him. American penology is really quite simple. We have just three means of punishment: probation, incarceration, and death. We have four principal justifications for punishment: rehabilitation, deterrence, containment, and retribution. Let us see how death as a means of punishment serves these goals and means. Looking at each possible justification, it becomes clear that both society's motivation and the penological justification for the death penalty are simply to impose retribution—we are "getting even."

First, *rehabilitation*. If there is one thing the death penalty surely does not do, it does not rehabilitate the person upon whom it is imposed. It simply takes one's life. Death does not rehabilitate. Thus, rehabilitation is not a consideration in the death option.

The second, *deterrence*, is also quite problematic. As earlier noted, deterrence is coercion through fear. Unfortunately, few criminals are afraid. Statistics uniformly show that condemned offenders did not pause before killing to consider the possibility that they might die for what they were about to do. Some may have felt that the death penalty lacked certitude because it might not be imposed, or they simply felt that they would not get caught. Others may have considered the consequences of killing, and refrained. The latter possibility has not been sufficiently researched. We simply do not know much about this possible aspect of deterrence. What incomplete data we possess indicate that, of those who kill and are caught, few feared the consequences. Obviously, those who killed in jurisdictions with the death penalty were not deterred by the threat or prospect that they too might die for their acts.

Again, there are exceptions for, among others, the pathologically motivated acts. Gary Gilmore became notorious, not for the two innocent persons he murdered execution-style but because he participated in his own punishment. Gilmore refused to appeal, rebuked attempts by others to help him, and insisted upon dying. He even tried to commit suicide twice. As Mikal Gilmore says of his brother, Gary:

> He made [the death penalty advocates] not just his allies, but he also transformed them into his servants: men who would kill at his bidding, to suit his own ideals of ruin and redemption. By insisting on his own execution—and in effect directing the legal machinery that would bring that execution about—Gary seemed to be saying, "There's really

nothing you can do to punish me, because this is precisely what I want, this is my will. You will help me with my final murder".[3]

According to Thucydides, in the Athenian debate over the punishment to be given rebellious citizens, Diodotus, the opponent of severe sanctions, argued:

> Men have gone through the whole catalog of penalties in the hope that, by increasing their severity, they may suffer less at the hands of evildoers. In early ages the punishments, even of the worst offenses, would naturally be milder, but as time went on and mankind continued to transgress, they seldom stopped short of death. And still there were transgressors. Some greater terror then had yet to be discovered; certainly death is no deterrent.

We simply cannot conclude, either based on historical experience or the evidence we have developed over the past 200 years of American jurisprudence and penology, that by killing one person, we will deter others from killing. Too many variables compete here, and that which deters has not been statistically isolated.

Beccaria, too, believed death ineffective as a general deterrent.[4] Writing at a time when death was the usual penalty for all but the most petty crimes, Beccaria concluded that popular reaction to executions was intense but soon forgotten. He believed that, although executions were a public spectacle designed, at least in part to deter, most observers felt compassion for the person executed, or were just repulsed by the horror of it all.[5] The *real* message of a public execution, even where capital sanctions are commonplace, is lost on all but a few because fear of death is displaced by other attitudes or merely forgotten in the moment of the crime with the criminal's certainty that *it won't happen to me.* As for the rest of society, observing a criminal facing a life sentence may provide an ongoing reminder and a deterrence that one more execution does not. As one of the women in the "Manson family" who slaughtered several persons in some sort of a ritualistic killing replied when asked about the murders in which she participated, "I think about what I did every day of my life." She is serving a life sentence in a California prison. Intuitively we know, and clinically we have discovered, that the potentiality or possibility of punishment, however it is imposed, does deter some. We cannot say at this time, though, that what we refer to as general deterrence philosophically justifies so permanent a solution as the death penalty. The fact is that we have never in any scientific way isolated just what works, what does not, and why.

David Von Drehe, in his book, *Among The Lowest of the Dead: The Culture of Death Row,* is direct in his appraisal of whether death is an effective deterrent:

> In a sense, the whole exercise is fundamentally ridiculous, because it rests on the notion that the hyperrational tools of mathematics can measure the irrational brain of a murderer. The problem with deterrence, as applied to aggravated murder, is that it assumes killers calculate risk and reward. The reality, with few exceptions, is that murderers are not clear-thinking people . . . [t]hey kill out of mental illness, or sexual perversion, for instant gratification or sheer bloody-mindedness. Some murderers actually seem drawn toward the death house.[6]

Then too, there is the further question of whom the government should kill. Answering this question, our death penalty laws permit almost totally parochial and hence arbitrary results. Nearly ninety-nine percent of those who commit homicide are not sentenced to death. For some reason, or perhaps for no reason at all, prison is sufficient to protect society from most killers. Local prosecutors usually have the first choice whether to prosecute an accused murderer's trial as a capital case. Locally selected juries are thereafter in control, and sentence but few to die. Persons who commit identical crimes do not receive identical treatment or identical sentences, because every prosecutor and every jury is different. Finally, according to the NAACP Legal Defense Fund Death Penalty Project, even after the prosecutor's decision, the jury trial, and the sentence, nearly half of all death sentences or the underlying convictions are reversed on direct appeal. In reality, the number of persons actually sentenced to death is not statistically significant, and statistics are insufficient to support most arguments favoring the death penalty.

Under *specific deterrence* theory, with the desired impact upon the person being punished, no one would deny that death works perfectly in its macabre fashion. Indeed, the person executed can never commit another crime. Death is permanent and specific, but *deterrence* is not an accurate term. More accurately, we have given up on this person and are simply exterminating him. The further question, however, is whether the death option is necessary at all for specific deterrence.

All current statistics indicate that it is, first of all, more expensive to execute a person than to imprison him for life. Indeed, the figures are astounding. *The Miami Herald* reported that between 1973 and 1988, Florida had spent over $57 million to execute 18 people, or $3.2 million per death. *The Philadelphia Inquirer* reported that it cost Pennsylvanians an average cost of $3 million per death, or approximately three times what it would cost for a life sentence without possibility of parole. In other states the figures are higher. In Kansas, the legislature rejected the death penalty as too expensive. They estimated it would cost $10 million in the first year, and that they would spend over $50 million before they could actually take the first life. The economic cost was simply too high to justify the deterrent value, whatever it is, of the death option. Life imprisonment was the most economically viable option for protecting society from further criminal acts by the offender.

The future may, however, present the obverse view. The death penalty may become more commonplace, the cost of each death may decline with fewer issues to decide, fewer persons excited by the death penalty, or, government may find more expeditious and less expensive ways to kill. It is difficult to say if, or when, the death option would become cheaper than a life in prison. In the event that it does, and as we commit as a society to eliminating procedural protections, we may reap the economic reward of bringing the cost of executions down. I trust, nonetheless, that we, whether penologist or citizen, would not become so inhumane or callous as to kill offenders simply because death is cheaper than other options open to us.

Although specific deterrence will support the death option penologically, many theorists reject both general and specific deterrence as legitimate justifications for the death penalty. Many traditionally have done so because death is not necessary. Increasingly, theorists reject the death option because it is the antithesis of the nonviolence we officially espouse. Internationally, we purport to deplore violence and do not hesitate to expend our diplomatic energies and money to condemn violence elsewhere, and to encourage and even require that others seek peaceful solutions to their disputes. Yet in response to crime, ignoring the cultural and social cost of official killing, the spiral of violence in which we participate, and the cultural paradox of a social system that ostensibly wishes to temper actions and calm violence, we nonetheless kill.

Containment, in the death penalty debate is also philosophically problematic, because, as with other penalties, it punishes the offender for something as yet not done. We use the crime he committed to predict, sometimes without further data, that he will perform a criminal act again. Unquestionably, although killing the offender does in a grim and final sense contain, and thereby protect society from potential future criminal acts against it, the next question would be is it necessary? A sentence of pain, punishment, or even treatment, beyond that which is necessary, cannot be philosophically justified. For after the proper measure of the sentence is administered, the rest is only revenge, and the punished becomes the criminal justice delivery system's victim. There simply are no data by which we can determine even the appropriate duration of a containment sentence—that is, one sufficient in length to endure beyond the projected time when the offender will commit another crime let alone to justify death. *Containment,* again an inappropriate term to describe the act, is simply irreconcilable with a sentence of death. Death is not necessary to contain most offenders. Penologists recognize that one can be effectively and economically contained in a prison. Even the Geneva and St. Petersburg Conventions forbid "unnecessary suffering."[7] That is to say, an implement of war that is deemed to inflict unnecessary suffering upon the enemy is an illegal act of war. Hence, most theorists also reject containment as a justification for the death penalty.

This leaves only *retribution*. Among those who favored capital punishment in a 1984 Media General Poll, the primary reason given was revenge.[8] Revenge by death is the ultimate payback. As a retributory tool, death works wonderfully. The desire for revenge is the dark secret in all of us. It has, I suppose, been so since the beginning of time. It is human nature to resent a hurt, and each of us has an impulse to hurt back. Before society depended upon law for order, the fear of personal reprisal may have been all that kept some from committing physical attacks and property crimes against others. With the rule of law, cultures sought to limit personal revenge by substituting official punishment, meted out in a controlled and detached fashion by the sovereign. The Mosaic and the Hammurabic Codes and later, Islamic law, although severe, were the sovereign's attempt to temper and preempt personal vendettas by assuming responsibility for punishment, thereby repudiating and curtailing personal reprisals.

The ideal American citizen is not like a Grangerford or a Sheperdson, the two feuding families in Mark Twain's *Huckleberry Finn*, or like a Hatfield or a McCoy, the feuding families of American folklore whose names have become charactonyms for the recriminatory idiocy in society. We know that revenge between citizens is antithetical to civilized society. It invites a greater retaliation, which in turn invites counter-reprisal, which again invites more revenge. It contributes to a spiraling escalation of violence between citizens, and between culture and the criminal counterculture. Leaders know, and have known for centuries, that civilization requires restraint, and that open personal revenge is socially destructive, cannot be permitted, and indeed must be renounced. Official revenge is no better, the results are no less odious, and it sends a paradoxical message to society. By using revenge-motivated sentences, government declares to its citizens that vengeance is acceptable behavior—it is just that *you* cannot do it. Hence, when government does not control crime, or is not vengeful enough to suit the demands of its citizens, they lust for more. Vengeance is our conditioned response to crime. It is also, after all, the official response to crime. By exacting revenge upon criminals, however, society drops to the social stratum of its dregs.

We are then playing on the offenders' terms, by their rules, and we cannot win.

Unfortunately, although our government knows better, it is ruled by the tides of public opinion. Following folklore instead of science, government has deigned to respond politically to the base passions of society rather than act as statesmen upon the sociological necessities of our civilization. Vengeance requires a victim, and in punishing a criminal, our government gives us a culturally acceptable one. Ignoring conclusions reached over the centuries by philosophers, penologists, psychologists, and theologians, and the practical wisdom practiced by parents, our government has legitimated notions of vengeance. *Paying back*, although destructive to culture and family alike, is politically popular. For that reason, and perhaps no other, it is the law.

There is a psychological overlay to society's actions which is what institutionalized killing is doing to our attitudes towards ourselves and our culture. As Victor Hugo said, "[D]eath has a way of its own of harassing victory."[9] As a judge, I have seen the defiant and unrepentant murderer and know how easy it is to identify only with the innocent and injured. Nonetheless, should not Christians strive to exemplify the grace and mercy of Jesus? Recall with me that Peter, unresponsive to the pacifistic admonitions of Jesus, still wore a sword, and in the Garden of Gethsemane drew it and severed an ear from the Roman guard. Nonetheless, Peter did not suffer the "ear-for-an-ear" retaliation that would be expected from the *lex talionis*. Jesus did not condemn him or cut Peter's ear off. Instead, according to the Scriptures, Jesus healed the Roman. Should not Jews strive to exemplify the spirit of *teshuva* and atonement, and follow the teachings of nonviolence? Should not humanists strive to protect their nominal tenet, human life? Confucius, when asked about the death penalty, answered:

> What need is there of the death penalty in government? If you showed a sincere desire to be good, your people would likewise be good. The virtue of the prince is like unto the wind; that of the people like unto grass. For it is the nature of grass to bend when the wind blows upon it.[10]

Should we not desire these positive qualities likewise in our society? I think so. And, if so, then we cannot abandon these same positive qualities in determining appropriate treatment or punishment for offenders.

In the hours leading up to a recent execution, the news reporters hovered around the prison like flies over a dunghill. One newspaper published the details of the condemned man's last meal and devoted three pages of its Sunday edition to such things as a full-color, front-page picture of the gurney upon which he was to die. One television station gave death-watch "updates" every half-hour during the count-down to execution. A Florida anchorperson was quoted as saying, "This is just the kind of break we needed for our ratings." Indeed it was. His station had won a lottery drawing to witness the execution.

It is difficult to feel pride in a culture that has become so inured to violence that death is an acceptable medium of commercial value, or worse. In Florida, on the eve of a scheduled execution, the crowds gathered outside the prison to await a condemned man's death, and at the fateful hour, they cheered. In a culture wherein criminal sentences are to assure safety and to preempt civil strife, the death penalty creates a paradox. We ostensibly deplore violence. Government ostensibly seeks to quell violence. Nonetheless, we deem it acceptable by calling for our government to kill killers. The shameful truth is that society, by urging vengeful punishment, exposes its own desire for violence. I have concluded that it is shamefully improper for government to give vent to this base desire.

The great essayist Michel de Montaigne said, "Malice sucks up the greatest part of its own venom and poisons itself." The harm resulting from vengeance does not end when the offender is executed. The evil of vengeance here is terminal and extends beyond the actual killing. It cannot be undone. It lingers on, and simply creates another cultural sore and cheapens the humanity that we realize we are called upon, by our individual faiths and morality, to practice.

In an aberration from the normal routine of sentencing by our legislatures or the judge, our laws require that we place the onus of this terrible decision upon twelve citizens selected at random. We give the most difficult sentencing decision, the choice between life and death, to an *ad hoc* group of lay citizens, selected at the moment of the trial. Ordinary citizens sitting on juries are the ones who condemn their fellow citizens to death. Aside from the psychological damage this may do to the jurors, I also believe this is certainly not the best method to minimize arbitrariness and mistake. Some people would argue this is the best method of ensuring community standards of decency in sentencing. It, however, is not. Because the law then denies the jury the option of exercising intuitive mercy, or of declaring the death penalty to be cruel and unusual, outside what they consider to be the evolved standards of morality and decency for their community. Community standards are trumped by the law.

Without considering the psychological burden borne by the jurors, or the cultural damage we do by making our citizens killers, we instruct them on the law and require that they decide who lives and who dies. I agree with Kalven and Zeisel, who have stated:

> Whatever the differences on which this decision hinges, they remain demeaningly trivial compared to the stakes. The discretionary use of the death penalty requires a decision which no human should be called upon to make.[11]

I seriously doubt that we as a society can kill others without doing psychological damage to ourselves and real social damage to our culture. And, I have concluded that our political system, our social system, and, indeed, our religions, cannot with intellectual honesty condemn private killing and simultaneously condone killing sanctioned and performed carefully and deliberately by the state. The positions are mutually inconsistent.

> The death penalty cannot be useful, because of the example of barbarity it gives men . . . . It seems to me absurd that the laws, which are an expression of the public will, which detest and punish homicide, should themselves commit it, and that to deter citizens from murder, they order a public one.[12]

Still, the death penalty *is* constitutional. Our Supreme Court has said so. Moreover, Carris received a fair trial and his full measure of due process on appeal. I know, because I reviewed the record and was on the court that declined to stay his execution. Nonetheless, whether the death penalty is constitutional and the trial is full and fair, who are they who we thereby select to kill? First, of the approximately 20,000 to 25,000 homicides committed each year in the United States, only a handful of the killers will be sentenced to death. Killing all killers would, of course, be abhorrent to us. So, we kill only a few. But are we killing the right ones? In sufficient numbers? Indeed, should we kill any? The death option creates more questions than it answers.

What does all this mean to you and me, who must decide whether to support death as a penalty and to vote for legislators who pass laws establishing it, and legislative candidates who profess to support it? First, we, the thinking citizenry who elect the delegates in this republic, are not mindless reactionary fools. It just seems that we talk that way when it comes to crime. Instead we should think pragmatically about our whole culture, and what the death penalty is accomplishing compared to what it may be destroying.

I believe that anyone who has experience with training others or in meting out discipline, whether as a parent, psychologist, supervisor, or employer, knows that prevention is the key. With violence and criminal offenders it really is no different. There is a reason why Americans kill each other in numbers unmatched in the world. We do not, however, know why. Should we not find out? I think so. Does the death option function in any way to stem this flow of blood? Preliminary evidence indicates that it does not. The fact is that the death penalty may hurt our culture. Nonetheless, we plunge ahead with more executions and kill those whom we should be studying like dreaded diseases to find out why they behaved as they did. I view this as the height of governmental, penological, and scientific irresponsibility.

Indeed, some who should know better do not appear to want to understand why offenders behave as they do. For example, U.S. Attorney General Janet Reno in her press conference of May 4, 1995, when asked if she understood why the Oklahoma City bomber did what he did, stated, "I could never understand what made those people do what they did in Oklahoma City."

We should not confuse feeling compassion for offenders, which is more than society can ask, with the notion that we should always endeavor to find out why, and to fully understand why one commits an offense, any offense, so we can possibly prevent another. It would be both irrational and unproductive were the surgeon angrily to smash the excised tumor on the operating room floor simply because it is cancerous. The cancer of crime is little different. We must, as I have said, study our offenders like dreaded diseases to determine what caused them to err. But we seem reluctant to do this. If we did, perhaps we would discover that certain practices and prejudices of our culture are destroying the capacity in some of our citizens to feel compassion for others. Perhaps we do not wish to because we are afraid to discover other things we do not want to know about our culture and about ourselves. Perhaps some of us simply do not care to understand the reasons why an individual commits a crime, because it is easier to punish him if we do not know the reasons. Understanding why an offender committed a crime might personalize the offender and make it more difficult to treat him inhumanely.

Albert Camus tells of Bernard Fallot, who had worked for the Gestapo, and confessed to many war crimes. Fallot was put to death after he declared himself to be beyond hope. "My hands are too red with blood" he said to a fellow prisoner. And, he had been adjudged both by the tribunal and public opinion to be irredeemable. Camus says he too would have classed him as such had he not read one astonishing piece of evidence. After having declared that he wanted to die bravely, Fallot told the same prisoner: 'Do you know what I regret most of all? Not having known sooner about the Bible they gave me here. If I had, I wouldn't be where I am now.'[13]

Fallot may indeed have deserved to die. Perhaps other war criminals and terrorists do too. We have an obligation, however, to find out why people commit crimes, that we may prevent other crimes. Knowing the real "why," however, may upset myths about both our increasingly godless culture, and the ease with which we hate both "sin and sinner." We may be surprised to find that knowing the *why* may point to historic values on the one hand or spiritual poverty on the other, as being among the real determiners of human behavior.

We are a government of the people. As Montesquieu, Locke, and Beccaria (each of whom supplied elements of the philosophy from which our political scheme was developed) observed, government is a contract or the result of a contract with society, and no one will contract to be dealt with more severely than necessary. Beccaria observed directly that, life being the greatest right, no one would accept a contract that may result in the loss of his own life.[14] He concluded that the social contract we call government would never grant to state authorities the power to take life. His argument is that because man is not the creator of his own life, he cannot confer the right to take life upon his government. Hence, he concluded that the death option is inherently unjust. Camus believed that no government is wise enough or innocent enough to claim the moral authority to kill.[15] In a very thought-provoking essay on death, Helen Prejean states:

> I would not want my death avenged. *Especially by government* which can't be trusted to control its own bureaucrats or collect taxes equitably or fill a pothole, much less decide which of its citizens to kill.[16]

Decisions at the highest levels are not supposed to be the result of public opinion polls but too often they are. They should be the result of detente among science, law, philosophy, anthropology, sociology, psychology, and indeed all the sciences, contextualized into problem-solving situations, but too often they are not. We citizens are obliged to scrutinize the reasons our society, and hence our government, behaves as it does. Indeed, if we are to support a government that kills, or candidates who supports the death option, we must know why it does, or they do, and be satisfied that the reasons are reconcilable with our philosophical, political, cultural, and religious tenets. Are they, when society kills for revenge? Each of us must answer for our self.

As Lady Wooton, the noted British criminologist, has observed:

> Science can undoubtedly examine the effects of sentences with a view to improving their future effectiveness in particular directions though always

with the exception that the purely retributive value of any sentence necessarily lies outside the field of scientific inquiry; for all the science in the world cannot measure whether a man has been punished as much as, or more or less than, he deserves.[17]

In the final analysis, is there a penological place for the death option? The answer is probably yes. I say *probably*, because we have yet to explore fully the notions of a true CBS system and we have yet to discover and act upon the reasons for violence in our culture. First, Beccaria recognized, as do most who oppose the death option, that in certain cases the death penalty may be a necessary response to counter an act of war, or its civilian equivalent, terrorism. Terrorism is like an act of war. It, like other acts of war and treason are exceptions to any discussion of criminal penalties, for the reason that they entail different and separate considerations from issues typically found in criminology and penology. Different from crimes that are usually motivated by either passion or greed, acts of terrorism, treason, and war are typically motivated by political or religious zeal, and must be treated as a different genre than crimes generally.[18] Being different from other crimes, terrorism and other acts of war, demand other remedies. For the political or religious zealot who marches to the beat of another's drum, and for other instances when only the threat of greater terror or extermination will stop him, the drastic and permanent measure of the death penalty, is defensible.

There is also in our culture, like other cultures throughout history, a percentage of citizens who are totally outlaw, cannot be corrected, and cannot be intimidated into socially acceptable behavior, by our prisons. They will always be a menace, even to the corrections mechanism while incarcerated. Willie Bosket, a fourth generation criminal, was, as was his father, first incarcerated at age nine and has spent his entire life as a social predator or in prisons. He claims to have committed two thousand crimes, including two hundred armed robberies, twenty-five stabbings, and several killings, all of which he laughed off bragging, "I feel nothing," proclaiming himself to be "a monster created by the system." While serving a sentence which will last several lifetimes, he stabbed a prison guard with a stiletto he made from a part taken from his typewriter. He stated that his only regret is that he failed to kill the guard, and "spit on his corpse." There is nothing the system can do to or for him to prevent him from committing crimes—even prison has failed.[19]

> I have not presided over nor reviewed a capital case in which actual innocence was the issue. But the fear of executing an innocent person is my constant companion in any death penalty case. Ronald Jones spent eight years on death row in Illinois before DNA tests proved that he could not have raped and murdered a Chicago woman. He was freed in 1999. Since 1973 there have been 12 persons executed, but 13 condemned persons exonerated, in Illinois alone! Throughout the United States, since 1973 over 80 people have been released from death row because of evidence of their innocence. Others have not been so fortunate. The American Civil Liberties Union reports that researchers, Radelet and Bedau, found 23 cases in which innocent persons had been executed.

But death, if that is society's option for the outlaw, should be more akin to Beccaria's notions of death as the final solution, but excuses neither our failure to find out why one kills, nor our failure to place greater emphasis on crime prevention. In the final philosophical analysis of death rationales, individually and collectively we must question whether we, who did not create life, can cede to a government the right to take it away.[20] Even if we are to assume that all persons convicted of capital crimes are guilty (and I am not so naive as to assume they are). They are, nonetheless, humans. As such, the death penalty, if America is to have one, would be reserved for those for whom neither correction nor containment will work. Death, stripped of all philosophical jargon, then has a solitary penological justification of simple extermination.[21]

In penology, the notion of extermination is too brutal for Americans to accept or consider as a response to a crime. Because to make an informed and calculated decision to kill another human requires that we consider a person's human worth, decide that it has been reduced to zero and deliberately, and without euphemistic labels for our motivation, kill him. This, outside the theater of war, I doubt we will do. For, as Sam Keen says, "To be effective killers we must dehumanize the enemy so that we will not be burdened by guilt nor crippled by compassion."[22] Dostoyevsky's Raskolnikov first rationalized that he was doing humanity a favor by killing the wealthy woman who "deserves to die," before he could bring himself to actually take her life. He thus convinced himself that he was righting the injustice of her having great possessions while others were in want. Having thus dehumanized his victim, Raskolnikov felt morally right in ridding the world of her.[23] I doubt that we can so completely dehumanize offenders that we feel justified in coldly and matter-of-factly exterminating them. That would place too great a burden on our consciences. We need the cushion of anger, legislative legitimation of revenge, and the myth-like rituals of a criminal trial to separate us from the decision.

For society to kill, it must insulate itself with myth and euphemism. Extermination of criminal offenders is too personal and does not allow us the myths and rituals, which dehumanize the offender, insulate us from what we are doing, and assuage our guilt. Only the depersonalized setting of the trial ritual allows us to divorce ourselves from the awful realization that we are killing another human. The ritual endorses the act by separating *us*, the nonjurors, the nonjudges, from the decision to kill and the act of killing another, leaving us unaccountable for what we have done. The myth of punishment rationalizes the motivation, so we can kill another from the lofty view created by a noble fiction that by doing so we avenge the innocent.

ENDNOTES

1. Victor Hugo, *Les Miserables* 13 (Lascelles Wraxall and Chas. E. Wilbour trans., Donohue Bros.)

2. Francis E. Devine, "Cesare Beccaria and the Theoretical Foundations of Modern Penal Jurisprudence", 7 *J. Prison L.* 8, 17 (1981).

3. *Id.* at xi.

4. Cesare Beccaria, *On Crimes and Punishments* 45-52 (Henry Paolucci trans., Bobbs-Merrill 1963) (1764).

5. As was Camus, I might add. *See* Albert Camus, *Reflection on the Guillotine* 5-6, in *The Literature of the Law* (Louis Blom-Cooper ed., Richard Howard trans., 1965).

6. David von Drehe, *Among The Lowest of the Dead: The Culture of Death Row* 209 (1995); *see also* Antonio R. Damasio, *Descartes' Error: Emotion, Reason and the Human Brain* (1994).

7. See International Committee of the Red Cross, *Status and Treatment of Protected Persons, in Commentary IV Geneva Convention: Relative to the Protection of Civilian Persons in Time of War* 199-231 (Jean S. Pictet ed., 1958); *see also* Francis R. Boyle, *The Legal Distortions Behind the Reagan Administration's Chemical and Biological Warfare Buildup*, 30 St. Louis U. L.J. 1175, 1181 (1986).

8. Lois Forer, *A Rage To Punish* 101 (1994).

9. Hugo, *supra* note 2, at 5.

10. Quoted in Huston Smith, *The Religions Of Man* 252 (1992).

11. Harry Kalven, Jr. and Hans Zeisel, *The American Jury* 448-49 (1966).

12. Beccaria, *supra* note 11, at 50.

13. Camus, *supra* note 12, at 440.

14. Beccaria, *supra* note 11, at 12-13 & 45-55.

15. See Camus, *supra* note 12, at 441.

16. Helen Prejean, C.S.J., *Dead Man Walking: An Eyewitness Account of the Death Penalty in the United States* 21 (1993).

17. Barbara Wooton, *Crime and the Criminal Law: Reflections of a Magistrate and Social Scientist* 97 (1981).

18. Devine, *supra* note 7, at 17.

19. Fox Butterfield, *All God's Children: The Bosket Family and the American Tradition of Violence* (1995), *Id.* at 324.

20. Of necessity, the law must preserve some individual power over life and death decisions, such as when it permits one to kill in self-defense or the defense of others.

21. Beccaria, *supra* note 11, at 45-55.

22. Sam Keen, *Faces of the Enemy: Reflections of the Hostile Imagination* 70 (1986).

23. Fyodor Dostoyevsky, *Crime and Punishment* (1866).

Crime, Pain, and Punishment: A Skeptic's View

This essay was presented in lecture form in Erie, Penn sylvania as the first lecture in The Pennsylvania State University 1997-1998 Lecture Series, and again in Macon, Georgia as part of the 1997 Middle Georgia Educational Foundation Lecture. This article is the combination of both lectures, portions of which were omitted from each. Part VI is a compilation of the questions and answers that followed the lectures. I have included them because the comments and questions following any lecture are significant, first, because they give me a Rorschach-like insight into my audience, and second, because they indicate what the audience heard, which is more important than what I said.

I. Introduction

One of the first matters I attended to upon becoming a judge in 1981 was to preside over the trial of an offender who already had an extensive criminal record. I then sentenced him to prison for assault. One of the last matters I attended to before leaving the trial bench to take my position on the U.S. Court of Appeals was to preside at the trial and sentence of the same offender to prison again for, among other acts, assault. Each crime was deliberate, and each time there was little doubt that he would be caught. Somehow the certainty of detection and the punishment he knew he was certain to receive was not a deterrent to him. His is not an isolated case. This same scene is reenacted day after day in courtrooms throughout the United States. It seems that all-too-many offenders are not learning a behavioral lesson from punishment. It seems that the criminal justice delivery system is failing to learn the same lesson that punishment, without anything more, is an insufficient response to crime. Over the course of the years, I have become convinced that there *is* a better theory to follow than the "crime equals punishment" equation that is now so thoroughly ingrained in our penology, our politics, and our popular culture. I believe that the failures of this equation require that we embrace a new philosophy and take a different approach. This new philosophy, which those who organized the Pennsylvania State University Lecture Series call the Skeptic's View, must first and foremost seek to explain *why* we sentence criminal offenders and the *purposes* we seek to serve by each sentence. Moreover, in applying this new theory to practice, we must ensure that our actions are both consistent with the purposes of the theory and that they advance the social ends we wish to achieve.

Recently there has been a reduction in violent crime. According to many it is because we have finally committed our criminal justice system to the simple equation "crime equals punishment." Under this theory, if an individual commits a crime, there is but one response, punishment. Thus, the theory goes, as the crime becomes more serious, the duration of the punishment should be increased or, perhaps, the offender should be put to death. One of the ironies of this formula is that many of us (professionals and laypersons alike) believe that it fully accounts for *why* we punish, and the *purpose* behind the decision to punish offenders. But is it *really* that easy? I do not believe so!

I suspect many of us have not thought much about why the criminal justice delivery system punishes criminal offenders. Perhaps this is because the answer seems clear. Again, I do not believe so. My position is that contemporary penal theory does significantly more harm than is necessary. I believe that the criminal justice delivery system should strive to produce hope, not despair; that it should be an instrument of social harmony rather than discord; and that it should prescribe remedies for offenders that are not socially corrosive. This essay will consider such deceptively simple questions as Why *do* we punish? What purpose does punishment serve? What are the goals of punishment? What are the appropriate means of punishment? Finally, should we punish at all?

Consider the following true story as related by author Robert Penn Warren. In the mid-1930s, Warren attended a murder trial in

Louisiana. The case being tried involved an old man who had shot
a young woman for, as he said, "talking meanness against his baby-
girl daughter."[1] The man had shot and killed the young woman
using both barrels of a twelve-gauge shotgun at a range of eight feet
while she was gambling. A dozen people witnessed the execution.
Incredibly, before shooting the young woman, the old man waited
thirty minutes on a stump outside the building where the craps game
was taking place because a friend had asked him to hold off so he
could win back six dollars that he had lost to the condemned victim.
Once the friend won the money back, the old man entered the
building and "went to work." Warren's discussion of what subse-
quently happened is worth quoting:

> He [the old man] never denied what he had
> done. He explained it all very carefully, and why he
> had to do it. He loved his baby-girl daughter and
> there wasn't anything else he could do. Then he
> would plead "Not Guilty." But if he got tried and
> convicted and they couldn't fail to convict, he would
> get death. If, however, he would plead guilty to
> manslaughter he could get off light. But he wouldn't
> do it. He said he wasn't guilty of anything. The whole
> town got involved in the thing. Well, they finally
> cracked him. He pled guilty and got off light.
> Everybody was glad, sure they weren't stuck with
> something, they could feel good and pretty virtuous.
> But they felt bad, too. Something had been lost,
> something a lot of them could appreciate . . . . It took
> him [the old man] three days to crack, and when he
> cracked he was nothing. Now, we don't approve of
> what he did, a status homicide the sociologists call it,
> and that is the worst sort of homicide, worse than
> homicide for gain, because status homicide is
> irrational, and you can't make sense of it, and it is the
> mark of a low order of society. But because status
> homicide is the mark of a low order of society, what
> are we to think about the old man's three-day struggle
> to keep his dignity? And are we to deny value to this
> dignity . . . ?[2]

What shall we make of the above story? It seems simple enough. One human brutally murdered another for what appears to be no rational or justifiable reason. Indeed, if we all went around shooting people "for talking meanness" against someone we loved, we would find ourselves in a culture that only the Hollywood movie industry considers normal. Clearly, under the "crime equals punishment" equation, severe punishment is called for. But as Warren and the Skeptic's View conclude, it is not that simple.

First, despite the unanimous agreement that the old man has committed a violent crime, he steadfastly refuses to accept that what he has done is wrong. Instead, the old man insists that he is "not guilty." His perspective, in turn, makes the members of his community uncomfortable because he is, in effect, challenging the community's collective concept of *right* and *wrong*. Indeed, the old man's refusal to admit or even recognize that his actions are wrong cuts to the very foundations of the "crime equals punishment" equation. We punish in reaction to wrong actions. *Wrongness* is a collective judgment of society, and laws are the political manifestation of society's collective moral ideals. *Here*, however, we are left to wonder whether because the old man does not accept, or believe, that what he has done is "wrong," does his community lose its desire to avenge the killing of another of its citizens. If so, what purpose will punishing the old man achieve?

Notice that despite the community's belief that the old man committed an awful crime, they offer him the option of receiving a much lighter sentence if he confesses. Indeed, the community appears to *need* him to confess. There are two primary reasons, and perhaps a third ancillary reason, for this need.

First (please follow me philosophically and then in the penological sense) punishment is ineffective against the offender who does not recognize the wrongness of his act because punishment then is, to him, an injustice, leads him to reject the authority of the law, and simply serves to harden his resolve not to accept blame. The old man's community recognizes that, as does Warren. Second, if the old man confesses, the community members are reassured by his fictitious admission that the man's moral perspective is ostensibly the same as theirs. In other words, if the old man concedes that his actions were wrong, the community is reassured that its collective judgment about his act is correct. Thus, its desire to punish him for his wrongful actions is legitimized.

A culture is less concerned with social or political theory than with its own insights. People understand the meaning of justice only when they can relate its demands to the rest of what they believe to be true about *their* cultural milieu. Secondarily, by offering the old man the option of *mercy*, the community expresses its discomfort with the rigidity of the *crime equals punishment* equation and eases its severity. Even though the old man has committed a brutal killing, the community believes that he is entitled to some leniency or compassion if he admits his action was wrong. In this way, the community gets the best of both worlds. The old man admits his *wrongness* (even if *he* does not believe it) and is punished, and the community tailors the punishment to meet both the particular circumstances of the case and the community's parallax view of punishment.

But there is more to this lesson: the community feels a sense of loss when the old man finally confesses. How can this be explained? My guess is that the members of the community have a latent grasp of all the considerations omitted from the *crime equals punishment* equation. Warren suggests that the old man's "three-day struggle to keep his dignity" is worth some respect and has some value. I agree. I also believe that members of the community implicitly understand that applying the straight *crime equals punishment* equation in this case ignores such realistic and relevant issues as the old man's love for his daughter, the absence of a coherent frame of reference from which to evaluate this crime, and the difficulty of balancing "justice" and other competing values they prize as human beings (mercy, forgiveness, self-respect) and in a word, humanity. And perhaps the community also believes that the old man really is not a "bad guy" despite that fact that he murdered a woman.

Why is this story relevant? In my view, the story illustrates both the complete incoherence of the crime equals punishment formula and its failure to account for the reasons *why* we sentence or the *purposes* served by our sentencing decisions. Indeed, the crime equals punishment equation disregards all the complex and varied factors relevant to the criminal justice delivery system, and replaces them with an apparently easy-to-apply, one-size-fits-all, mindless approach to sentencing criminal offenders. The crime equals punishment equation is in reality the perfect complement to American consumerism and the pop, fast-food, get-it-while-you-can culture into which we have devolved at the end of the twentieth century—make it easy, make it fast, don't make us think too much, and, above all, remember that we have a short attention span.

Our current system is not driven by a coherent plan but instead by a myth that fails to fortify the social commitment necessary to challenge, and defeat, the power of the developing criminiculture. Simply stated, crime equals punishment is not an integrated philosophy and contributes little in terms of advancing our efforts to promote a safe, fair, and just system that serves both the community and offender.

The crime equals punishment equation instead does significant harm. By relying on this reflexive, unthinking equation, we are deflected from the essential question that we should be asking: Does our present criminal justice system ensure the safety of the citizenry? This fundamental question will not disappear merely because we choose to adopt the easy-to-execute "crime equals punishment." Instead of the ready-made, drive-thru crime equals punishment scheme, I suggest that we need a full-service philosophy that seeks to answer the question of whether our existing criminal justice system protects the citizenry and then proceeds to ask and address other issues of the criminal justice system.

Moral life does not thrive well in the absence of a socially meaningful existence. We need an *understood* philosophy that accounts for why we behave, why we err, why we punish those who err, and the *purposes* served by our punishment. Society must know *of* it, know *it, and* understand it or society will resist it. This essay outlines the parameters of just such a theory.

II. Should We Punish at All?

Americans are caught in a parallax position between the facile myth of punishment, to which our penology clings, and the reality of life, which we are all-too-content to ignore. We have an enormous investment in the status quo, and confessing error is difficult. Nonetheless, we must. Our preoccupation with causing pain to the offender and keeping the pain within constitutional limits creates an unnecessary philosophical tension. Nonetheless, the shock of really questioning our fundamental beliefs is too much for some of us to bear. Thus, the attitude prevails that if a sufficient number of people are content with a simple response to criminal behavior, and banished prisoners are so easy to ignore, why should we challenge the myth? I respond: pragmatics. Because, like all myths, this one is failing the test of both science and reality.

As I have earlier written, historically, we have relied on four explanations for why we punish offenders: deterrence, containment, rehabilitation, and retribution. At various times throughout American history, each theory was used as an explanation and justification for why we punish. And at various times each theory provided rational support for the punishment inflicted upon criminal offenders. None of these theories, I submit, survives contemporary critical scrutiny. Let us review them briefly for this discussion.

A. *Deterrence*

There are two different types of deterrence, general and specific. General deterrence proceeds from the idea that by punishing one offender for his acts we thereby discourage others from doing the same because they will, theoretically, fear the same result. In other words, by making an example of one offender, we hope to ensure that others behave. Specific deterrence relates to the impact that punishment has on the behavior of the punished individual. We punish an offender for one act to convince him that he must refrain from doing it again so to avoid suffering the unpleasant consequences he now associates with that action.

Empirically we know that deterrence works because we each have at some time feared something that caused us to alter our behavior. But we do not know how it works, nor do we know what it is about the rule or law itself (the detection, arrest, trial, and/or punishment process) that actually deters. As such, neither general nor specific deterrence can successfully function as a full-service theory that accounts for why we punish and the purposes to be served by the decision to punish.

B. *Containment*

When the criminal justice delivery system imprisons offenders to prevent them from committing other crimes, that is containment. In other words, we punish offenders for the criminal actions that we *believe* they will commit. Underlying this theory is the premise that once an individual commits a crime, the perpetrator forfeits any presumption of future innocence.

As a baseline, I am troubled by a theory that justifies punishing offenders for something they have not done and may never do. Indeed, containment rationalizes the continued incarceration of criminals based on sheer speculation that those who have previously committed crimes will continue to do so. As a consequence, this theory results in unnecessary containment because we incarcerate those who may already be corrected, those who need no correction at all, or those who can be corrected less expensively without incarceration. In fact, there is mounting evidence that the incarceration itself may perpetuate ill behavior.

C. *Rehabilitation*

Under the rehabilitation theory, the purpose of punishing criminal offenders is to modify their behavior. At one time, many believed that rehabilitation was the future of the criminal justice system. Unfortunately, earlier rehabilitation theory was based upon a flawed premise, that we could change *them*. Those who favored this theory understood neither *how* to rehabilitate nor *who* was capable of being rehabilitated. Moreover, earlier experiment with the theory was scrapped too soon.

Today, rehabilitation is all but dead. Prison itself rehabilitates few, and criminal sentencing has dissociated itself from the goal of rehabilitation. Most criminal offenders who change for the better do so in spite of prison, not because of it. Clearly, rehabilitation does not rationalize what we currently do to offenders.

D. *Retribution*

Retribution is revenge plain and simple. Retribution comes from the same place in the heart as revenge and in the same place etymologically. *Re* means back, and *tribuere* means to pay. Retribution and revenge are "Humpty and Dumpty," and when they philosophically fall, they will shatter identically. We punish offenders who violate the law because we are angry and want to get even.

Retribution is about power. It is about force. It is about repression. Under this theory, the offender's *violation* of the law legitimates our vengeful punishment and absolves us of any injustice or transgression we may commit upon him because the offender *deserves* some suffering for violating the social order. However, power creates the cruelty of indifference, and force sacrifices justice to achieve peace. Any peace gained by these means, however, is always an uneasy one that is lost when the force of power is not present.

We rationalize punishment by various means. But when the penological smoke clears, punishment is psychologically for the punisher. We like to punish, and our rationale for doing so is really quite simple. The ugly truth is that we punish because it makes us feel good to get even. The Skeptic's View is opposed to any penological expression of revenge.

III. What Is the Skeptic's View?

Essentially, the Skeptic's View is that we must move from an offense-based theory, that is to say, punishment exclusively based upon what one has done, toward a correction-based system, with an outcome-graded accountability that strives to isolate the *reasons* for criminal behavior, imposes remedies that seek to correct or palliate, and then accounts for its results with the goal of preventing future harm. Hindsight is a ruthless critic. There is no other way to truly understand crime and the criminal offender except to identify and analyze all the factors that affect behavior and then do something about them and account for our actions in terms of the outcome.

The most significant aspect of this perspective is that it challenges us to stop thinking about the criminal justice system as relevant only after the offender has committed an infraction and we have a victim. Instead, it commands us to re-conceptualize antisocial behavior as a location upon a continuum along which lie the rule or law, the temptation, the opportunity, the infraction, the disposition, and *then* the remedy and post-remedial response. The Skeptic's View requires us to concern ourselves with potential offenders' behavior pre-trauma, *before* they become criminals, and with crimes, *before* offenders commit them. It requires that we stand outside a behavioral event and its given conditions, consider them as contingent related facts, find out what went wrong and where, imagine how they might have come out otherwise, and then begin to change the predicate actuators.

Moreover, the Skeptic's View also demands that we play an active post-crime role in the lives of offenders. In my view, sentencing should not be an end, but a journey. Society cannot leave offenders to deteriorate socially and psychologically in prison. The Skeptic's View would devote substantial efforts and resources by providing offenders with the necessary incentives and tools for *them* to correct *their* behavior and to repair their lives. I have no difficulty telling offenders, "You are all screwed up and you are here until you change." But I would also willingly add, "And we are here to help you." The criminal justice delivery system should recognize that it cannot *make* change happen, but it should acknowledge that we can seek, expect, and facilitate positive change.

A. *The Role of the Victim in the Skeptic's View*

The Skeptic's View would place the victim near the center of the criminal justice delivery system, but for reasons other than the superficial *argumentum ad misericordiam*, which only provides an opportunity to vent a desire for revenge. I view victim participation as substantive; indeed, partially supplanting the state as the eminent party at trial, and requiring that the system and the offender confront the *consequences* of the crime and account for it in the sentence.

Government determined long ago that the true victim of an offense is the state, not the one who actually suffers. The victim instead becomes society's surrogate. Ostensibly, the purpose of having the state as a party was to intercept the potential for vengeance and recrimination that would accompany violation of a victim. Actually, it may have been to usurp the monetary restitution that would flow to the victim, in favor of a mulct that would flow to the state. Theoretically, we are supposed to be content with the state's taking authority from the victim and controlling the balance of the act. In reality, the fines go to the state, and revenge is taken by the state. The victim is forgotten unless we use the experience to discover something new. How else can we palliate the pain imposed upon the extended circle of victims and prevent future harm to others?

The victim is often emotionally, and sometimes physically, traumatized. I want victims and victims' rights groups to *participate* because having a real role in punishing offenders is not only helpful to the sentencers and correctional personnel, but is also therapeutic to the victim. I believe that psychologically, sentencing should be the rough equivalent to the funeral and interment of the deceased, which allow the bereaved a significant event to put the emotional trauma behind them. This cannot happen unless participation is actual. Participation should not merely be a forum in which to express emotions that may or may not affect the sentences.

Under the present "crime equals punishment" equation, few resources are devoted to research the root causes of crime and criminal behavior, and even the causes are discovered, little is done about them. Ignorance will serve us just fine if punishment and vengeance are our primary goals. However, ignoring the causes of crime and criminal behavior has taken us to a point where prisons are a significant growth industry; we have a whole segment of our economy built around crime and fear, and our recidivism rates have run off the charts.

Understanding human behavior is largely a matter of understanding the multiple forces and powers that work together, or struggle against each other, to affect the course of events. Consequently, the Skeptic's View would study crime and criminal behavior as if they were dreaded diseases of a healthy culture, in an effort to change the course of events. The Skeptic's View would require using scientific method, not political rhetoric or myth. Getting "tough" on crime is an empty slogan that does not work. Almost anyone can meet and master pain. To change, however, is both challenging and frightening. We need to get more than tough; we must get "smart" on crime so that we can confront crime in all aspects of social life and then demand change.

Discovering and understanding the root causes of crime and criminal behavior permit us to move to the second aspect of the Skeptic's View: dedicating our social systems to intervention, palliation, and prevention. In my vision of the twenty first century,

the criminal justice system will look more like a "Health Maintenance Organization" than the current "second wave"[3] farrago of
functions which operate neither systematically nor accountably for
their contributions to safety. The HMO has a designated population
of potential patients and has a single purpose as its mission: *keep
them healthy*. I suggest that the twenty first century criminal justice
system will resemble a "Safety Maintenance Organization." It
may, as it now does, comprise police, courts, probation officers,
judges, prisons, and parole boards. It must also encompass social
scientists, physicians, educators, health and zoning administrators, and other professionals from numerous other disciplines. It
should also rely on other social institutions and professionals for
pre-offense intervention and prevention, post
-incarceration behavioral modification and post-release observation and support. The SMOs I envision will likewise have a
population of citizens and be given as their mission: *keep them safe*.

Behavioral technology requires that we consider how the
criminal justice delivery system of tomorrow will interact with the
individual at several distinct times in the criminal justice delivery
process; how it will interact with other social institutions; and,
importantly, how it will interact or interface with the allied sciences. Currently, the criminal justice system does not get involved
in the life of the individual until after he has committed an offense.
Informed by scientific research about the predispositions of potential offenders, or the risk posed by the influence of certain environments and conditions, will this remain the case? I hope not.

Setting out a preemptive role for the criminal justice delivery
system, however, raises a number of issues. Is each component of
the system, the police, the prosecutor, probation and parole, the
prison, the court, willing to cede sufficient portions of its power that
an integrated criminal justice delivery system can be developed? Is
the system willing to recognize the importance of other disciplines
and institutions, academicians, physicians, educators, and psychologists? Does the criminal justice delivery system have the
institutional capacity or resources to engage in preventive action?
Is there a public will to develop preventive measures? Is this a role
we want the system to be performing? Should we be concerned
about stigma in the process of targeting would-be offenders and
offering therapy, counseling and education? And, what are the
constitutional implications of all this?

> I suggest that it makes absolutely no sense to return uncorrected offenders to society; and if one is ever to be released, the effort should be to do what is necessary to assure the law-abiding public that it is safe when the offender is released. This is not now being done. Indeed, we can fairly accurately predict that a sizeable percentage of offenders are being released to prey upon society again. This is stupid.

In the Skeptic's View, the role of the criminal justice delivery system in the post-offense time frame will also be different. It will move toward a theory of sentencing that emphasizes correction and not punishment, and then towards the ideal which is prevention. The components of the criminal justice delivery system and its personnel will be taught to deal holistically with offenders as morally, educationally, socially or biologically deficient individuals. In practice, this means that sentences will be less focused on incarceration and more focused on methods designed to return corrected offenders to a society whose security and safety is not threatened thereby. Clearly, as recidivism rates indicate, this is not a task at which the present system has been particularly successful. Indeed, given the overwhelming emphasis on punishment in today's penology, it would be fair to say that policy makers do not know how to correct offenders; or knowing how, do not have the will or the means to do so; or, nonetheless choose a politically more popular stance, such as a mindless "toughness" on crime without regard for what is truly tough on crime, for fear that doing something productive would place them perilously close to the political quicksand of being considered soft on crime.

In the Skeptic's View, the system cannot consider itself *just* unless it is administered by officials who are fair, impartial and wholly committed to the ethos that gives their culture its order. If we want a criminal justice system that values either humanity or its own citizen's safety, the whole scheme must be changed. Neither excessive nor inadequate punishments are just. Punishment, when therapy could be of greater value, is unjust to the offender who would benefit from therapy. Likewise, mercy and leniency, when severe punishment is indicated, are unjust to the public which needs to see its deviants reproved. And, all of it is both senseless and unjust if with pragmatic and preventive effort we could have superseded and precluded the criminal act and saved a victim in the first place.

B. *The Skeptic's View of "Experts"*

Justice must be therapeutic for the immediate victim, for the extended spectrum of victims, for society, and for the offender. Under the Skeptic's View, sentencing should emphasize prevention, intervention, and correction with punishment only one element of the exercise. In concrete terms, this means that the components of the criminal justice system and its personnel should be taught to deal holistically with criminal offenders and confront them as morally, educationally, socially, or biologically deficient individuals. Such a system, would seek out that which can possibly be corrected and those for whom correction could be required. The Skeptic's View would uncover what is possible to change and change it. It would recognize what is beyond the scope of our knowledge and our tools and initiate a palliative response.

Towards this end, I would transform the sentencing phase of the criminal proceeding into a *meeting* of experts from many disciplines such as: sociologists, education professionals, psychologists, victims and victim support organizations, ministers, priests, rabbis, and even urban planners. These experts would become the court's resources and would convene as the court's jury to help the court and each other formulate an integrated social and penal response to infractions based on a holistic view of the entire ecology of the crime. Together, the courts and the panels would, where deemed possible, work to develop appropriate remedial programs that present offenders with *real* obligations and *real* opportunities to change their behavior and to achieve the end goal of correcting the behavior of criminal offenders at *all points on the continuum between pre-offense and post-release*. As a consequence, this means that sentences would be less focused on incarceration as an end in itself and more focused on incarceration as a *means* to apply methods designed either to return corrected offenders to society or, if not released, as a means of humanely retaining them. Indeed, incarceration would diminish as punishment, in an inverse relationship to its increased significance as an institution for behavioral research on how to prevent crimes, first and foremost, and how to prevent recidivism, secondarily. Importantly, the Skeptic's View recognizes that we can learn as much from failure as from success if we recognize failure, account for it, adjust to it, and seek to learn from one infraction how to prevent others.

C. *The Skeptic's View and Political Rhetoric*

Outcome is one of the magic words that surfaces in any contemporary reform effort. When we combine raw materials and effort, we want to know whether that which comes out is better than what went in. Even more elementary, however, we must know what we want to come out, what we want from offenders, if we are to confront them with what they must become before they can be reintroduced into society. We must have a CBS plan and an image of the end product we desire, or we have no suitable measure of success. Significantly, under the Skeptic's View, the criminal justice system can be built neither upon some concatenation of moral abstractions nor upon hollow political rhetoric. Instead, the criminal justice system must be part of a solid foundation for building a workable community out of the raw human material given it, and then it must, with other social elements, be required to account for the results. If I were asked what has happened to any of the thousands of persons whom I have sentenced, I would have to answer, "I don't know." How did they do in prison? "I don't know." Did they improve? "I don't know." Did they commit other crimes? "I don't know." If the criminal justice delivery system were required to account to the public for its results, a revolution would have to take place in it.

A criminal justice delivery system must be *accountable*. Unlike today, where the criminal justice system need not account for the future actions of its offenders, the Skeptic's View demands that we treat each crime and criminal offender as part of a never-ending research process. In this respect, every sentence and every offender must be followed closely to determine what worked and what did not, and the results must be made part of the data used to make future sentencing decisions. Through this process we can avoid repeating sentencing mistakes, and, importantly, we can keep the pressure on offenders to behave. Indeed, by demanding that both the system and the offender account for sentencing promises, progress, and decisions; acknowledge their failures; and study the reasons why particular sentencing decisions result in particular outcomes, the Skeptic's View moves us toward the end goal we must demand of our sentencing philosophy: the correction of criminal offenders and the prevention of criminal behavior.

D. *The Skeptic's View of the Death Penalty*

The ultimate penalty in the context of punishment is the death penalty. We are most at peace with law when it comports precisely with our individual visions of morality. If society condemns as illegal that which we condemn as immoral; if society's manifestation of justice coincides with our practical notions of fairness; if society imposes only those sanctions that we in good conscience could personally impose; then the rule of law is easily understood and largely auto-enforced. When legislators consciously observe these bounds, laws thus enacted enjoy wide acceptance and a stamp of legitimacy.

Most of us feel an obligation to obey laws because, psychologically, we seek equilibrium with the norms around us and desire order and logic in our lives. We are, after all, constituent elements of the government that enacted the laws. If the legal duty imposed is also perceived to be a moral duty, that obligation acquires the force of an imperative. If, however, the law threatens, challenges, or contravenes a moral tenet (or if the sanction for violators responds only to a passionate demand for revenge or other infirm motivations) the law itself creates a tension between civic duty and moral conviction and will spawn an anxiety that is certain to erupt at cultural fracture-points. Nowhere is this tension more evident than in our reaction to end-of-life issues and legalized killing issues such as abortion, euthanasia, physician-assisted suicide, organ and tissue farming, and the dissection of clones. Likewise, no other penal issue is as socially divisive in this last decade of the twentieth century as officially sanctioned death.

The death penalty is the ultimate sanction and brings the philosophy of punishment sharply into focus because of its drastic and irreversible consequences. The death penalty is more, however, than just a penological debate which few enter. It is also more than just a morally divisive issue. The death penalty is more because it has become the surrogate for society's frustration with government's failure to protect it. Philosophers, theologians, psychologists, and sociologists struggle with the propriety of killing criminal offenders. The dilemma reaches each of us, and in the face of it, we must reconcile our innermost moral, cultural, and penological beliefs, all of which seem inextricably intertwined. Some people may decline to express an opinion about the death option. No one, I submit, is truly neutral about it.

The only *traditional* justification for the imposition of the death penalty that withstands critical scrutiny is retribution. Society puts criminal offenders to death because it wants revenge against those who have committed heinous crimes and shattered the safety and peace of society. Revenge is the reason most given by people who support the death penalty;[4] in some studies, one hundred percent of the sample questioned gave revenge as the reason for supporting the death penalty.

The Skeptic's View is Beccarian. Cesarre Beccaria reasoned that the death penalty is probably penologically supportable, not in an attempt to even the score, but to terminate the life of an offender who has an unresectable evil of such dimensions that civilized society can tolerate no lesser response. In other words, viewed in its naked reality, the death penalty is extermination. Thus, to kill, the state must be prepared to evaluate a human life, place it at zero, and take it. The state may be wrong in taking the life of some offenders, but under *penological* scrutiny, the error is not the killing of criminals and the taking of the lives; *that* is a moral and a sociological judgment. Rather, the error is in following a practice that fails to serve its penal purpose. Hence, the ultimate sanction may be penologically supportable when nothing else works. Let me give you examples of two such situations.

The first example arises in response to acts of terrorism, genocide, or war, situations in which the killer denies the wrongness of terror or killing itself. Indeed, he most likely believes it the right thing to do for the cause he is defending, and an act for which he will receive a sort of heroic acclaim or in the case of "holy wars" an eternal reward. Most crimes are motivated by greed or passion.

Terrorist acts are different. They are like acts of war and motivated by factors that have little in common with criminality. Accordingly, our best efforts to discover the causes of criminal behavior and the dedication of our criminal justice system to the treatment and correction of these causes are unlikely to have any impact on preventing terrorist acts. Indeed, terrorists often march to the beat of another's drum and are prepared to sacrifice even their lives for whatever cause it is in which they believe. As such, terrorists are unlikely to respond favorably under any theory of punishment or corrections, and neither nor correction will likely be effective. Moreover, were we to do less than impose death in such massive acts of violence against culture, the public would retch at the injustice.

The second example arises when, despite our best efforts to treat and correct the behavior of criminal offenders, there remain offenders who are totally outlaw, incapable of correction and who present a continuing threat to the safety and well-being of the citizenry. In such cases, where we have exhausted our efforts, where the offender has committed a heinous crime and presents a continuing menace to society, the death penalty is penologically justified because there is nothing more we can do to fulfill our mission of civil safety.

E. *The Skeptic's View and Criminal Insanity*

For more than 100 years, the American criminal justice system has struggled with such misleading terms as *insanity* and *diminished capacity* to mark the boundaries between certain offenders who will be treated with compassion and others who will be punished with vengeance. Under the Skeptic's View, however, we can put an end to this nonsense.

I suggest that we place the primary emphasis about state of mind and receptivity to remedial measures where it belongs at a hearing to determine what *remedy* is to be employed and what containing, correcting, or punishing measures are to be borne by the offender. Indeed, in keeping with the treatment-based approach of the Skeptic's View, the issue of mental capacity is most relevant to the issue of *how* we treat and attempt to correct the behavior of the criminal offender, not *whether* the offender is guilty of a crime.

We all lie somewhere along a mental continuum. On one end of it, beings are wholly incapable of rational acts and on the other end, theoretically, beings are entirely rational and calculating. A person's position on the continuum means little to the equation of safety. We are all capable of antisocial acts. Where an offender's mental condition does matter significantly, however, is in determining if and how he can respond to punishment and/or remedial measures and how the penological system can best ensure that he presents no future threat to either himself or society. This is the social high ground that the Skeptic's View attempts to take and secure.

IV. Why the Skeptic's View is Needed

Something is desperately wrong with our criminal justice system. Recidivism, in some prisons running more than 80 percent, is evidence that prison prepares its "alumni" for crime while failing to impress upon them that they should not return to, or remain with, their criminal behavior. If we had an educational system with failures running at this rate, we would demand change. If our doctor used nineteenth-century theories, science, and practices, we would not tarry long in that office. Change, in both theory and practice, is overdue.

When everyone is trying to behave, almost any criminal justice theory will do because offenses are fewer and sentencing mistakes are more easily ignored or suppressed. But as the percentages change and the numbers of those who have "beaten" the system increase, the focus on what we do and why we do it becomes more acute, and finding a more precise answer to the question of what to do about crime becomes critical. Law in civilized society is a surrogate for force, and every culture has norms that all must obey for a peaceful progress. How we punish offenders must have a legitimate reason, a defensible moral and philosophical basis, and be focused upon simple and understandable goals like public safety and obedience to the law. This is the essence of the Skeptic's View. I submit that any legitimate theory of justice must satisfy these fundamental requirements.

I do not intend here to present a conclusive argument for my beliefs. I cannot because I, too, do not have the data, the research results, and the knowledge. The question *why punish*, cannot be answered on *a priori* grounds. It can be answered only by studying the social consequences of our sentences. Reality is always more complicated and varied than the theories by which we attempt to render it coherent. I speak as a searcher, and I have tried to present a developmental, transitional, and evolutionary model open to, anticipating, and welcoming our developing understanding of human nature. It is not easy. Yet, at the same time, my Skeptic's View is simple: Correct if we can and contain if we must.

The Skeptic's View is not about prisoner's rights, although I do not deny that prisoners have some rights. It is not about some *bleeding heart* plan for saving the poor lost souls in prison, although I firmly believe that prisons contain many such people. It is about community security and the obligation to strive consistently towards that which makes it safer. The Skeptic's View may not be the place to end the inquiry. It is, however, a place to begin.

V. Conclusion

Robert Penn Warren's observations are still true today. Upon close examination, the *crime equals punishment* equation is too simplistic to account for the myriad of motivations, emotions, and the deeper sociological and psychological trends that account for human behavior. Let us not be fooled by short-range statistics into the facile assumption that all is well. All is not well. There is now such a volume of crime that it has its own momentum and a life of its own. Success therein is when you get away with "it," whatever "it" is. Our prison system has become like a vast university with a student body that is nearly two million strong. This system counter-educates its wards in anti-social and counter-cultural skills and holds graduations daily. What are you going to do when one of their graduates moves into your neighborhood? Think about that now! Time is running out.

We need to reexamine our theory of criminal justice from its philosophy up. I have outlined the parameters of just such a theory today. A new credo referred to as the "Skeptic's View". I do not seek utopia. However, I do seek an escape from dystopia. I believe that to see beyond the immediate horizon requires an imaginative frame of reference. Accuse me of being a penological idealist if you wish. To that, I plead *nolo contendere* (no contest). Daily, however, I am a pragmatist. I want to know what works, and I reject any scheme that settles for less than what is possible. The time has come for a new philosophy, one that comes from a blueprint of wisdom, that is built upon a foundation of knowledge, which is carried out by humane means, that seeks corrective ends, and which strives for the purpose of securing the public's safety. The Skeptic's View is big enough to be benevolent, it is secure enough to be kind, it is honest enough to see failure, and pragmatic enough to do the necessary.

In closing, let me leave you with one illustration that sums up what I stand for, and, in a most awful circumstance. Think with me—Who really is this person Timothy McVeigh? Really? We know that:

> One day he was conceived by a mother and a father;
>
> One day he was born;
>
> One day he learned to crawl;
>
> One day he learned to walk;
>
> One day in diapers;
>
> One day in pants;
>
> One day he left home for school;
>
> One day he left school for work;
>
> One day . . . one day he detonated a bomb . . .
>
> at the Federal Building in Oklahoma City and he killed 168 innocent men, women, and children, fellow humans whom he did not even know, and, for which,
>
> One day he will be put to death.

The question I keep asking over and over and over is this: What happened to the baby boy? What happened to all the baby girls and boys? We lost them, somewhere, and we are continuing to lose them, with disastrous consequences. I do not plead for a terrorist who *knows* why he committed his evil deed. I plead for an America that *does not* know why. And I weep for an America that doesn't care. Francis Bacon said, "for in revenge a man gets but even." That is not good enough for me. We control the house and the game, and I want better odds. I think we need to come out ahead. Dispensing punishment, causing pain to offenders is not enough. Killing Timothy McVeigh is not enough. We must employ means to avert pain, to save victims, and to prevent crime in the future. I am skeptical that the current system can accomplish such goals. This is the Skeptic's View.

VI. Questions and Answers

The following is a compilation of the question and answer sessions following the lectures upon which this essay is based. Some questions were duplicates, or quite similar, so I have combined them. In doing so, however, I have strived to express precisely the language of the question, and the mood of the questioner.

Questioner: I have two questions: Do you think we will ever allow the condemned to simply take a pill and end their own lives rather than face execution? And what do you think of victimless crimes?

Nygaard: To the first question, no. As long as we seek revenge and punishment for our offenders, we will not allow them to take their own lives. This is not Socrates drinking hemlock tea. Please understand, in today's scheme we are not just trying to end a life but to avenge a killing. Recall with me that recently, in another jurisdiction, a condemned man tried to commit suicide. He was rushed to the hospital and resuscitated only to be executed later. We want revenge. To allow one to gain the control over his own life to the extent that he can control its termination frustrates that desire.

As to the second question, one usually refers to such crimes as, for example marijuana use and prostitution, as victimless crimes. This first, marijuana use, is currently too overlaid, and for that matter overladen, with moral and political overtones to be dealt with undetachedly. These factors must be dealt with before the issue can be approached jurisprudentially.

The second example prostitution, is *not* a victimless crime. Indeed, this crime is unusual in that, in my view, the defendant is also the victim. Where is the crime? I think we must question what right does anyone have to *buy* the body of another? This to me strikes at the heart of the hypocrisy of our macho, male dominated criminal law system. The buyer of the body is the real criminal, isn't he? But that's a whole new lecture, isn't it?

Questioner: How does rape fit into your theory?

Nygaard: I am not sure I know. I have always answered letters I received from prisoners, and I have quite a collection of them. An analysis "from the inside" if you will, is that rapists cannot be corrected and spend their time plotting how they will do it again. I don't know whether this "peer review" is accurate. I do know that rape is one of the most complex of crimes, with moral, power, psychological, and maleness/gender social overlays, with our cultural sexual hierarchy thrown into the confusing equation. Many rapists may be amenable to nothing. But any analysis must cope with these psychological, emotional, moral, and emotional overlays.

Questioner: I didn't understand your answer.

Nygaard: My response to specific *crimes* is that I don't know. I would have to ask "what rape" or "what rapist?" My theory is that the penal response should be tailored to the specific offender. It may be that we cannot release him. Safety is the key.

Questioner (follow-up): How about chemical castration?

Nygaard: I think we have more to learn about that. I suspect, however, that if we study offenses and offenders, we will find many alternatives to just "doing time." These may be more pragmatic and, indeed, prevent subsequent offenses. Many of them may be chemical. We are controlling a lot of behavior that way now. Pharmacology, it is called. Schizophrenia, for example. Again, the point I keep hammering on is research, testing, and accountability for the results. Look beyond the immediate crime to prevent others. Chemicals of many varieties may hold a key and play a role.

Questioner: Aren't you concerned that you may be accused of messing with people's minds; mind control?

Nygaard: I hope so. That is what correction should be about. Look, we require that children attend school, and we mess with their minds for twelve years. We call it education. We teach science, mathematics, etc. Then we give them philosophy and ethics in college, long after it can do much good, I must add. I suggest that we begin to teach ethics and, yes, law in grade school. Many laws are merely the embodiment of fundamental moral injunctions anyway. I suggest that if we are going to require people to obey the laws, it would be easier if we inculcate the morality that underlays them and teach them as social expectations and requirements to be performed, not just as laws requiring outside enforcement. Social skills and knowing cultural expectations are as important as many other skills taught to our youngsters. Yes, I want the criminal justice delivery system to mess with people's minds.

Questioner (follow up): But you seem to refer to intervention before they commit crimes.

Nygaard: I am. But there are many ways to do that. A friend of mine has done considerable research into urban planning and architecture to prevent crimes. This is the ecology of crime I refer to. But more, the Supreme Court recently decided a very interesting case, *Kansas v. Hendricks*.[5] By this decision, the Supreme Court authorized the retention and treatment of one who had served his sentence after the state showed that, if released, the offender posed harm to himself and/ or others. When we decide to treat, not merely to punish, new options open to us. I think this case is of enormous importance to sentencing reform.

Questioner:　I have been a physician for twenty-six years, sixteen of them as a psychiatrist, and I question your premise that we can change behavior. I have worked with juvenile offenders, and I have made such a minor percentage of change that, well . . .

Nygaard:　At what age do you think we have to get to them?

Questioner:　Very early. Maybe by one. It may just be genetic.

Nygaard:　First, I must say up front that I have a fundamental disagreement with you. I think we *can* change behavior. My basis is empirical. I have seen it in my sentencing. But therein lies my frustration also; the sentencing judge has insufficient tools. Prison alone, punishment alone, is not enough. That's my point! Many, perhaps most, sentences are now determined in the halls of some legislature far removed from the crime and the criminal; the judge merely imposes them. If we are to progress, that, at a minimum, must change.

Let me say that I would love to work with someone like you to fashion real remedies that treat real people. The specialist with the knowledge, the judge with the authority, and an institution in which to do it.

Questioner (follow-up):　What happens if you fail? I mean, if I make a mistake, I can be sued. What happens if you do?

Nygaard:　Nothing. That is one of my points. We must account for our actions, reactions, and remedies. Right now we do not. No part of the system really does account for results. I think we should start to do so. And when I say we, I include the legislatures, which now have great control over the sentences—sometimes fully determinative control.

Questioner (follow-up): I agree with you there. I have been a physician for thirty-two years. I am very dismayed that in your lecture, not in the Warren story or anywhere, you don't talk about the victim. How about the victim?

Nygaard: You weren't paying attention! What did I say my panel of experts would comprise? Not only victims but victim-rights organizations. I said the victims would be the centerpiece of the sentencing decision and not for superficial reasons. But I will readily add that my focus is beyond the person who has already been victimized. I view my most salient goal being to prevent other victims.

Questioner (follow-up): I also wonder about changing; my view is that it is all the influence from the family.

Nygaard: Fine. You may be right, or . . . (gesturing to the doctor who felt it was genetic). How then do we create or recreate family or some surrogate for it for the children who have none?

Questioner: That's just it, you cannot.

Nygaard: I'm not going to give up that easily. First, we can continue to guess and just take stabs at what we consider to be the problem. That is foolish. Or we can, as I suggest, empanel experts like you folks and really look for answers rather than trying to manipulate results according to our own predilections. That's what I want. I'm talking about a complete overhaul of the whole system.

Finally, there is mounting evidence that the family, while paramount, is only one integer in the equation, and social milieu may play an even greater role. Perhaps we could better invest our education dollars in the four years before kindergarten rather than the four years after high school. Maybe our PhD's should teach pre-school and grade school. That is something to think about. Perhaps we could create a cultural family to teach social rules and skills to those for whom the traditional family had defaulted. Research, research, research, and more research. Study and experiment. That is what I keep pressing. The reasons for crime may be as legion as viruses. But I suggest that we begin isolating them, one at a time if necessary, and look for ways to treat, palliate, or cure.

Questioner: I have spent many years in the ER (Emergency Room). I have seen the [injured] victims. Have you ever done that? Have you ever seen a murder victim die?

Nygaard: No, I never have. But what does that add to the equation? I am against revenge. It is counter-productive. My view is that someone must stand back from the event, take a pragmatic look, and see how we can do better to prevent other crimes. This is the most complex of questions to answer, usually asked out of pity. But that is not the point. We can only hope to palliate her suffering. Pity is laudable, but it does nothing for the penologist in terms of discovering causes and reasons for crime.

Questioner (follow-up): You sound like you have spent so much time with the criminals that you are taking their side. Are you sure you aren't doing that?

Nygaard: No, recall what I was saying. I am trying not to take sides at all. I want a system of delivering justice for the victim, for society, and for the offender. I will admit that I believe the pressing need is to begin to deal effectively with the offender. He is the one who will present the future threat to society. Look, if we do not deal justly with the offender, whatever we do to him cannot be the most productive because it will likely just harden him. We can't do anything about the past. The lessons of history are worth nothing unless we use them to inform the present and prepare for the future. I have compassion for the victim, but I do not let that cloud my judgment of what must be done now to prevent other victims. I have an abhorrence for what some offenders have done. But I try not to let that cloud my judgment. We must learn from one offender how to prevent other crimes, how to prevent other persons from becoming offenders. It is not much different from what you doctors do. Do you not hope that in losing a fight to save one patient, you can learn something about the disease that may save others? Sure you do. That's medical research. Physicians and research hospitals are a paradigm for what we can do. I want to see the same thing in penal research.

Questioner (follow-up): I think when someone kills another, that he forfeits his right to life.

Nygaard: Let's analyze that. We have 22,000 to 25,000 homicides each year in America, and we sentence a minor percentage of them to death. Whom would you kill? How many? All of them?

Questioner: (Pause) Yes.

Nygaard: (No response).

Questioner: I think we behave out of fear. I mean that I do what's right because I am afraid of the consequences if I break the law. Isn't that why we obey: we are afraid?

Nygaard: I am absolutely astounded! I think you are dead wrong. As I said, deterrence accounts for something, but we don't know what. Let me say that most people obey out of a sense of duty, because it is the right thing to do, not out of fear of going to jail. I disagree fundamentally with your premise. I think most of us try to do what is right out of perhaps compassion for others or a sense of shame of ourselves if we cheat on the rules of society. I think that if we fear anything, it is that if we screw-up, we will be exposed; as a result, our self-image and, I suppose, our reputations will suffer.

But first, let me be fair, and let's step aside from this question for a minute. Please, do not make the mistake of thinking of all criminals as *them*, bad guys from the other side of town. Sure, we have our share of *them*, and the pathological offender too. But many crimes are committed by people who have shiny shoes, who live in our neighborhoods, wear ties, and work in air conditioned offices. Many offenders are predators, yes. But many people just err. And remember, all were at one time first-offenders, perhaps when we could have done something to and for them.

Let me ask you, do you remember the ring of Gyges from Plato's *Republic*? Gyges removed a magic ring from the corpse of a giant. He discovered that by manipulating it, he could become invisible. By the power of anonymity, he murdered the King, seduced the Queen, and seized the throne. This is power! You could walk into a jewelry store and take anything you wanted. You could do anything you wanted. What would you do? Are you virtuous or vile? Don't answer, please. Think about it though; with the opportunity to perform good or evil, anonymously, what would you do?

One more thing while we are here, not all the crooks go to jail. In fact, very few of them do. You look surprised. Think with me about this. In 1990, Americans committed 35 million crimes, and we sent only about 500,000 offenders to jail. Two years ago the figure was 42.7 million and not many more went to jail. A lot of folks didn't fear anything. Right? Look, we can't have a cop on every corner. We can't even depend upon the concept of law enforcement to protect us. That's why I said we need a whole new approach. A whole new philosophy. We need change from the bottom up and the top down. We need to instill a desire or a duty to obey, not depend upon a fear of disobedience. We need to think about preventing 40 million crimes, not just punishing 500,000 offenders.

ENDNOTES

1. Ralph Ellison and Eugene Walter, *Warren on the Art of Fiction, in Talking With Robert and Penn Warren* 25, 49 (Floyd C. Watkins et al. eds., 1990).

2. Ellison and Walker, *supra* note 2, at 49-50.

3. Alvin and Heidi Toffler, *The Third Wave*, 53 (William Morrow 1980).

4. *See* Lois Forer, *A Rage to Punish: The Unintended Consequences of Mandatory Sentencing* 101 (1994).

5. 117 S. Ct. 2072 (1997)

ESSAY 7

The Insanity Plea,
Mental Defenses, and Punishment

[E]xcept for totally deteriorated, drooling, hopeless psychotics of long standing, and congenital idiots—who seldom commit murder or have the opportunity to commit murder—the great majority and perhaps all murderers know what they are doing, and the nature and quality of their act, and the consequences thereof, and they are therefore "legally sane" regardless of the opinion of any psychiatrist.[1]

Zilboorg

The term *insanity* no longer means anything useful either scientifically or legally, and should be stricken from our legal vocabulary. Nor are *diminished capacity,* and the few other terms we in law use to denominate the myriad states of mind, of much use to describe either the social danger or the remedial needs of an offender. Yet such misleading terms continue long beyond their useful years to mark the boundaries of criminal responsibility between certain criminal law offenders who will be treated with compassion, and the others who will be punished with vengeance.

It is fundamental to any enlightened legal system that each of us must be held to account for our own actions. And in any moral or ethical system, most acutely in the American criminal justice delivery system, the basic concepts of *right* and *wrong* mean little if each individual is not required to account for applying them in the conduct of his or her own affairs. Our system shares with most other systems the prerequisite to culpability for crimes, that the offender not only have *done* the act that the law forbids, but that he also have a threshold mental capacity to have done so with a specific or requisite will. That is to say, that he had the requisite free will to do other than commit the crime, and that his behavior was not somehow determined by a mental disorder.

That which the law calls "insanity" is an excusing condition that negates the voluntariness of an act, without which there can be no conviction or punishment. Mental elements or conditions necessary to establishing criminal "responsibility" are, in law, supposed to provide a bright-line division between offenders whom we call guilty (who are then held to account and receive condemnation, pain, and punishment for their transgressions) and those for whom we make various insanity declarations (who are relieved of responsibility and receive compassion, treatment, and care). Except in rare instances, the line is not clear and instead, *responsibility* or *insanity* tests have become at once both devices for avoiding punishment and uselessly unscientific tests for those who truly need help. They also reveal the ill-will and hatred that are the dark secret at the heart of our sentencing philosophy.

Insanity, whatever that term means, originally served to define a whole range of psychological and organic mental disorders and socially deviant behaviors. The term has disappeared from our scientific vocabulary, replaced by a myriad of descriptive terms used to qualify the various forms of mental illnesses and behaviors. The word insanity anachronistically survives in our legal vocabulary, notwithstanding the fact that this construct has no medical counterpart. It is defined in law as "that degree or quantity of mental disorder which relieves one of the criminal responsibility for his actions."

I posit that it is time to remove this line-drawing based upon semantic nonsense of sanity/insanity and responsibility/nonresponsibility that is cast in a concrete, nonscientific theory, defined by arcane nineteenth-century terms that, scientifically and jurisprudentially, are obsolete. It is also time to remove the determination of the accused's mental health from the procedural theater of the criminal trial and the *ad hoc* groups of lay citizens whom we call upon to decide issues of guilt.

The idea of using a panel of experts instead of jurors to determine an offender's state of mind is one alternative. First proposed by Dr. William White in 1911, many professionals from the health care disciplines have joined him. In 1964, Judge Joseph Weintraub, addressing the Annual Judicial Conference of the Second Circuit, proposed that insanity as defense should not bear on adjudication of guilt, but rather on determining appropriate sentencing remedies following conviction. Karl Menninger, M.D., stated in *The Crime of Punishment* that lawyers and psychiatrists are miles apart in their thinking on human behavior. Norval Morris, in his article, *Psychiatry and the Dangerous Criminal*, posited that psychiatrists do not function as successful healers of mental illness in criminal justice system, and that those prominent in criminal justice system reject the idea of insanity as a defense.[2] I agree with all four of them that we should place the primary emphasis about state of mind and receptivity to corrective or punitive measures where it belongs, with a panel of professionals, and at a hearing to determine what therapeutic remedy is to be employed, or what containing, correcting, or punishing measures are to be borne by the convicted offender.

Ascertaining the accused's basic mental capacity is significant to a threshold determination of who is capable of possessing a guilty mind at all. *Mens rea*, or a *guilty mind,* remains a consideration in guilt, otherwise the process under most current laws, may become constitutionally infirm. But the concept of intent is a rather low threshold. An offender's state of mind, among many other factors, should become of greater significance. I suggest, in determining the reasons for the crime and, to answer what should be the predominating question in the process—what shall we do with *this* person? The offender's sentence is supposed to be the remedy that will provide a safeguard for society against further predations by the offender, and it theoretically must be related to the gravity of the damage that would ensue if the criminal act or acts are repeated. Unfortunately, in reality, sentencing does not accomplish this objective. American penology is simply content to punish and seek revenge, without regard for either the reasons for the crime, or the consequences of the sentence.

Americans have an uneasiness about their penology, and for good reason. The vindictive nature of our sentencing policy has created a triangular tension between our revenge-based punishment on one point, the basic call to humanitarian consideration for our fellow citizens we claim to heed on the second point, and the need for incapacitating remedies for those who have made a decision to commit crimes on the third. The rancor, so evident in our sentencing scheme, adds nothing positive to the equation we should use to determine what to do with the criminal (including the calculating or career criminal).

The entire trial procedure is cloaked in myth and formalistic ritual, by which we seek to instill dignity and order in such important decisions as dealing with criminal guilt or innocence. But the calm of the trial is in stark contrast to the psychological and physical cacophony that will follow for the convicted criminal in prison. And surely the concept of retributivism, which is in reality revenge, runs counter to the predominant American faiths, enlightened notions of human cultural growth and social intercourse, the moral bookkeeping so fundamental to any rational correctional system, and, significantly, the discoveries of science.

Another such legally incapacitating condition is age. Juveniles are usually not found guilty—instead they are declared delinquent, based upon the theory of responsibility. The juvenile lacks maturity, biologically and emotionally, and often is not considered to be legally responsible for his or her acts. Like insanity for the adult, age often provides the juvenile a defense to legal guilt. Public outrage over some heinous acts performed by juveniles may sometimes cause prosecutors to prosecute the juveniles as adults. The motivation is the public's desire for revenge, which overcomes the sympathy otherwise felt for children.

There is no logical reason why one offender who is just short of a critical birthday should receive treatment different from one who has reached it. Chronological age simply does not matter except as it relates to the brain's development, and to the extent time has exposed one to the information necessary to make responsible decisions. Some people simply have not been given, or for various reasons have not developed, the psychological, mental, or social equipment necessary to make responsible, pro-cultural decisions. Some people never do.

This uneasiness is most acute in the manner with which the criminal justice system copes with offenders who suffer from some mental impairment, or neurological or brain dysfunction, and who violate the law. Peter Marzuk states that "[i]n the last decade . . . the evidence showing a link between violence, crime and mental illness has mounted. It cannot be dismissed; it should not be ignored."[3] None of us wants to be considered a bully for having taken advantage of either a mentally retarded or deranged person, or one who suffers from some recognized mental disability. It is no surprise that we neither want to execute the mentally disabled, nor place them in physical peril through imprisonment. We draw the line at doing something so outrageous. Our compassion for the mentally impaired has, nonetheless, nothing to do with whether the accused *did it*, or whether he is dangerous. Although a mentally disabled person may be as, or more, dangerous than the *normal* ward of the criminal justice delivery system. Most of us do not want to be known as so callous that we would kill or imprison a mentally deficient or similarly disabled person.

Theoretically, our policy is rationalized by contending that before punishment is inflicted upon one of our fellow citizens he must be truly capable of being held to account and responsible for his acts. But under scrutiny, the line-drawing in which courts engage to determine who will be killed, imprisoned, hospitalized, or freed, the underlying theory and the policy become bizarre. The court's methods to decide upon a person's state of mind (the tests and how they are applied) are a professional, philosophical, and humanitarian nightmare, and a cultural embarrassment. The law uses the fiction of what is essentially a yes/no answer to an offender's *responsibility*, to avoid punishing the mentally deficient offender, and from it no end of problems ensue.

Unfortunately we do not have legal tests for insanity to make sure that the offender is capable of profiting from a sentence. Our rationale for having these tests confirms that we are involved in sentencing with the most base of penal theories. Let us again briefly examine the four main philosophical rationalizations by which we justify our punitive sentencing, deterrence, containment, rehabilitation, and retribution, and see how mental condition play out in each.

Apologists for the general deterrence theory argue that by sentencing one person we will by example cause others who would not otherwise do so to behave out of fear of the consequences. Under this theory, however, punishment of the mentally disabled offender is justifiable because it would still influence others to refrain from similar activity. Under this theory, it would be irrelevant that the punishment did not affect the insane offender's behavior because punishing insane offenders would have positive consequences overall as a result of the exemplary effects on other persons.

Under specific deterrence theory, a sentence is rationalized by its effect on the offender actually being sentenced, and its goal of deterring him from committing other crimes. With respect to the mentally impaired, however, even the simplest minds are capable of feeling fear. Research reveals that individuals, wherever they lie upon the mental continuum, can think in some degree for themselves and learn lessons in differing degrees from experience. A study by the Royal Commission on Capital Punishment regarding the mentally disabled and the law reveals that "the great majority of the patients in mental hospitals, even among the grossly insane [and the psychotic], know what [conduct] is forbidden by the rules [of the hospital] and that . . . [breach of these rules may result in the] forfeit[ure of] some privilege,"[4] and hence, could theoretically be deterred.

As rationalized by the *containment* theory, we incarcerate offenders to prevent them from committing other crimes. Containment, however, would work in substantially the same way on all offenders regardless of mental capacity. As such, containment cannot be relied upon to account for our decisions whether to punish (criminals) or treat (the mentally deficient) as a justification for sentencing them differently.

Finally, that *rehabilitation* would be a systemic result from punishment is absurd and has been largely abandoned as a philosophical justification for sentencing. At least as it is now, when the sentence is intended as a form of punishment, and is executed by imprisonment. Charles E. Torcia says that rehabilitation does not "attempt to intimidate [i.e., punish] the offender" but rather to "instill[] . . . the proper values and attitudes, by bolstering his respect for self and institutions." I add it is simply incorrect to call rehabilitation punishment because in rehabilitation efforts the emphasis is not to make the offender suffer, but to make his life better, more productive, law abiding, and more pleasant.

Under the first three penological theories, the mental capacity of the offender is completely irrelevant. Only under the retributivist theory does it matter if the offender is mentally, biologically, or emotionally impaired, or wholly rational, because retribution is for the punisher, not the punished: Americans punish their offenders because they are angry and want to "get even." Judge Lois Forer writes in *A Rage to Punish* that:

> [K]illing by government no longer evokes a sense of revulsion in many law-abiding Americans who roundly denounce crime and violence. Vengeance as an appropriate response to wrongdoing is no longer shunned. It has become respectable.

I am afraid that she is correct. And, simply put, our humanitarian concerns do not permit us to pay back, get angry, or get even with a mentally disabled person who draws sympathy and understanding, rather than anger and hatred, from us. So, an offender who may be truly dangerous but who falls short of our unscientific and artificial mental criterion is deemed by our legal standard to lack the necessary state of mind to permit us to consider him "guilty" and subject him to our punitive sentencing measures.

Currently, in offense-based sentencing, the law punishes an offender based upon the offense he committed. It is not being intellectually honest, however, to claim that the "punishment fits the crime." Serious penologists cannot make such assertions without crossing their fingers behind their backs. First, there is neither theoretical nor empirical data to support any sort of "fit." Second, if the punishment were to fit the crime, as opposed to the individual, it would not matter whom we are punishing (mentally responsible or otherwise) if this individual actually performed the prohibited act.

I fundamentally disagree with the concept of proportionality—that a criminal sentence must be proportionate to the crime for which the defendant has been convicted. Philosophically, proportionality is a necessary premise to define the outer limits of penal pain. Current sentencing policy, however, has flipped this reasoning on its back and made proportionality the reason-in-fact for the sentence. Rather than using proportionality to limit punishment, it is used as a test to make sure the criminal gets his full share of pain for having violated the law. Thus, in our sentencing jurisprudence, proportionality confirms that punishment is driven by what one has done and, by a social desire for retribution.

By providing a "sane/insane" mental "loophole" for some offenders and for some crimes, American sentencing policy tacitly acknowledges that which it otherwise tries to deny, that individuals are truly different and should be treated differently. Seymour Halleck observed that in our current political climate, the pressure is toward eliding the psychological issues related to culpability, by narrowing the insanity defense or simply doing away with the diminished capacity doctrine. He notes that by providing a loophole for dealing with the worst possible cases [in the usual context, murder] the insanity defense acknowledges a distinction in our law for individuals, in the recognition that at least some offenders *are* different.[5]

But the binary option between sane/insane, diminished capacity or full, is like a teeter-totter, all up or all down. And, to make it worse, the fulcrum of this teeter-totter is moved around according to the vagaries of the individual trial and jury, and the persuasive ability of the experts who testify. Consequently, this most important decision of the trial and sentencing becomes arbitrary and nearly meaningless for an accurate and scientific determination of mental capacity or impairment. It is meaningless as well as to determine the degree to which one's behavior is capable of being changed, and the appropriate remedy for changing it. It is high time that we in penology abandon the unscientific concept that there is a bright line beyond which some individuals, the mentally, or otherwise, incompetent, lie. Rather, we should recognize that there is a mental continuum upon which all persons lie, each having our own deficiencies, diseases, predilections, actuators, and environments, that predispose some of us to culturally offensive behavior. Offenders need their own brand and degree of behavior modification before being released into society again.

Far removed from a scientific determination of who is legally *responsible*, and thus required to bear the full brunt of prison and retribution, mental condition has become a battleground in the adversarial guilt-determination process of the criminal trial, in which we have totally lost sight of the preliminary notions of criminal law which is safety and behavioral control. It is not even useful, when deciding upon guilt, to speak in terms of sanity or mental illness. Mental health or capacity cannot be divided into two categories, one for the fully rational and one for the totally irrational. It no longer makes penological sense to construct criminal law theory on such a simplistic, nonscientific distinction. The mental or emotional component of behavior is far too complex and too pervasive. Mental health services are now a significant part of most hospitals' programs and, indeed, of many services now provided to employees. A President's Commission on Mental Health found that one-fourth of all American citizens suffer from some form of "severe emotional stress."[6]

As Lady Wootton points out:

> Nature knows only infinite gradations in both the physical and the mental differences between members of the human species, and it is even probable that not only does one individual's responsibility for his actions differ from that of another, but that the sense of responsibility in the same individual may also vary from time to time.[7]

Psychologists from the National Institute of Health have stated that almost no family is free of some form of mental disorder. Perhaps none of us is.

It is too great a simplification to say that not all mental defectives are criminals, and correspondingly, that not all criminals are mentally defective. Although it is true that those who break the law are often "psychologically atypical," offenders are different from the law-abiding by the presence or absence of other shared characteristics. Some people, mentally sound or not, are neither sufficiently inhibited by the law nor by a concern over consequences to refrain from performing antisocial acts. Others do not have sufficient social skills to cope with temptation or to resist acting out their aggression. Still, others are pathologically incapable of remaining within the cultural bounds set by our civilization. It is to this last, the third category, that I direct your attention.

Criminal laws are premised on the notion that all are capable of free and rational choice between alternative modes of behavior, and that those who *choose* to commit crimes are culpable. Unfortunately, this simplistic formula, dividing offenders into just two groups, culpable and not culpable, loses sight of the myriad of actuators that may come into play in any behavioral decision. The Anglo-American tradition of relieving the onus of criminal culpability from this amorphous group of mentally disabled persons by reason of *madness* or *insanity* stems from developments during the reign of Edward III (1326-1377).[8] It was then that the main test for what was then (and unfortunately in law is still) called insanity, was enunciated. The test comes from the famous *M'Naghten Rule* announced in 1843 by the House of Lords in *M'Naghten's Case.*[9]

In January of that year Daniel M'Naghten shot and killed Edward Drummond, who served as private secretary to the British Prime Minister, Sir Robert Peel. M'Naghten shot Drummond in broad daylight and in the presence of a policeman. Investigators reported that M'Naghten approached Drummond "from behind in the open street, and in the broad face of day." M'Naghten shot Drummond in the back with one gun, and prepared to shoot him again with a second gun when a policeman, who had witnessed the event, seized him. It was later discovered that M'Naghten thought he was shooting the Prime Minister, whom M'Naghten, in his deluded state, thought was tormenting him. When asked by police inspector if he knew who he had shot, M'Naghten replied, "Yes: Sir Robert Peel." M'Naghten believed that Sir Robert Peel, the Prime Minister and leader of the Tory Party, was heading a conspiracy to persecute him.[10]

English common law had a tradition of taking an offender's mental state into account when deciding upon guilt.[11] Children, the mentally retarded, and insane persons were generally not held criminally liable. The law held that an offender could only be punished for an offense committed with a "guilty mind." Early English common law allowed insanity as a defense to common law felonies. The policy behind allowing the defense was that a felony required *mens rea* and an insane person did not have the capacity to have the requisite *mens rea* and thus, could not be punished. A lunatic, [the term used in that day for the mentally retarded or insane] it was said, "is punished by his madness alone."[12]

Because it appeared that M'Naghten was surely insane, and there was no desire to punish him, the primary object of the trial seemed to be that of establishing a connection between M'Naghten's insanity and the shooting. Nine expert witnesses testified on M'Naghten's behalf that he was insane at the time of the shooting, including, indirectly, Dr. Isaac Ray, whose just-published book on insanity and the law was presented at trial as relevant authority on the issue. Before introducing the contents of Ray's book on M'Naghten's behalf, counsel for M'Naghten held the book in the air, exclaiming, "I hold in my hand perhaps the most scientific treatise that the age has produced upon the subject of insanity in relation to jurisprudence." The expert testimony was so convincing as to M'Naghten's insanity that the judges cut the trial short and promptly submitted the question of M'Naghten's sanity to the jury. The jury easily established the connection between M'Naghten's insanity and the shooting and Daniel M'Naghten was sentenced to spend the rest of his life in an insane asylum.

That, however, was not the end of the case. The verdict in M'Naghten's trial received sharp criticism in England. Newspaper editorials claimed M'Naghten had been "profitably insane," feigning insanity to escape punishment. Others criticized the court for being too lenient and even naive. The Queen entered the fray by writing a letter to the Prime Minister (who was, coincidentally, the intended target of M'Naghten's bullet) criticizing the M'Naghten verdict. The Queen's letter prompted the House of Lords to consider the parameters of the insanity defense by reviewing the M'Naghten verdict.

Following review by the House of Lords, the fifteen judges of the English common law courts developed their tradition into a legal doctrine defining the bounds of the mental abnormality defense to criminal prosecution. This doctrine sets forth three conditions for a successful insanity defense: the accused must have suffered from a defect of reason at the time he committed his act; the defect must result from a disease of the mind; and that as a result of this defect the accused did not know what he was doing, or if he knew what he was doing, did not know that it was wrong.[13]

Specifically, what Lord Chief Justice Tindal formulated, and what would become known as the *M'Naghten* test as follows:

> [T]o establish a defence on the ground of insanity, it must be clearly proved that, at the time of the committing of the act, the party accused was labouring under such a defect of reason, from disease of the mind, as not to know the nature and quality of the act he was doing; or, if he did know it, that he did not know he was doing what was wrong.

Courts and criminologists have struggled since to decide whether this means *moral* or *legal* wrong. Some courts have taken the view that a defendant must simply not know that the act performed was morally wrong. Other courts have required that a defendant not know that the act was legally wrong. This latter view is clearly the view in England, where *M'Naghten's Case* is now interpreted to require that a defendant must lack the knowledge that the act was legally wrong.

The significance of this distinction between *morally* wrong and *legally* wrong is best illustrated by a classic hypothetical. If A kills B, knowing that he is killing B, and knowing that it is illegal to kill B, but under a delusion that God has commanded him to kill B because the salvation of the human race depends upon A killing B, then A is guilty if the word *wrong* is taken in its legal sense, but A is not guilty by reason of insanity if *wrong* is understood in its moral sense.

That the test even survived is amazing. It was quickly denounced, primarily because it failed to take into account the myriad other reasons why one may breach the rules, knowing them to be legal or moral injunctions, but having insufficient ability to resist breaching them. With the focus only upon punishment, even early critics decried how in a civilized system we could punish others who, although not mentally deficient, *could not* have obeyed the rules. Moreover, applied literally, the rule required total incapacitation of the offender's cognitive faculty, for him to escape responsibility and punishment. The test is based on a scientifically obsolete and a factually misleading conception of the nature of mental disease. In reality, mental disease (insanity) does not affect the cognitive or intellectual faculties only, but affects the whole personality of the patient, including both the will and the emotions. A mentally ill or deficient person may therefore often know the nature and quality of his act, and that it is wrong and forbidden by law, but yet commit it as a result of the mental disease. Under current tests, however, the offender simply must not have been able to *know*. This is an unworkable, intellectually dishonest, and scientifically absurd rule.

One year after *M'Naghten*, in *Commonwealth v. Rogers*, a Massachusetts judge expanded the doctrine to include some who *were* able to distinguish right from wrong. Rogers was a convict who had killed a prison warden by stabbing him in the neck with a knife. He claimed he had been insane at the time of the act, and extensive expert testimony was introduced on the matter. The judge instructed the jury that if it found that "the disease existed to so high a degree, that *for the time being* it overwhelmed the reason, conscience, and judgment" and that the defendant "in committing the homicide, acted from an irresistible and uncontrollable impulse" then the defendant's "act was not the act of a voluntary agent, but the involuntary act of the body, without the concurrence of a mind directing it." He instructed his jury that they could acquit the accused if the mental disease "overwhelmed the [defendant's] reason, conscience and judgment," and if the jury found that he was acting "from an irresistible and uncontrollable impulse."[14] Thus the irresistible impulse test broadened the range of mental disease that could excuse an offender by adding a defect in *volition* to the purely *cognitive* defects allowed by *M'Naghten*.

In 1859 the courts added another wrinkle to the *responsibility* fabric, when a jury acquitted Daniel Sickles[15] of killing his wife's paramour, finding Sickles to be suffering from *temporary insanity*. The trial of Sickles involved a sensational case that became known as the Sickles-Key Affair. Sickles was a United States Congressman in Washington, D.C., who had become friendly with Philip Barton Key, a United States Attorney who was also the son of Francis Scott Key, the author of the *Star-Spangled Banner*. Sickles had aided Key in getting reappointed as a United States Attorney. Not known to Sickles, however, Key was having an affair with Sickles's wife, Theresa. Key would come to the Sickles house waving a white handkerchief to signal to Theresa that it was time for a rendezvous.

When Sickles became aware of the affair, he waited for Key to arrive and, upon the wave of the handkerchief, Sickles emerged from his home and gunned Key down. At trial, Sickles advanced the defense of temporary insanity. It appears from the acquittal that the jury accepted Sickles's claim that he had been overcome by an irresistible and uncontrollable impulse and had been temporarily insane when he shot Key, notwithstanding his uncontested premeditation. Later other modifications were proposed to this largely unworkable doctrine of responsibility to make it conform to the facts of the more troublesome cases. But as with all rules of law, this one did not change quickly. Indeed, considering the tremendous advances made in the fields of medicine, psychiatry, psychology, and sociology in the past 150 years, the law virtually has stood still.

The next significant change came in 1871 when the New Hampshire Supreme Court rejected the *M'Naghten* rule as inadequate in *State v. Jones*. Jones also killed his wife after learning of her infidelity. The court reasoned that "[i]f the defendant had an insane impulse to kill his wife, which he could not control, then mental disease produced the act. If he could have controlled it, then his will must have assented to the act, and it was not caused by disease, but by the concurrence of his will, and was therefore a crime." The court promulgated a new rule: "[T]he verdict should be `not guilty by reason of insanity' if the killing was the offspring or product of mental disease in the defendant."[16]

This formulation did not attract attention until 1954 in the case of *Durham v. United States*.[17] The court in *Durham* adopted the "product" approach originally enunciated by the New Hampshire court in *New Hampshire v. Jones*. Durham had a long history of mental illness and was appealing his conviction for housebreaking, claiming that the test for criminal responsibility applied at his trial was obsolete. The court found that the *M'Naghten right-wrong* test, even when supplemented by the *irresistible impulse* test, was inadequate because it was too narrow. Instead, the court held that a person is not criminally responsible if his unlawful act was the *product* of a mental disease or mental defect. Instead, under the *product* test, an offender will not be held responsible if his act, while otherwise criminal, was the product of a mental disease or mental defect.[18] Relevant inquiry under *Durham* is directed toward medically informed concepts of mental health, rather than lay conjecture as to the defendant's total incapacity to make moral judgments.

Later, the Model Penal Code recommended further practical revisions to the rule of responsibility. According to the Code: "A person is not responsible for criminal conduct if at the time of such conduct as a result of mental disease or defect he lacks substantial capacity either to appreciate the criminality of his conduct or to conform his conduct to the requirements of the law."[19] The most significant difference between the Model Penal Code approach and the *M'Naghten* and *irresistible impulse* tests is that the Model Penal Code presents a much less rigid threshold, requiring merely a lack of substantial capacity to understand that the act is illegal, or an inability of an individual to conform his behavior to the requirements of the law.

In *United States v. Currens*,[20] the United States Court of Appeals for the Third Circuit criticized both tests as being too rigid for assuming that the mind "can be broken up into compartments, one part sane and the other insane," instead of "determining the total mental condition of the defendant at the time he committed the [criminal] act." Instead, "The jury must be satisfied that at the time of committing the prohibited act the defendant, as a result of mental disease or defect, lacked substantial capacity to conform his conduct to the requirements of the law which he is alleged to have violated." It should determine the "total" mental condition of the defendant at the time of the alleged crime. Therefore, it is not the mental defect, but the "total personality" which, as a result of mental illness, is responsible for the lack of control.

All of these tests made important and needed changes to the rules of responsibility. Now, throughout the states, several variations on these main themes guide jurors in the critical decisions they must make with respect to a person's mental capacity. Although *Currens* comes closest, none of these tests confronts the reality that clear and definite rules, so necessary for jurors who must decide these weighty issues, cannot account for the human psyche's myriad of variables nor for the offender who is defensively using these definitions as a strategy to escape punishment for his criminal acts.

Then Congress stepped in, creating the Insanity Defense Reform Act, which states:

> It is an affirmative defense to a prosecution under any Federal statute that, at the time of the commission of the acts constituting the offense, the defendant, as a result of a severe mental disease or defect, was unable to appreciate the nature and quality or the wrongfulness of his acts. Mental disease or defect does not otherwise constitute a defense.

Congress thus scrapped the volitional aspect of the insanity test and recodified the *cognitive* predicate of M'Naghten's case, bringing American jurisprudence full circle, back to 1843 and the House of Lords.

In reality, emotional and mental condition and the psychological components of behavior are more liquid than solid. Moreover, none of the doctrines now used in the criminal law recognizes that trained professionals should be the ones who determine a defendant's mental capacity, not lay persons who must sift through masses of conflicting, often incomprehensible, or at least uncomprehended, data to make life and death decisions.

A part of the problem is philosophical: sentencing relies upon the myth of punishment as the panacea for crime. This triggers a host of constitutional considerations that treatment does not. In reality, however, inflexible rules and myths can neither adequately educate jurors nor adequately differentiate between the varying personal motivations an offender might possess or actuate when committing a crime. It is the ambiguity of a mental test that would permit a court to transmute the test to fit each case or would permit a court to simplify an otherwise incomprehensible explanation for a lay jury. This, however, is precisely that which Congressional rulemakers have sought to eliminate.

With contemporary psychiatric and psychological data, the legitimate experts, who must testify about mental conditions, are unable to make accurate and scientific determinations fit into the rigid legal definitions the law imposes. Our current process systemically eliminates what is psychiatrically sound or psychologically workable, leaving us with a test for responsibility that may have no relationship at all to whether the offender needs help, punishment, confinement, or a combination of all three. Research indicates that offenders committing the same crime may differ greatly from one another with respect to the chronicity of their offenses, the role played by substance abuse, the danger they pose to themselves and others, and the needs for mental health therapy. Despite the results of scientific research, legislators are increasingly eager to propose simplistic solutions. Moreover, it is my experience that, contrary to the law, jurors filter out the law's jargon, and on the basis of their intuitive sense of justice simply decide whether, irrespective of expert advice and testimony, they think the offender is "nuts."

Trials in which a jury must decide upon the accused's guilt based upon the contradictory testimony of experts results in a "battle of experts" and virtually assures arbitrary outcomes. As I used to advise my juries: "No one is smarter than one expert. No one is dumber than two." With the freedom of the accused, and the safety of society, at stake, this sometimes arbitrary decision a jury must make as to which expert to follow, is simply not good enough. I have urged and continue to urge that sentencing practice and theory abandon the myth of punishment as the *raison d'etre* of the criminal trial. American criminal law needs to discover causes and motives of crime. And it needs to begin to provide therapeutic resources to rehabilitate offenders, rather than simply to build more prisons to contain them. We must begin to think of penology as an adaptable and multi-disciplinary process that can examine, accept, and implement proposed solutions derived from scientific discoveries if those solutions will help us reach a realistic goal, in this instance, public safety.

The current practice of determining responsibility and state of mind as a predicate to culpability is, however, in great tension with science and practical reality. American penal theory was developed 200 years ago and reflected the eighteenth-century theories of mind-body dualism, with the mind or soul as the source of behavior. It still does. Modern science, contrarily, is beginning to view the brain and the body more as a holistic biological system that expresses itself within and with a complex social ecology.

Antonio Damasio, in his book *Descartes' Error: Emotion, Reason, and the Human Brain,* gives the case history of Phineas

Gage, a twenty-five-year-old construction foreman whose entire demeanor and personality changed when an explosion sent a steel rod through the front of his brain, exiting through top of his head. Gage, a five-foot-six athletically built man, worked for the railroad, laying down tracks in Vermont. While preparing to detonate large rocks, Gage was distracted by nearby conversation and accidentally tamped the explosive powder with an iron bar, causing the powder to ignite. The ensuing explosion was so fierce that the iron bar flew through Gage's hand, entered his left cheek, pierced the base of his skull, traversed the front of his brain and exited through the top of his head at high speed, landing more than one hundred feet away. That Gage was not killed instantly was truly amazing. What was even more shocking was the account of the incident reported by the *Boston Medical and Surgical Journal*: Following the explosion, Gage exhibited a few convulsive motions, spoke within a few minutes thereafter, was carried onto an ox cart in which he sat erect during the trip to a nearby hotel and got out of the cart himself with some assistance from his co-workers. He was pronounced cured in less than two months (he was, however, blind in one eye).

Although Gage survived this ordeal, he no longer was the Phineas Gage his friends and colleagues had come to know. One account of Phineas Gage's recovery noted that although he had no speech or language problems, "the equilibrium or balance, so to speak, between his intellectual faculty and animal propensities had been destroyed." He often used language so foul that women were advised to stay away from him. Employers could not work with him, and he was routinely dismissed for poor discipline or, instead, quit in a "capricious fit."

According to Damasio:

> Gage's example indicated that something in the brain was concerned specifically with unique human properties, among them the ability to anticipate the future and plan accordingly within a complex social environment; the sense of responsibility toward the self and others; and the ability to orchestrate one's survival deliberately, at the command of one's free will.

Before Gage's experience, scientists' understanding of the brain was quite limited. Following Gage's ordeal, however, scientists came to realize an exceptional truth: "The observance of previously acquired social convention and ethical rules could be lost as a result of brain damage, even when neither basic intellect nor language seemed compromised." They discovered that there existed in the human brain systems that were dedicated to the personal and social dimensions of reasoning. Gage had once had a sense of personal and social responsibility, exemplified by the ways in which he had advanced within his employment, cared for the quality of his work and related to his employers and colleagues. Nevertheless, following his accident, Gage lost all respect for social convention, violated all sorts of ethical standards and made decisions without regard to his best interests. If nothing else, the story of Phineas Gage reveals just how complex the human brain truly is, and that we still have much to learn about the role it plays in our social development and existence [21]

I am not sure whether science can prove that humans have a "mind" or a "soul," or describe fully the thought processes of the brain. It does, however, show that each of us have a brain, nervous system, and genes that make us the individuals we are. I am not sure whether a judge can adequately describe "insanity" or "mental illness" so that they are workable concepts that a jury can use when assessing the guilt of an accused. If, however, physiological diseases, pathologies, and brain or neurological dysfunctions exist in the offender, science can establish specific diagnoses.[22] Then brain defects, mental illness, retardation, emotional stress, or genetics, if they are the reason for the offending act, can provide solid scientific bases for treatment or penal options, rather than simply allowing juries to reach a verdict upon conflicting bits of evidence that lead to what may be an arbitrary decision by, followed by another almost-arbitrary decision on how to sentence the offender.

Science is an enterprise to discover, to propose solutions for, and to provide at least probabilistic answers to ultimate questions such as these. New discoveries about the physiology of human behavior can also be used to prevent crime. Scientific tests have discovered, for example, that people who are violent are often low in the neurotransmitter serotonin (a product of amino acids which can be gotten from diet or from health food stores). Violent offenders have also been shown to have abnormally low levels of nutrient minerals, and abnormally high levels of toxic minerals such as lead, cadmium, mercury, and aluminum.

Other tests from a California study involving prison inmates revealed excessive levels of manganese in hair samples taken from them. Cocaine releases and then depletes the dopamine and serotonin supplies in the brain. All this is to illustrate that it is time to bring law into alignment with reality and science. Mental health is not an either/or status. Knowing an offender's mental state, nonetheless, helps point to the likelihood that his behavior is the product of his mental deficiencies. Science can help the criminal justice delivery system to determine whether the offender presents a moral problem, or a medical problem to be rectified.

All the retrospective approaches to the accused's state of mind as preconditions to a ritualized passage through the criminal justice system, in order to rationalize punishment are absurd. Indeed, these approaches successfully divert our attention from appropriate, prospective, problem-solving, and therapeutic approaches to behavior control. I submit that each traditional philosophical justification for punishment is seriously flawed, not just from difficulties of proof and the realities of misuse, but because nothing in a convicted offender's past can fully justify what is *now* done in the form of a prison sentence for any offender who will be released. The past is useful only as a portion of the diagnosis by which the criminal justice delivery system must determine how to correct, or how long to contain, the offender, and what must be done to prevent future infractions.

As I have suggested, it makes no sense at all to consider "sanity" when deciding culpability. All humans lie along a mental continuum some place between Zilboorg's "drooling idiot" and the theoretical, entirely rational, and calculating being. A person's position on the continuum means little to the equation of criminality. All of us are capable of antisocial acts. I suggest abandoning the concept of sanity as solely a function of determining culpability, and instead turn full attention to an examination of mental condition and capacity after the factfinder has determined, in a *whether* portion of a trial, that the accused *did it*. The court, aided by panels of professionals, can then determine *why* the offender committed the act, and employ the findings to develop the appropriate punitive, remedial and/or corrective measures. "Sanity," "diminished capacity" and "insanity," are only bits of semantic nonsense that should be removed from the trial. Crimes should be redefined so that mental condition is left to the decision of what must be done to an offender after it has been determined that he has violated our criminal rules and is a danger to himself or to others. I suggest that a complete mental examination by a panel of impartial experts be required for all persons accused of serious crime, regardless of whether they are raising the issue of criminal irresponsibility (provided, of course that all procedural protections of a criminal proceeding are made applicable to the examination and the results).

I also suggest that we consider revising our penal codes and trial procedures to limit the extent of the initial trial or plea of admission to whether the accused performed an act that fits the legal definition of a crime. A positive finding or a plea of admission on that issue would then bring the accused to a status that would require the court to consider remedial and/or therapeutic measures to be employed, such as containment, punishment, therapy, release, or some combination of those measures. Dr. Carol Barash calls our penal theory incoherent, drawing, as it does, a dichotomy between mental condition as a mitigating (resulting in less punishment) and as an excusing (wholly exculpating) condition.[23] I would go further and set both aside and look at the offender's *condition* wheresoever it lies on the mental health continuum as a basis to fashion a remedy.

The criminal justice delivery system should deal with defendants who claim a mental deficiency by bifurcating, or dividing their trials into two stages: a trial phase to determine whether the accused performed the forbidden act, followed by a second phase to discover the reasons why the offender committed the act and whether it was a product of the will, or determined in whole or part by genetics, emotional stress, mental defect, or any combination of reasons.[24] The first phase would focus solely on whether the government has proven beyond a reasonable doubt that the defendant performed the crime for which he has been charged. Mental capacity would not be an issue during this initial phase of the trial. Rather, in this portion of the trial, the finder or finders of fact are to "look at the defendant's actions and rely on their own perceptions, experiences, and common sense to determine whether the defendant formed the specific intent necessary for the crime."[25]

If the prosecution is able to establish beyond a reasonable doubt that the defendant performed the act, or if the defendant pleads guilty, the case would proceed to the second phase, devoted entirely to considering not only the defendant's mental capacity, but the full ecology of the crime and the criminal, with a view toward finding the reasons why the offender performed the prohibited act, and toward determining an appropriate remedy for him. Under my proposed revisions, line-drawing to determine responsibility need not preoccupy us. In the second phase of the trial, the finder of fact must determine the full extent of the defendant's mental capacity, not just the capacity to form the intent to commit the crime with which he has been charged. It would also enable the court to make other findings germane to the remedy, such as the *extent* or *degree* to which mental derangements or infirmities may have contributed to the crime. In this phase *all* reasons for the crime and *all* deficiencies of the offender would be explored to determine a corrective response to his act. Here, the court would not concern itself with requiring the social or physical scientist's analysis to fit into the legal system's definition of "insanity" or "mental disease of defect," or other similarly cloudy and often psychologically meaningless terms. Arbitrary sanity/insanity lines would be rejected, and each offender would be described in terms of whom he is, morally, mentally, emotionally, and genetically; what shall be required of him before he is released; and what the health, mental health, correction, or penal systems must contribute to support the process. The court, at this phase, would admit whatever expert and lay testimony "is competent and relevant to show the defendant's cognition, volition, and capacity to control his or her behavior," and not be limited simply to a binary yes/no finding about sanity as an exculpating condition. The goal being to devise a humanitarian response to an offender who is a danger to society if left untreated or untended. Although we must say to the offender, "You are all screwed up and must change." Again, I also know that we must add emphatically, "And we are here to help you."

This is not to say that the two phases could not be recombined in a structured plea. This would enable the defendant to know what remedy he faces when he enters his plea. Indeed, few trials are real "whodunits," in which the defendant pleads and contends that he is totally innocent. I suggest that degrees of guilt and technical defenses, the "stuff" of most trials would diminish as trial issues, if the defendant knew that excess punishment and revenge was out of the question in his sentence, and that he faced a no-nonsense, remedial or therapeutic sentence with known proportions.

I do not diminish the need to show an accused's basal capacity to form intent. I do, however, suggest that currently the tests used for intent are unscientific and unrealistic. I do also suggest, that given the myriad of actuators that come into play in human behavior, this phase be expanded to become the basis for remedial decisions for all who transgress the law. One who lacks the requisite mental capacity, whether due to mental impairment or some type of brain dysfunction, may not be found "guilty" in the contemporary sense, but may nonetheless require some form of commitment to protect society from further predatory acts.

Under my suggestions criminal law must abandon its preoccupation with punishment and direct its attention to devising pragmatic and humane remedies for all offenders. An offender who lacks the requisite mental capacity to "intend," and thus does not have a "guilty mind," may nonetheless require considerable help. The system should not be a screen to filter out those whom it does not want to, or feel it cannot, punish. There are many people passing through the criminal justice delivery system who just plain need help, regardless of whether they plead their mental condition as a defense. The almost wholly arbitrary decision as to who knows *right* from *wrong,* and hence, the decision whether to label an offender either mentally ill or criminal, results in a gross disparity: one offender gets treatment in an atmosphere of safety if deemed to be mentally defective, another gets punishment in an institution of danger if adjudged to be normal. Any intelligent and responsible parent and anyone else who has had experience in child rearing knows that behavioral problems are not merely a matter of the child failing to know right from wrong. From a very early age, children begin to discern what is expected of them behaviorally. When parents seek professional help to correct a child, especially one with a serious problem, it would be foolish indeed to limit the counselor to deciding whether the child knew better. We would want answers about the whole child. We would want solutions for the child.

I want answers and solutions for the criminal justice delivery system because the criminal law corrections mechanism is similar. It is, or at least should be, all about behavior. Behavioral control requires that we consider a myriad of actuators and motivators, and be prepared to respond to them. As Dr. Philip Q. Roche says, "Our criminal law is a child rearing system for grownups."[26] It matters little to public safety whether a person who committed a crime "knew better." Rather, it matters that a law has been broken and that an offender needs to be contained until corrected or treated so that society may once again become safe from further breaches of the public order by him. Whether an offender is a psychopath, sociopath, rational criminal, or simply a bumbling fool, he should not be on the street until controlled, cured, or otherwise corrected.

Finally, I note that the test for insanity and responsibility is most often employed in a most crucial sense, where it is probably least appropriate—in trials on a charge of homicide. Here, the procedural interplay is between the accused, who is at risk of losing his life for taking another's, and a public, whose paranoia over crime is at the site of its deepest roots, the loss of a victim's life. It is also here that we intuitively conclude that an offender must be at his most antisocial and inhuman limits because he actually took another's life. That makes he who would be so callous as to take a life seemingly the most fitting for the ultimate act of revenge. This may not be so, however, because here we also find offenders who are the least stable emotionally, morally and culturally. As Bernard C. Glueck, Jr. observed years ago in the twentieth century's most stable decade, the 1950s "It is my personal opinion . . . that no person in our society is in a normal state of mind when he commits a murder."[27]

Yet, it is only he who has killed whom we in turn would kill for committing the crime. Is the person who has committed a killing when mentally out of control, suffering from some brain dysfunction, or experiencing a life crisis, worse than the person who makes a calculated decision to become a career dope peddler, importer or manufacturer? Should not the passionate offender be easier to deal with dispassionately than, for example, a person or corporation who commits mass destruction of life, liberty, and property, coolly, deliberately, and to make a profit? And do not these deliberate and businesslike offenders really deserve worse? I answer, "no," "yes," and "yes."

> Pamela Blake and her associates examined 31 murderers and found none of them "normal in all spheres," and in 20 of the 31 they found more than one neurologic diagnosis. Evidence continues to accumulate that neurologic and psychiatric diseases may be at the root of significant numbers of violent crimes. She reviews other literature indicating that violent behavior often results from malfunctions in brain centers within limbic system and temporal lobes.

I suggest that upon close examination we will discover that we must personalize sentences. To provide essentially the same remedy to all offenders, regardless of their physical, biological, mental, or social condition, but who have committed the same crime is equivalent to prescribing the same treatment for all ill persons, whatever the kind or degree of illness. Offense-based punishment is like placing a bandage on the lesion while ignoring the bacteria, or equivalent to putting a balm on the open sore while ignoring the infection causing it. Every offender's sentence must treat him for his mental, personal, and social deficiencies, and not be simply a blanket treatment identified by the rule he violated. The sentence cannot, however, be personal unless the sentencer knows everything about the offender that the physical and social sciences can tell, and unless the criminal justice delivery system is prepared to engage all contemporary technology to model for it the appropriate remedial goals, means and tests for progress and compliance.

Although mental or other circumstances may explain crime, they do not excuse it. I believe in full accountability. Each offender must account for his actions, and to the degree to which he has the capacity or will to perform voluntary acts or refrain from them. This accountability cannot function fully in an all-or-nothing, sane/insane determination, in which the determination is merely whether the offender is responsible or excusable, and from which a decision must be made whether to send the offender to prison or a mental ward.

I believe that the criminal justice system should react to infractions of the law by imposing a treatment, a punishment, or both, that is proportionate to the needs and deficiencies of the individual being sentenced, while being consistent with the overall goal of public safety. It must make offenders realize that they as individuals are morally accountable and, if mentally and morally capable, hold the keys to their release—by conforming to the norms and goals of free society. In addition, it must view every sentence as a death-rebirth experience, a chance to bury an offender's past and create a responsible, productive citizen. Thus, it must call upon expertise from all the sciences in reforming and transforming the behavior of our social deviates.

In the event of an airplane or train accident, the cause is normally sought by intense investigation by numerous federal agencies, who thoroughly examine all the circumstances of the event. They look into any underlying physical or psychological abnormality in the persons concerned. And all is performed with the utmost thoroughness. Americans spend much time on that which may well be spectacular, but whose ramifications and pain touch comparatively few lives, and yet it expends little effort to discover the causes and cures for crime, which bring grief to an entire culture.

As Wootton concludes about the investigation of crime:

> The nature of the disease is not understood, and
> the treatment therefore palliative rather than curative:
> and the same could be true of criminality. At the
> same time a more sinister interpretation in the case of
> criminality is also possible—namely, that the treatment
> itself aggravates the disease.[28]

The conclusion is obvious to me. The criminal justice delivery system must look for causes, explore cures and accept, rather than manipulate, answers to the question, What works? The preliminary decision in sentencing at present is; Who should be incarcerated and for how long? As it now stands, courts for the most part impose determinate sentences set by a legislature far from the factual scenario of the individual case, and in a procedure that is wholly ignorant of the victim, the ecology of the crime, and the person to be sentenced. That cannot productively determine either whether he is a danger, or if so, what is necessary to neutralize his danger, nor can it determine when he will no longer be a danger and is once again capable of being replaced at liberty in society. This makes both the sentence and its duration nearly arbitrary. Determinate sentences, unless followed by and coupled with an indeterminate, goal-oriented period of corrective effort, bear almost no relationship to guiding the productive principles of penology.

An article entitled, *Prevention Versus Punishment: Toward a Principled Distinction in the Restraint of Released Sex Offenders,* published in 109 Harvard Law Review. 1711, 1713-15 (1996) discusses legislation requiring offender registration, community notification and DNA collection and registration. One such law enacted in New Jersey is known as "Megan's Law." It was enacted following strong public outcry resulting from the murder of a seven-year-old by a pedophile who had recently been released from incarceration. The opponents of "Megan's Law," which is intended to inform residents of the identities of convicted sex offenders living in their neighborhoods, argue that the law indefinitely strips the sex offender of his fundamental rights based solely upon an unreliable assessment of the convict's predilection to commit future sex crime

Another such law resulted from the killing of a twelve-year-old by a "career criminal." The large public outcry led to California's swift implementation of the "Three Strikes and You're Out" law. The general "Three Strikes and You're Out" law puts a three-time felon in prison for life, without a thought for rehabilitation.

Sentencing theory must take all that science has discovered about human behavior and, as in science, carry its discoveries out to the next decimal, and the next. The system must begin anew to amass empirical data on crimes and offenders with a view toward developing new sentence formulas, modeled upon all the data it can accumulate, and while keeping a watchful eye on the product—safe and productive citizens.

The simple get mad. The average get even. But the wise come out ahead. I suggest that sentencing policy start emulating like the latter. I am certain that there is no one formula that will solve all of the problems that cause crime. However, by progressing scientifically, by sharing data between court, the police, the prisons, and our probation and parole boards, and by honestly accepting answers, I believe the criminal justice delivery system can begin to renew the correctional system to respond to the deficiencies of the offender, whatever his crime, with a remedy that is designed to assure public safety. This requires that the simple responsibility/ nonresponsibility dichotomies be abandoned, and instead adopt a wide range of options for individualized sentences responding to the remedial needs of offenders wherever they lie on the continuum between Zilboorg's "drooling idiot" and the compassionless, calculating criminal.

ENDNOTES

1. Dr. Gregory Zilboorg, *Mind, Medicine and Man*, 274 (1943).

2. Published in 41 S. CAL. L. REV. 514

3. Peter Marzuk, *Introduction, 53 Archives of Phych.* 481, 481 (1996).

4. Royal Commission on Capital Punishment 1949-53 RPT 103 (1953). [hereinafter Capital Punishment].

5. Hans Toch and Kenneth Adams, *The Disturbed Violent Offender* 162 & n.7 (1994). Seymour L. Halleck, *The Mentally Disordered Offender* 61 (1986)

6. President's Comm'n on Mental Health, *II Report to the President From The President's Comm'n on Mental Health* 27 (1978) (Report of the Task Panel on Mental Health).

7. Barbara Wootton, *Crime and the Criminal Law: Reflections of a Magistrate and Social Scientist* 91 (2d ed. 1981).

8. John Biggs, Jr., *The Guilty Mind* 83 (1955).

9. 8 Eng. Rep. 718 (H.L. 1843). See Richard Moran, *Knowing Right From Wrong: The Insanity Defense of Daniel NcNaghten* (1981).

10. Biggs, *supra* note 29, at 98

11. For a discussion of insanity under English common law, see BIGGS, *supra* note 29, at 81-110; 1 Nigel Walker, *Crime and Insanity in England* (1968); F.A. Whitlock, *Criminal Responsibility and Mental Illness* 12-34 (1963); Homer D. Crotty, *The History of Insanity as a Defence to Crime in English Criminal Law,* 12 CAL. L. REV. 105 (1924). *Id.* at 110.

12. *See* BIGGS, *supra* note 29, at 81 (noting requirement of "guilty mind" or *mens rea* at English common law); Whitlock, *supra* note 33, at 55 ("'For some centuries, English law . . . has made liability to punishment for serious crime depend, not only on the accused doing the outward acts which the law forbids, but on his having done them in certain conditions which may broadly be termed mental . . . [which] are commonly, though rather misleadingly, referred to by lawyers as *mens rea*.'") (quoting H.L.A. Hart, *Punishment and the Elimination of Responsibility* 20 (1961)); Crotty, *supra* note 33, at 110-11 (noting English common law required *mens rea*).

13. *M'Naghten's Case*, 8 Eng. Rep. at 722. 2 Sir James Fitzjames Stephen, *A History of the Criminal Law of England* 149 (1883).

14. *Id. see* Wilson and Herrnstein, *supra* note 27, at 504.

15. For the transcript of the Sickles trial, see *The Trial of Daniel E. Sickles for the Murder of Philip Barton Key*, 12 Am. St. Trials 494 (1859) [hereinafter *Trial of Daniel E. Sickles*].

16. 50 N.H. 369 (1871).

17. 214 F.2d 862 (D.C. Cir. 1954), overruled by *United States v. Brawner*, 471 F.2d 969 (D.C. Cir. 1972).

18. *Durham*, 214 F.2d at 875. For a discussion of the "product" test adopted in *Durham*, see LaFave & Scott, *supra* note 14, at 286-92 (discussing workings and elements of *Durham* test); Edward de Grazia, *The Distinction of Being Mad*, 22 U. Chi. L. Rev. 339, 342-48 (1955) (same); William O. Douglas, *The Durham Rule: A Meeting Ground for Lawyers and Psychiatrists*, 41 Iowa L. Rev. 485, 488-95 (1956) (discussing *Durham* from psychiatrists' point of view); Herbert Wechsler, *The Criteria of Criminal Responsibility*, 22 U. Chi. L. Rev. 367, 368-76 (1955) (criticizing *Durham* test).

19. Model Penal Code § 4.01 (1985). For a discussion of the Model Penal Code approach, see LaFave and Scott, *supra* note 13, at 292-95. LaFave and Scott, *supra* note 13, at 330. A number of courts of appeal have adopted some variation of the Model Penal Code approach. *See, e.g., Brawner*, 471 F.2d at 973 (overruling *Durham* and adopting Model Penal Code rule while supplying its own definition of "mental disease or defect"); *United States v. Smith*, 404 F.2d 720, 727 (6th Cir. 1968) (leaving duty of determining precise wording of jury instruction to trial court, but requiring that three questions based on Model Penal Code be answered); *United States v. Chandler*, 393 F.2d 920, 926 (4th Cir. 1969) (praising Model Penal Code formulation but refusing to require any uniform instruction); *Wion v. United States*, 325 F.2d 420, 430 (10th Cir. 1963) (adopting essential elements of Model Penal Code formulation).

20. 290 F.2d 751 (3d Cir. 1961).

21. *See* Antonio R. Damasio, *Descartes' Error: Emotion, Reason, and the Human Brain* 3-14 (1994).

22. *See generally* Pamela Y. Blake et al., *Neurologic Abnormalities in Murderers*, Neurology, Sept. 1995, at 1641-47 (reporting results of neurologic study of thirty-one murderers between 1989 and 1993). Dr. Blake, along with Dr. Jonathan H. Pincus and Dr. Cary Buckner, established specific neurologic diagnoses in twenty of these thirty-one subjects. *Id.* at 1643.

23. Carol Isaac Barash, "The Insanity Defense: Legal Incoherence Equals Conceptual Confusion", in *Philosophy of Law, Politics, and Society* (Proceedings of the 12th International Wittgenstein Symposium) 128-31 (Holder-Pichler-Tempsky eds., 1988).

24. *See, e.g., People v. Wells*, 202 P.2d 53, 65 (Cal. 1949) (en banc) (stating that where insanity is pleaded as defense to criminal charge, trial is broken up into two sections or stages, but in eyes of law there is still only one trial); People v. Villarreal, 213 Cal. Rptr. 179, 181 (Cal. Ct. App. 1985) (outlining procedure for employing bifurcation); *Lucas v. United States*, 497 A.2d 1070, 1072 (D.C. 1985) (explaining bifurcation process); *Novosel v. Helgemore*, 384 A.2d 124, 129 (N.H. 1978) ("In the normal course, . . . the not guilty plea coupled with an insanity defense should be bifurcated upon request of the defendant."); *State v. Brink*, 500 N.W.2d 799, 802-03 (Minn. Ct. App. 1993) (discussing system of bifurcation required in accordance with Minn. R. Crim. P. 20.02 whenever defendant pleads "not guilty" and also raises defense of insanity).

25. *Brink*, 500 N.W. 2d at 803.

26. Roche, *supra* note 95, at 108.

27. Bernard C. Glueck, Jr., *Changing Concepts in Forensic Psychiatry* 45 J. Crim. L. & Criminology 123, 130-31 (1954); *see also* Blake et al., *supra* note 67, at 1641-46 (conducting study of murderers and finding brain dysfunction at root of their violent behavior).

28. Wooton, at 4.

ESSAY 8

The Rise and Flaws
of Law Enforcement

*The aim of every society must be a state of
affairs in which every man is his own constable,
until at last none other is required.*

Hippolyte Taine

I can recall with the clarity of a current event, the words of
my high school American History teacher, Harold
Richards, who admonished us:

> If Americans lose their respect for the law, or
> ignore their responsibility to obey the law, we are all
> in trouble. Laws simply cannot be enforced,
> regardless how efficient the police are. *You* must
> obey the law, and *you* must see to it that others do too.
> If it ever becomes stylish to disobey the law,
> democracy is sunk.

I was a junior in high school, and that was 1956. When I
returned from the Navy and entered college in the '60's, I began to
wonder: riots, open drug use, disrespect for the law and the police,
and indeed, an aversion to anything that was "establishment,"
indifference by many who had some institutional authority, made
it seem as if his prediction was being tested, or perhaps, was coming
true. I sometimes still wonder. Something in our social system did
change in that decade. Now, something in our social system must
change again. Because, socially we do not seem to have recovered

the sense of respect for the law and respect for each other that is necessary for social order.

The theory that punishment can function well as the primary component of the American response to crime causes everyone to suffer a little. Some, such as the actual victims of the criminal act, suffer greatly. Others, such as the victims' and the offenders' families, often suffer, too. Another, usually forgotten, class of victims of our dysfunctional criminal justice delivery system are the persons whom we have misnamed our *law enforcement officers*. It is to them we believe we can and must turn for protection from a host of dangers, difficulties, and threatening situations. This belief is problematic and is a part of the Hobbesian myth of punishment that has evolved into America's contemporary unsystem of criminal justice. Something more than law enforcement by police officers, and punishment for those whom they arrest is needed to maintain public order.

A primary question of governance that must be faced by those who would prescribe forms of government is how it will make people behave. Thomas Hobbes was among those who held a low estimate of humanity and believed that people are largely self-seeking, that what people understand best is force, and that fear of punishment will provide sufficient motivation to behave. Hobbes was from the philosophical school labeled realists. Like Hobbes, the realist believed that the answer to crime lay in laws with teeth in them. Hobbes created an elaborate system of punishments and rewards, with long and detailed laws. Early America subscribed to this theory, but, as we now see, at great expense.[1]

Today I doubt that police *protection* or law *enforcement* is a possible, or even a plausible, concept given the conditions of our culture, the attitude of its citizens, and the current state of our justice delivery system. For certain, I mean no disrespect to our police officers. I have the utmost respect for them as the most overtaxed, underrated, misused and misunderstood components in the entire criminal justice delivery patchwork. Daily they face the very real possibility that violence may be used against them at any time. Indeed, police scientist William Ker Muir, Jr., observes that police officers are the most frequent victims of this direct form of violence.[2] And we all depend upon them. The primary problem I see is in the criminal justice delivery *non*system itself and its underlying philosophy. Secondarily, America simply cannot defer the task of law enforcement to the police, and thereby elide the responsibility every citizen has to exert their collective pressure on others to obey the rules. It is not with the police officers who diligently try to accommodate the chores that our government has given them to perform within this flawed system.

Nevertheless, police officers stand among those who are the most beset and are consequently nearly crippled by the deficiencies of this system. Our criminal justice system fails to correct offenders, but the police officer is told to arrest them. By the very government that promises equality but delivers frustration, the police officer is told to go out and keep order. In a social system that perpetuates crime, and an economic system, a portion of which thrives on it, the police officer is asked to control it. In a culture that perpetuates violence, the police officer is asked to keep the peace. They are given laws that lack public support and told to enforce them. At election time their support is sought eagerly and is coveted greatly by politicians who, after the elections, just as quickly forget them. They are on the fulcrum between, on the one side, a culture that fails to prevent crime and an obsolete, post-act response to crime that fails to correct offenders before it releases them. On the other side of the fulcrum is a growing crimini-culture, fed by official violence, nurtured by failed social theories, and whose members are in desperate need of far more than the uniformed sentries of a city can provide. I am convinced that the common factor in all this is that the police department of today has been given an impossible mission to accomplish, and insufficient tools and support to deal with the certain failure that follows.

We give the police officer a nightstick and sue him if he uses it. We give him a weapon that is designed to kill people, and then relieve him of duty and thoroughly investigate him if he uses it for its intended purpose. When he fails to make an arrest, we criticize him. When he conducts a successful, but flawed, investigation and uncovers incriminating evidence, we, in a fantasy land bit of nonsense called the *exclusionary rule*, suppress it. Politicians boldly declare war on crime. But woe to the cop who behaves like a soldier. We feel a vicarious thrill of vindicating victory when someone *makes* Clint Eastwood's day. But just as quickly, we condemn the cop who behaves like Dirty Harry and *blows away* some creep, regardless how much better off the world is without him. Finally, and most significantly, when the officer makes an arrest, and irrespective of whether we imprison the offender, we release the offender without correcting him, all-too-often to violate the law again, prey upon society, and, perhaps (one would hope) to be arrested again. This is an absurd and vicious cycle that must be broken.

In sum, we have given our police officers a job (law enforcement), that no person or single agency is even capable of performing. We have built into this position great citizen expectation, great official responsibility to perform a function on our behalf, but without sufficient legal, cultural, or moral authority to perform it. No group can perform on our behalf unless we deputize them to do so. Americans are republicans to the core. And, if we perceive that our delegates or representatives in government have overstepped their delegated boundaries, we become indignant and rebellious. Hence, even the police officers' acts must be empowered by and enjoy the support of the culture they are deputized to protect. We have given the police officer more of a burden than can be reasonably borne. Then we recoil in horror at the *unreasonable* but certain results, low morale, psychological problems, high divorce and suicide rates, great frustration, and occasionally, as we saw from the Rodney King incident, catastrophic reactions. But, I ask myself: When officers must daily deal with people who are behaving at their worst, how can we expect them always to behave at their best?

I abhor violence in any form, and do not seek to excuse unnecessary force, even if employed by the police. But with *brutality* such a common cry of alarm, and from many and diverse places, it is evident to me that there is at least *a* common cause, or *a* systemic reason, perhaps there are many. If excess use of force is inevitable under current conditions, then conditions must change. If something is missing, supply it. If something must be removed, remove it. And I query. What have we done to this great symbol of safety and order, the peace officer, when the offender goes free and the arresting officers go to jail? There is a reason or, more realistically, there are reasons why. One of them is *not* that we hire psychologically flawed individuals to staff our police departments.

It is *not* that there is something fundamentally wrong with the individuals to whom we give the uniform, the gun, and the badge. There are many symptoms to indicate that we have culture-wide unsolved, and indeed, unaddressed social problems and that something is basically and terribly wrong with our *un*system of justice that is damaging the very individuals whom we hire to operate it. What are we doing? And why?

Most Americans tend to believe that the police officer's job is to *crush* crimes and catch those who commit them. When the crime rate goes down we give the police credit, which, from a critical and misunderstanding society, they are understandably all too happy to receive. This is probably undue. But so is the obverse. When the crime rate goes up, the police do not deserve the blame. The fact is that police are only one integer in the total equation of crime control and prevention, and the evidence indicates overwhelmingly that we will not control crime simply by enforcing laws and punishing those caught violating them. Former New York City Police Commissioner William Bratton states, "The goal of the criminal trial system is to seek truth and justice." "But," he adds, "in actual practice the goals of both the defense and the prosecution are to win. In the competition over who wins and loses, the truth is often left without a guardian."[3] As I have so often said to new judges: "You may be the only person in the courtroom who truly desires justice. Because unfortunately each side, defensively or self-righteously, just wants to win. Without a strong judge on the bench, *the truth* and hence, *truth* will lose."

Most of what policemen do has little to do directly with what concerns a fearful and insecure public, and what the statistician calls *real* crime: robbery, rape, burglary, assault, and murder. Most of what police officers do is actually in response to situations and complaints that statisticians deem minor (auto accidents, family quarrels, traffic, neighborhood disturbances). In other words, *the public peace*; events that may well be, however, the most important elements of social cohesion and control, and the most important function of the police officer. The law enforcement *response* to crime is by definition *after* the fact. Few criminals are caught in the act by police. With *real* crime, the average police officer's role is generally limited to mundane matters of filling out reports to be turned over to others who investigate the crime and who will, one hopes, at some point make an arrest. Few crimes are prevented by the presence of a police officer and, unfortunately, approximately 90 percent of property crimes go unsolved. So for 90 percent of property-crime victims, the system provides no relief and, for 90 percent of property crime offenders, the system provides no penal deterrent.

It is becoming clear that contemporary police, if limited to their role as law enforcers, have only a partial, albeit important, supporting role in crime prevention. As Professor Jackson Toby said, it is "the socialization process [that] keeps people law-abiding, not the police."[4] The relationship between civil disorder and violence is well documented. James Q. Wilson found that neighborhoods generally become vulnerable to street crime after they become disorderly. He found that a person's expectations about civil order diminished as general disorder prevailed.[5] Hence, peer pressures to conform to civil order become inoperative, and counter cultural opportunities and temptations become more attractive to potential offenders when persons are permitted to be personally offensive, when the streets remain dirty, when graffiti is allowed to remain, when the houses become run-down, and when the prevailing perception is that pride is gone, and that others no longer care. These conditions are neither under the control of, nor are they the responsibility, of the police. The persons and institutions, whomever they are, who encourage peace and maintain order do more to prevent crime than the law enforcement officers.

I am convinced that safety and civil peace are a result of a culturally integrated civic, social, medical, educational, and religious response to misbehavior. All individuals, agencies, and elements of society functioning together toward a single goal of civil peace and safety. We can prevent crime only by activating a whole system, culture-wide, dedicated both to safety and civil peace, and to seeking truth and justice. Society can only control crime if the criminal justice delivery system requires and promotes change in the individuals who transgress our rules, if the totality of social institutions promote obedience and duty among all citizens, and if we can offer a promise of peace among people who obey.

Some politicians dramatically call their programs a *war* on crime. The battle concept is flawed, because we fail thereby either to prevent crime or to destroy or catch a sufficient number of offenders. It is flawed because in the business of crime, or the crime of business, one cannot easily discern who is on which side. It is flawed, too, because when our mind set is fully for war, the arts of peace and prevention are of no use, and peace-makers are ignored. It is flawed because they who use or accept the concept forget that in any war both victor and vanquished sustain battle casualties. Pyrrhus said after the costly victory at Asculum, "Another such victory over the Romans and we are undone!" Although he had won victory after victory in battle, he lost so many troops in each battle that he despaired winning the war. The police are arresting and the justice system is imprisoning record numbers of offenders, but we do not seem to be winning the war. When the two million offenders now in prison get out, I despair that we too will lose the war. Then, too, the troops in *this* war are our friends, neighbors, children and spouses. They are not composed of expendable warriors operating alone. Our municipal troops are too precious to sacrifice in some ill-defined concept of war. We need a full-court, social press, not a war using troops whom we deem expendable. The *thin blue line* should simply be considered as one color in a whole spectrum of institutional hues comprising a tartan-like pattern that should be a criminal justice delivery system. But something is going wrong.

The concept of a civilian police began approximately 150 years ago when police departments were developed as a component of a total social system whose by-product was peace and order in the city neighborhoods. Police were not primarily engaged in *law enforcement*, they were proactive as peace officers.[6] When the police were watchmen of the town, as the visible tip of the civil peace and order-control function and the obvious tip of the coordination function, they were successful. Alexis de Tocqueville ascribed the success of crime prevention in America to the public interest, stating: "In no [other] country does crime more rarely elude punishment. The reason is that everyone [in America] conceives himself to be interested in furnishing evidence of the crime and in seizing the delinquent."[7]

Then, the police officer did arrest persons, did enforce laws, but they represented more, much more.

But over the past three decades a subtle change has occurred. The cop on the beat with intimate knowledge of his and her subjects is all but gone, replaced by mechanized "patrols," who incidentally patrol, but essentially respond to calls from victims for assistance. Their essential role until this change began was really to maintain the social order and to reinforce the other instruments and institutions of social control operating in our culture. The causes and effects of both crime and control differ little today. Where other institutions of control are functional, and the public interest and cooperation with authorities is high, police work will appear to be effective. Where few or no other social control mechanics are operational in a neighborhood or city, (or are counter-functional) the police, no matter their numbers, will be able to do little to control crime, and able only secondarily to respond to reported crimes and possibly arrest the offenders. This reactionary method may place the police officer at the crime scene long after the crime has been executed. This is crime *reaction*, not crime *enforcement* or *prevention*. It is a system that guarantees that there will be victims. And it is absurd.

Setting aside crime for a moment, the notion law enforcement or after-the-fact reaction to offenses, pervades in other areas as well. Think with me of the Highway Patrolman or Trooper, who has discovered the best places to hide a patrol car on stretches of the highway where motorists are most likely to be speeding, then spends his shift writing tickets. This officer is tacitly and practically abdicating a responsibility to prevent speeding, by acknowledging that he or she either cannot or will not, and is only after motorists who have already violated the law. This practice accepts the notion that the law must be violated before acting. I recall one prevention-minded California Highway Patrolman, who, in patrolling a particular dangerous stretch of highway conducive to speeding and which produced a large number of accidents, hit upon the idea of simply driving down the highway, with lights flashing, at precisely the speed limit, allowing no one to pass. He wrote no citations for speeding. But, there were no accidents on his watch. That is not merely law enforcement. It is prevention at its finest.

> Although we cannot have a police officer on every corner, there is evidence, however, that perhaps we could have more foot patrols. Given the cost of installing and maintaining the necessary lights and equipment, some of which is now computer-controlled, the idea of officers in some cities and towns controlling intersections during the busy hours and stop signs controlling them at night, may be cost-effective.

The concept of *law enforcement* as a guiding, predominating police principle is a chimera. Realistically, we simply cannot rely upon detection and punishment to control behavior and assure safety. At least, we cannot rely on police detection and law enforcement. We cannot afford to have an officer on every corner. We cannot control the streets by might. As de Tocqueville summarized,

> There are no great men without virtue; and there are no great nations. It may almost be added, there would be no society without respect for right; for what is a union of rational and intelligent beings who are held together only by the bond of force?[8]

Rule obedience, civil peace, and public safety must come from the totality of social control institutions and mechanisms, from basic morals and social incentives, and from each citizen answering a call to duty and ethics, the call to obey, not from notions based upon post-violation detection and punishment. These institutions, morals, and obligations may be formed by greater social bonds in our culture. It has become apparent that they will not, however, be swaged by force. Immanuel Kant was right when he expostulated that ethics and moral performance generally must come from the notion of "duty" to obey or perform, not from self-interest or to avoid unpleasant consequences.[9]

On January 9, 1997, a Brinks truck spilled approximately a half-million dollars worth of coins, bills and food stamps, which were quickly scooped up by the residents of the poor neighborhood in Miami where the accident occurred. When asked by the authorities to return the money, the residents laughed, and nobody did so. The newspapers reported that one resident called it "a once-in-a-lifetime thing." I wonder, are these Miami residents really atypical? They may not be.

Because we have failed to detect and correct sufficient numbers of offenders, our legislators have offered overkill in the place of real progress. They hope the illusion of a powerful *tough* response, with greater numbers of law enforcement officers and greater punishment for those who get caught, will detract attention from the fact that we are really no safer. Because we catch so few, we cathartically hammer harder on them. As a consequence, some who really do not need punishment are punished and some who need but little punishment are punished too severely. As a result, all of society pays for the government's inability to prevent crime, or alternatively, its failure to catch and contain or correct the offenders. This method has never worked but has been tried over and over whenever it becomes unpopular to prevent crimes or difficult to catch offenders. As de Tocqueville also said, "[i]t has since [the middle ages] been discovered that when justice is more certain and more mild, it is more efficacious."[10] We did not learn the lessons from historical failure. We are not learning the lessons from current failures because no one is held accountable for the system's failures. Crime is still prevalent. The public still feels unsafe. And, no one is held to account.

Good behavior and self-control should be the end of all criminal laws, and must be so acknowledged. The key, however, is that social control and behavioral incentives to good behavior must be imbedded within the warp of our culture. Civil peace cannot be accomplished merely by politicians enacting criminal laws or declaring war on crime. Nor can it be accomplished by police officers expending even their best efforts to enforce the law. As long as we look only to a Hobbesian post-act enforcement of rules to *control* behavior, instead of preventive programs to *guide* behavior, we will never master the problem of *preventing* misbehavior. We cannot master the problem, and indeed, we know we cannot even analyze the problem, unless we begin to think of developing the teamwork of interlocking *systems* and related systems of behavior prevention, modification, development, capable of being studied scientifically for their successes, and, as a last resort, control by *post-hoc* punishment. The response must be a heuristic portfolio of different programs running in parallel towards a common goal, and, with a common vision.

In my vision of the twenty-first century, law enforcement will only be one integer in the entire equation by which we actively and proactively respond to crime. It will be a criminal justice *delivery* system. It may, as it now does, comprise police, courts, probation officers, prisons, and parole boards, but I predict that it will also encompass social scientists, physicians, and educators, and utilize other social institutions, in cooperation with business and private corporations for pre-crime intervention and prevention, and psychologists and other post-crime and post-incarceration therapists to support behavioral modifications. If the prison survives in its present form, its function will be limited to containing the cultural flotsam for whom all correctional efforts have failed or have been rejected, and who must indeed be severed from society. Finally, the system and its components will be called upon to account, individually and collectively, for results.

Then too, I see great value in relaxing the severe divisions of labor between the police on the street, the probation and parol officers, the staff in our courts, and the staffs in our prisons. I suggest that each element of this correctional equation or system would profit from a cross-vocational opportunity. Each should be intimately acquainted and involved with the other, at least at the staff levels. One of W. Edwards Deming's guiding principles is to "break down the barriers between departments."[11] He recognized in industry, as we must in the justice delivery system, that each element of the system will function better if it can appreciate what the others are doing, what others are contributing, and concomitantly, what is thus expected of one as a component of the system. This is Deming's *team concept*. It requires that each *walk in the others' moccasins*. My image of the criminal justice delivery system is labeled *safety*. Correction, detection and prevention are simply colors, forms and shapes in this safety picture. These various persons, however, are the elements of the safety delivery system who have the longest contact line with the offenders and potential offenders and stand the best chance for acquiring the knowledge necessary to provide a quality product—the public peace.

Hobbes was simply the wrong philosopher to follow or, more accurately, he is the wrong philosopher to follow today. We Americans simply do not respond well to a behavioral control system composed only of rules. We are independent, innovative, and respond to incentives and collectively established norms. Behavioral norms are not awful, arcane or fearful. But, they must be inculcated by a press of social sources. There are sufficient and known commonalities to establish the behavioral norms with which to begin: honesty, peace, respect for others' persons and property, and the list goes on. In *Religions of Man*, Huston Smith refers to what he calls a "water table" of humanity. It is that minimum threshold of values, which historically has permeated all cultures and their laws. Additionally, the tenets of all religions include some variation of a Golden Rule, "Do unto others as you would have then do unto you." See, e.g. ". . . thou shalt love thy neighbor as thyself." Or what Smith calls a Silver Rule, "Do not unto others what you would not have them do unto you."[12] Every segment of the cultural system must be a source of instruction and accept some responsibility for enforcing these common virtues. That includes employers and businesses, schools, synagogues and churches, neighborhood groups, and all cultural organs. Neither the power nor the duty to control behavior should be centralized, but instead personalized, individualized, and diffused into many systems, all working in parallel or series fashion to effect positive behavioral change, and all heading in the same direction, albeit, not all on the same routes.

These pathways to progress, however, are somewhat compli-cated by the fact that America has become one of the most traditionless cultures in history. This has come about by design. It is almost as if from the first instance we recognized that starting anew in the new world we should reject old traditions and should not depend upon a common ethos, or a common set of traditions, in the new world and the new government. Instead we, the practical realists, followed the notions of the theoretical realists and the *enlightened* like Hobbes and Jefferson, and instead proposed to be ruled by reason. That is to say, we believed that if we all had the information and education to reason well, we could be counted on to act sensibly both as leaders and followers, and the occasional misbehavior could be deterred by punishment. This has not worked. Perhaps I should say it is not now working. We are discovering that we need more. Traditions, whether the product of myth, religion, history or some combination thereof, are powerful instructors and operate subtly to induce right conduct. Traditions are indeed necessary.

Without, behavioral norms and traditions to guide society, nor this "full-court" press on the citizenry to behave, there is nothing save the threat of reprisal to discourage those who are otherwise tempted to misbehave. Force and threat of force is necessary for social cohesion because it must be called upon to suppress the self-interest that threatens the collective interests. But force *alone* is at once excessive and insufficient. It is excessive because, unless counter force has the full power of a police state, and unless repressive individual punishments are so massively and greatly coercive as to be socially repugnant, force alone does not assure peace. It is insufficient because history teaches us that the detection and immediacy of our response to misbehavior is the most significant deterrent, unless the force employed is massive. We have found however, that as traditions, and other institutions which follow them, diminish in importance in a culture, the voids have been replaced with an intensifying militia-like police presence.

For example, the Soviet Union's penal system was massive, excessive and brutal, but successful. It did control crime. While I was in Central and Eastern Europe providing constitutional and justice reform expertise, I found that Eastern Bloc citizens, who lived in fear of their government, had been, and had felt, relatively secure from harm by their fellow citizens. But how, why, and at what cost? These excesses and successes were both documented, and casually, but very matter-of-factly explained by a Russian procurator who said to me, "Under communism, one out of four persons was spying for the government. When you never know who would tell on you, you tend to behave." "And," he added wryly, "when we caught someone, it was very, very unpleasant." The moral order in the Stalinist legal system was set only by rules, which were strictly enforced and infractions of which were severely punished. This does work to a limited extent, but with awful consequences that are anathema to our liberal democracy.[13] Peace gained by force alone is uneasy at best because it is inherently unjust. Moreover, when the force abates, behavior deteriorates. Note the scale of cultural and legal unraveling that has taken place in Russia and some of the countries of the former Soviet Union. Social order dissolved when the police state disappeared. There were no traditions and behavioral norms, save the police state, and no institutions empowered to control or correct them outside of law enforcement itself. They had no philosophy to guide them. There simply was an insufficient concept of moral order and ethical duty to induce them to self-control their behavior. And as a consequence, Russia with plenty of laws to live by, lives instead in criminological chaos.

The law can describe the ideal, but it cannot guarantee it. That takes more. The law can outline consequences of misbehavior, but it cannot make us behave. That takes more. The law can define a marriage, but not the relationship. All this takes tradition. The police can crush rebellion, arrest law-breakers, and cause most of us to think twice about refusing to give due regard to each others' rights, but by doing so, they do nothing to create or define the *duty* we owe to each other as fellow citizens and neighbors. This too, is a element of tradition. Law helps, if it fully represents the will of the people, but it is not the whole answer. For this we need traditions. We have but few traditions, and, and now, we must recreate them.

Huston Smith states that without the spontaneous traditions that are developed over great time to accommodate the evolved notions of a culture, we must have deliberate customs.[14] This requires that we identify the values that are common and important to a society, the role the tradition must play in its culture, and then employ every institution to develop inculcate and internalize them. Confucian habits and traditions "were driven into the people by every possible means—temples, theatres, homes, toys, proverbs, schools, history, and stories until they became habits in daily life. . ."[15] These customs, habits and traditions must become what Walter Lippmann called one's *second nature*:

This second nature is made in the image of what he is and is living for and should become. . . Full allegiance to the community can be given only by a man's second nature, ruling over his first and primitive nature, and treating it as not finally himself. Then the disciplines and the necessities and the constraints of a civilized life have ceased to be alien to him, and imposed from without. They have become his own inner imperatives.[16]

Peace and order must come from within us. They cannot be acceptably imposed from without. As Confucius said in *The Great Learning*:

If there be righteousness in the heart,
there will be beauty in the character.

If there be beauty in the character,
there will be harmony in the home.

If there be harmony in the home,
there will be order in the nation.

If there be order in the nation,
there will be peace in the world.[17]

A government is legitimate only to the extent that it properly exercises the power delegated to it by the people. When government exceeds that delegation, although it may escape being held accountable for a while, the laws it enacts, to the extent they exceed the delegation, will not enjoy the support of those whom they are intended to control. The legitimacy of traditions, like laws, comes from, and is only as secure as, their actual relationship to the extent of control we as a people will accept or deem necessary. Unlike laws, traditions can evolve in such a way, and over such time as to remain relative to, and synchronized with, those needs. And, when so synchronized, traditions and the acceptance of the common ethos makes each of us a peace officer.

It is my firm conviction that law enforcement officers must become peace officers once again. To do so, they must become vulnerable to, and identifiable with those whom they serve and with whom they are to control. They must be neighborhood-integrated, know who is who, doing what, and why. They must be permanently assigned to neighborhoods and perhaps be required to reside in the neighborhood they serve. John J. DiLullio, Jr. points out that the Los Angeles police officer has the image of a *helocop* who swoops out of the sky, to visit the scene of a crime and in like fashion recedes. L.A., he notes, has become a high-tech game of cops and robbers, and the spectators are getting the worst of the game. Officers there are graded on how well they play the game, not on the crimes they prevent. This type of police department has become the paradigm of what not to be.

In contrast, other cities that have enjoyed relatively good police/community relations, have begun progressively to rethink their police role. Some cities have, without fanfare, quietly instituted neighborhood policing, and often have several of the city's police officers walking beats or patrolling on bicycles. The response to neighborhood policing has been entirely positive. Kansas City, MO., found out that when police officers got out of their police cars, good things began to happen. Street crime abated. People felt more secure. The officers felt greater psychic rewards from their work, and their relationship with the community improved.[18] From this and many other intuitive bits of evidence, we have come to realize that officers must have a lasting and territorial commitment and not simply be able to leave *the beat* behind them after they go off duty. As Nils Christie writes, the officer must have a sense of "vulnerability" to those whom he must police.[19] Police *stations*, as singular locations in a city, must diminish in importance and, in Toffler's terms, be "demassified." As Wellington said, "[T]he secret of success in war is to find out what is happening on the other side of the hill." That is also the secret to success in crime prevention. The officer must again become a part of, and find out, what is happening on the other side of the neighborhood. Laws must be enforced, of that I have no contrary illusion. But culture must run as much on *oughts* as *nots*.

For the police system to revert to its original vision and mission, however, will not be easy. The concept of law enforcement credits crime, because enforcement is graded, not on the peace it keeps, but on the number of arrests it makes. Police departments get institutional credit and police officers get psychic reward for solving a crime, for catching an offender. Among the public, until it is educated to the contrary, police officers will get a better rating for bravely fighting crime than quietly preventing it. We glorify that aspect in novels and films, and a macho culture of *crushing crime*, a mystique of the *blue knight* has paradoxically built itself around the quite authoritarian, but nonetheless heroic image. An example which Edwards Deming overheard in a seminar and gives:

> One gets a good rating for fighting a fire. The result is visible; can be quantified. If you do it right the first time, you are invisible. You satisfied the requirements. That is your job. Mess it up, and correct it later, you become a hero.[20]

The entire system of peace and justice delivery, judges, probation and parole officers, wardens and police officers alike, must be graded on success at safety and civil peace. Police departments (as indeed all of the system of social safety) must be rated or graded on the peace they maintain, not the people they arrest, convict and sentence, or indeed, not even the crimes they solve. Safety depends upon more than law enforcement officers. The entire criminal justice delivery system must be in constant dialogue with its police officers. The arrogance of ignorance does not enhance systemic coordination.

Police officers have been complaining about the courts and the prisons for years. We have ignored them to our detriment. It is time we start listening to them again. The vision of system must be of a teamwork process in which many take part, and in many stages, and in which no element is supreme. Penology must support this vision of the system by correcting or containing all offenders. The criminal justice delivery system that begins with law enforcement and ends with punishment and release, will fail to deliver either justice or safety. The system must grade each of its component parts on peace, safety and how well each component of the criminal justice delivery system produces safety. The system must grade itself and account for how well the system as a whole functions. A CBS, *outcome-based* system must be developed among all the coordinate sections of the system that should be called *protection*, a system that is accountable for its contribution to social safety. Or else, the police as enforcers of the law, and protectors of a culture will remain a myth.

The results of law enforcement are visible, and they can be quantified. In the sense of physical competition and law enforcement, crushing crime has greater drama, is far more exciting and, no doubt more fun as well. Peace officers, on the other hand, only get credit for low or no crime. Compare our notions of the contemporary law enforcement officer, with the institution of the *lensmann* of Norway. The lensmann is charged with the peace, and is credited with maintaining it. He or she attempts to prevent crime and to mediate disputes, rather than simply to make arrests.[21] Unfortunately, if you simply and quietly prevent crime, you are successful but invisible. Quite understandably it is also much easier to substantiate an increased budget or to argue with a city council for more officers if crime is up. It is far more difficult to substantiate staffing levels by telling the appropriating agency that crime is down. Nonetheless, only this second scenario shows real success because crime and victims are necessary predicates for law enforcement.

I think often of Mr. Richards, and that admonition he gave us in his American History class that day so long ago. I think of him when I hear of someone who turned their back on a crime because "they didn't want to get involved." I think of him when I hear of neighbors who banded together in watch groups because "they didn't want to lose their neighborhood to crime." I think of him when I lecture about our system. I thought about him when I set my goal and mission, to change the justice delivery concept and mission, for the whole system.

Mr. Richards is dead now. And so he will never know the impact that one statement had on me. But, I believe he would agree with me that peace was, and must become again, the real and acknowledged product of police work. He would agree that Taine was correct: we must work toward an ideal in which all members of society are constables of their own behavior. He would agree that the peace officer will have become totally successful again when the police log reads "Today nothing bad happened."

ENDNOTES

1.   Thomas Hobbes, *Leviathan*, Great Books of the Western World, Vol. 5 (1952) p. 145 et. seq.

2.   Charles E. Silberman, *Criminal Violence, Criminal Justice*, Vantage Books (1980), p. 316.

3.   "Notable and Quotable," *The Wall Street Journal*, Dec. 30, 1995, quoting from a speech given Nov. 14, 1995 at a symposium of the Harvard Law School's Criminal Justice Institute.

4.   Jackson Toby, "Is Punishment Necessary?", 55 *Journal of Criminology & Police Science*, (1964).

5.   James Q. Wilson, *Thinking About Crime*, Vintage (1985).

6.   Wilson, p. 74.

7.   Alexis de Tocqueville, *Democracy in America*, (1838), Henry Reeve text, Knopf (1938) p. 95.

8.   De Tocqueville, p. 244.

9.   Immanuel Kant, *Groundwork of the Metaphysic of Morals*, Trans. H.J. Patton, Harper (1964) p. 56-65.

11.   Deming, p. 202.

12.   Huston Smith, *Religions of Man*, HarperPerennial (1986).

13.   See Richard L. Nygaard, "A Bill of Rights for the Twenty-first Century," *Hastings Constitutional Law Quarterly*, Vol. 21, Number 2, Winter 1994 p. 189.

14.   Smith, P. 239.

15.   Chiang Monlin, *Tides from the West*, Yale Univ. Press, (1947), pp. 9, 19 (Quoted in Smith p. 239).

16.   Walter Lippmann, *Essays in the Public Philosophy*, Simon and Schuster, (1955) p. 137.

17.   Smith, p. 245.

18.   John J. DiLullio, "A Limited War on Crime That We Can Win," *The Brookings Review*, Vol. 10, No. 4, Fall 1992, p. 10.

19.   Nils Christie, *Limits To Pain*, Universitetsforlaget, Oslo (1981) p. 86.

20.   Deming, p. 107.

21.   Christie, p. 73-74.

ESSAY 9

Sentencing Guidelines:
Reform or Retreat

*I draw my idea of the form of government
from a principle in nature which no art can
overturn, viz that the more simple any thing is,
the less liable it is to be disordered, and the easier
repaired when disordered . . .*

Thomas Paine

L egislative control of criminal sentences is not new. The history of criminal laws, extending at least back into the eighteenth century, shows legislatures providing specifying sentences for specific crimes. Traditionally, however, these laws only provided maximum terms of imprisonment and maximum fines, leaving the minimum to be set but the judge. During the past two decades, this has begun to change. Legislatures, believing judges to have been too lenient, began to establish *minimum* as well as maximum terms of imprisonment, as *guidelines* for sentencing judges.

The U.S. Congress, ostensibly to correct disparity between sentences of different offenders for the same crimes, promulgated U.S. Sentencing Guidelines that in fact mandate (within a limited range) the term of imprisonment for each crime. Basically, the guidelines give a numerical point factor for each crime (the offense level). If specified aggravating facts are found by the court, it will add points to that level and, if specified mitigating facts are found, the court will subtract points. Unless the case presents atypical features, the final number is then compared to a chart that gives the sentencing judge the range in months of imprisonment or probation (and perhaps a fine) within which the offender must be sentenced.

The federal trial judge in reality has very little discretion in determining the duration of an offender's prison sentence. The sentences in significant measure are determined by Congress.

The concept of guidelines and mandatory minimum sentences has many detractors. I am not one of them. Inequities in sentencing practice and wholesale failures in American sentencing theory demanded action, and, Congress stepped into the breach. That having been said, I hasten to add that I believe the *current* United States Sentencing Guidelines, and many state guidelines, to be not only a colossal mistake, but worse—a missed opportunity. First, they represent a missed opportunity to make the U.S. system of corrections truly responsive to the real needs, not merely the momentary passions of society. Second, they represent a lost opportunity to make the federal system, which is a paradigm for many state systems,[1] not merely punitive, but in addition remedial and therapeutic, a correction-based system. To do either, of course, would have required that in fashioning remedies the sentencer look at more than what the offender did, or, more realistically, what he was caught doing. To fashion a remedial sentence, the sentencer must instead make the rather more difficult personal decisions required when someone looks into the character of the offender to discover where precisely the offender is deficient and what precisely is needed to correct him.

The current Congressional scheme is a mistake for another important reason, it violates one of the cardinal rules of a workable system, simplicity. Congress instead created a confounding farrago of technical rules. It lacks what in the computer age is called "user friendliness." I do not refer here merely to the myriad of rules, tables, equations, descriptions, comments, definitions and formulae in the guidelines themselves, all of which overly complicate the determination of a sentence (The Federal Sentencing Guidelines Manual is 1371 pages long). They are bad enough. But these clerical matters can nonetheless be largely computed by court functionaries from electronic spreadsheets, and often are based upon material and information supplied *extra curia*. The other and more important "user unfriendliness" problem I see is that this sentencing scheme is largely incomprehensible to the person for whom it should be graphically clear, the citizen and the potential offender. The guidelines' complexity also diverts attention from the simplicity of what should be the real goal of the criminal justice delivery system (safety), and the reproduction of an obedient citizen from a criminal law offender. The scheme keeps judges and probation officers so busy reviewing and so preoccupied with applying the forms and formulae, that they forget what the sentences are really to be about. Our sentencing philosophy, punishment, is simplistic to the extreme. Also the means of determining its duration and of parceling it out (the guideline sentencing scheme) is complicated to the ridiculous.

Some judges and theorists suggest that studies are necessary to determine if the guidelines are achieving their goals.[2] I take no quarrel with that. I believe that the criminal justice delivery system should fully account for its activities, and accept both credit and criticism where due. My questions, however, challenge the goals themselves. I would posit that every sentenced offender should be part of a longitudinal study that should question whether the system is deterring crime, and if so, how. Legislators, judges, prison superintendents, indeed the whole criminal justice delivery system should know whether offenders are coming out of the system better than they went in, and, whether we are containing offenders for the appropriate length of time to assure our culture of its safety from further predations by them. In other words it should question everything, and try to determine "what works," in our efforts to assure a safe society from the dysfunctional and misbehaving material that comes into the criminal justice delivery system.

Governmental inertia, ignorance about the consequences of poor corrections, and a lack of citizen interest, which translates into an issue that lacks political appeal for real reform, all conspire to present but few opportunities to examine and positively overhaul sentencing and corrections. The sentencing guidelines and the Sentencing Reform Act addressed only disparate sentencing (a laudable goal), but did nothing to address the root or reason of all sentencing, or consider the fundamental penological question: what do we want to achieve by the sentences, and what will be most effective in achieving our goals? Once we answer these questions and discover what works, guidelines will truly be helpful and functional.

I take no issue with some punishment. Indeed, it is the basic element of most successful corrections models, whether to correct a misbehaving child or a criminal law offender. But punishing criminal offenders by itself is not enough. Punishment requires nothing of the punished offender. In a punitive scheme, the punished offender has only to endure, and unfortunately, all-too-often merely becomes a more durable and culturally calloused criminal. Punishment may be considered a logical first step in penological plans and a step which may have been sufficient by itself when alternate institutions or elements in our culture effectively encouraged obedience and nurtured or coerced the punished offender back to social health. But it is no longer sufficient by itself. The alternative institutions and elements, family, school, church, synagogue, fraternal organization, that once performed that palliative function are weakened, failing, indifferent, defunct, or entirely missing, leaving only government and the punitive prison sentence at the terminal end of our criminal justice delivery system in their absence. Consequently, society feels it must increasingly turn to the justice delivery system to provide total readjustment for the maladjusted, total reclamation of the misguided, and total rehabilitation of the morally and socially debilitated. This may be possible if we proceed scientifically, and if we reemphasize and reempower all other cultural media to assist the system to prevent and control crime. But all this is more than can be done by punishment alone, which is both the universal remedy, and the current panacea prescribed by the sentencing guideline scheme for all offenses. The results are foreordained. The system has failed, is failing, and will continue to fail until it is completely overhauled.

For one thing, we err if we believe that by merely empowering government, and at the expense of alternative cultural media such as churches, synagogues, schools, scouting, fraternal organizations, sororities and other social organizations, it can cure crime. We err doubly if we accept government's solitary response, that by simply attaching an arbitrarily determined penal duration to the prison confinement it uses to punish offenders, it *is* effectively fighting crime. We err again if a sentence is not equivalent to the offender's need for containment or correction. No matter that it is equivalent to the sentences of others who have committed the same offense. Parity among offenders, however, is all the guidelines and mandatory sentences have done. This is the opportunity we missed by accepting, indeed participating in this half-a-loaf, or no-loaf-at-all, guideline scheme.

A theoretical and a practical problem with both mandatory minimum sentences and contemporary guidelines, as a solitary scheme for sentencing, is that our legislators who determine the sentence are insulated from both the situation and context of the crime and the recipient of the sentence. Currently the real sentencer is not even present at the critical moment of sentencing in our system. The sentence has been imposed long ago in Washington, D. C. or a state legislature. Sentencing has passed from the process where decisions are made by judges; professionals, formally schooled in the law, each of whom practiced and was selected from among his or her colleagues to be the sentencing specialist, the president of the trial. It has passed instead to the amateurs in our legislatures (no derogation intended), the citizen law-givers, who after all need no degree of any kind, let alone in law, psychology or sociology, and who are far from the actual proceeding wherein appear the victim and offender alike, and far from the first-hand view that the judge can give the crime, the offender and the victim. As Nils Christie states, "The judge [has become] only a tool, an instrument of destiny."[3] The expert on sentencing, the judge, has become only a functionary in the process. And as Sir Samuel Romilly observed:

> Every novice in politics is permitted, without opposition, to try his talents for legislation, by dealing out death to his fellow creatures; and laws of this kind commonly pass without observation or debate; whilst the most insignificant bill concerning money obtains repeated discussion.[4]

Viewed from the perspective of political science, sentencing now is primarily a legislative function. It has little to do with penology or sentencing philosophy, both of which are traditional concerns of the judiciary. Legislative sentencing by guidelines or mandatory minima is a political implement. Whether a sentence performs any utile function is far from the legislator/sentencer's minds. The legislator fulfills the wishes of the electorate, which now wants revenge, and enacts sentencing laws that have long mandatory minimum terms. The judge cannot decide to exercise mercy, shorten the prison term, sentence the offender to community service, or require that he accomplish remedial steps before release, even in an appropriate case, and must bear allegiance to the law, as set by the legislature. The executive is content to execute a sentence as inexpensively as possible, regardless of whether the offender is released from prison better or worse from the exposure. No one in this scheme is wholly responsible. No one accounts to society for failing to correct the offenders, who, upon release, now return to the system in frightening numbers. And, not surprisingly, little improves. No one in this scheme sets the goals or ends of punishment. No one now really determines what the end product should be, which we hope is a corrected individual, to see if anything truly has been accomplished.

British criminologist Barbara Wooton states:

> If we really want to get trained and efficient sentencers, the way to do it is to reduce to the minimum the number of people who have to be kept informed and trained, and to keep them in close touch with one another and with those who provide them with their information.[5]

Courtroom sentences imposed by *trained and efficient sentencers*, determined upon all factors, permit the judge to exercise mercy in a case where the pre-calculated sentence is too severe, unnecessary or counterproductive. Or, alternatively, permit the judge to impose a more severe sentence if the facts of the case and the character of the offender warrant it. Neither crimes nor offenders look the same on paper as they do in real life.

In the current sentencing scheme, the law has made it easy for a judge to justify her or his sentence. No deep philosophical reasoning is required. She or he must only recite a litany of reasons sufficient to show a consideration of elements deemed by our legislatures to be proper components of the nearly-preordained decision.[6] It is simple. The sentence with some discretion, is simply what the law requires, or in some cases, what the law permits. Sentencing guidelines have systematized sentencing, reducing each sentence to a quantifiable figure, drawn from a known and carefully developed, essentially offense-based formula. Designed to bring parity to sentencing, the guidelines opted for the law of averages and sacrificed efficacy for certainty. They have, as a result, made the sentencing procedure and the sentences themselves almost meaningless. Philosophical justification unfortunately is not required of our delegates in government who create the laws, of the judges called upon to apply them, or of the executive called upon to carry them out. Few are now concerned with the end product they create.

It is time that penology did not lean so heavily upon the slender reed of proportionality—that the "time must fit the crime," at least not for the major portion of a sentence. Denunciation and retribution may indeed be both a cultural necessity, and a valid philosophical support for sentences. I take no issue with some punishment if the primary positive function of retribution, hence punishment, is to make the victim and society feel vindicated by having the offender "repaid." I agree that some short, severe "shock treatment" type of punishment may well be necessary for the offender's correctional experience *and* for the law-abiding public's perception of the sentence. Our goal must be, first and foremost, social safety. But following the short and possibly *more* severe determinate sentence sufficient for the punitive purposes of retribution and denunciation, a sentence must follow a correct-or-contain-based plan that would require the participation by, and action of the sentenced individual.

Governmental retribution, by harsh and long prison sentences, contained in legislature-mandated sentencing, is also a failure in its other aspects as well. First, because the retribution is too remote in time and space. And, second because it is inadequate to purge the anger felt by the victim. The offender's impact upon the victim is now virtually meaningless to either the judiciary, whose hands are tied by the legislature's guidelines, or to the offender, who gains little by feeling compassion for his victim. Hence, although the victim may testify at a sentencing hearing, he or she does not really participate in the decision. "Victim impact" evidence may be used to enhance the duration of the sentence, but does little to add anything corrective or constructive. The trial, ritually should be to victimization and the concomitant anger; what the funeral, ritually is to death and its concomitant sorrow. Sentencing, like the committal and interment of the deceased, should provide a mythological end to the anger process of the victim and of society. Unfortunately, it is not.

As currently constituted neither the trial nor the sentencing are providing a full measure of this potential. Unless the victim is invited to participate in the process by which the offender is actually sentenced, and not just a ritual in which a sentence previously determined is imposed, the procedure deprives the victimized society, the victims and the offenders, of an essential factor in criminal justice which is an honestly constituted and fully empowered forum in which to express grief, anger and pain, to tell their version of the events of the offense with the prospect of a meaningful, not a merely cathartic, participation in fashioning the sentence itself. A confrontation between victim and offender in the sentencing hearing is as important to the healing function of the entire procedure, as the right of confrontation is to the truth-gathering function of the trial.

A pre-determined sentence, whether by guidelines or a mandatory minimum, also frustrates the ritual nature of the process and compromises its integrity. If a sentence is truly to correct, the victim must be a cornerstone of the proceeding. Not that the criminal justice delivery system should do what the victim wants done to the offender, but that the victim can thereby personally participate in the process by which she or he receives a measure of satisfaction, and by which the reality of the end of the unpleasantness is graphically marked. The ritual must require the offender to account for his actions to the court, in the victim's presence, and allow the victim the opportunity to rebut, correct or otherwise participate. Like the funeral, the trial and/or sentencing ritual must offer the victim and the victimized society the therapeutic opportunity to release authentic feelings of their grief and anger. If a sentence is to correct *and* heal, as I submit it must, the victim must participate meaningfully in the proceedings. That is not possible if mandatory minimum or guideline sentences are predetermined in the halls of some legislature or a committee room far detached from the ritual being performed in the courtroom. Hence, the sentencing process is neither satisfying to society (who want to feel safe) nor to the victim, whose feelings now mean but little to the sentence. It satisfies no one.

It is deceptively easy to say that if an offender "does the same crime," he should "do the same time," as other offenders. It is a nifty jingle for society that lives on one-liners and sound bytes. But, it has more sound than bite. Even crimes described alike, and which appear alike, are different. A serious deficiency of the most common form of guidelines and mandatory minimum sentences is the manner in which they determine sentences and their duration. That is to say, punishing people for what they are caught doing, not for what they are. This defies all we know of human nature, and, moreover, is simply not working. The first message of offense-based sentences to the offender is that it does not matter who you are, or how evil or good you are. You will all be basically classed the same. The second message is thus, that it does not matter how much you progress towards reform during the sentence, because its duration had already been determined by what you did. As Barbara Wooton further states:

> If the primary object of a sentence is to discourage further offenses at the cost of minimal interference with liberty, then the moment at which this discouragement is effective enough to justify the offender's release can hardly be forecast in advance: it must depend upon his progress.[7]

Even documented personal progress by the offender towards reenculturation would mean nothing for a mandatory sentence, or a compulsory guideline.

Release upon progress is a demanding scheme and requires much of both the system and the offender. It requires, before release, a full *resentencing* procedure, during which all factors would be reconsidered in light of how the prisoner has progressed in his correction. And, I submit, this novel "hearing for release" that I propose is more important than the initial sentencing hearing. The primary purpose of the entire criminal justice delivery system is, ostensibly, safety of the public. Hence, like the initial sentencing, resentencing release hearings would be charged with determining if the offender's correction has progressed to the point that he is safe to be reenculturated, or whether he must be returned to the institution for further containment. And, equally as important, the entire system must be held to account for its results (the product it produces) not the offenders it incarcerates, but the safe citizens it releases. Nothing less will do.

From this logic, guidelines and mandatory sentences are twice removed. Not only do we base our legislatively mandated sentences on unrealistic criteria, not only is little, usually no prediction made as to possible or expected corrective progress by the offender. On the contrary, the sentencing determination or what the system will do to the offender, is in fact made long before he is even called to the dock. There is no forecast, moreover, there is no follow-up to research the success of past sentences. Hence, we have no data from which to reconfigure future sentences to succeed where past sentences failed. The legislatively mandated sentence only looks back, as all retributive sentences do, at what the offender was caught doing. What happens in the future to the sentenced offender is both well-documented and totally ignored. Most often, he will get worse. Society will suffer. But, the legislator will get reelected. The noted criminologist, Professor James Fox, criticizes the American fascination with what he calls "the three 'R's of sentencing: retribution, revenge and retaliation." I do too. He also adds a fourth 'R'—reelection—as the expected result of legislation based on the first three.

The medical model provides an analog: the parallels are striking and dramatically illustrate the shortcomings of the criminal justice delivery system. Think with me of a simplified HMO system in which a provider is given an amount of capital, a population of potential patients and is told, "Keep them healthy. Your success (or salary) depends upon it." This concept is moving the medical response up the chain from therapy to prevention. Unfortunately, American penology is regressing and has overtly turned its back on therapy and has adopted a "leper colony" mentality with respect to its offenders. Treatment or therapy is not a priority with either the legislatures or the courts. Prevention is not even a gleam in their eyes. It is as if this HMO is run by undertakers.

I remember the days of which Judge Weinstein wrote in "Some Reflections on Seven Lean Years of Guidelines Sentencing."[8] Judge Weinstein recalls that in the days before the sentencing guidelines, at sentencing one discussed such moral concepts as *right* and *wrong*, such penal concepts as *responsibility* and *rehabili-*

tation. Like Judge Weinstein, I keenly rue their passing. Instead, today what one hears discussed at sentencing are numbers and grids, cross-references, and case interpretations. But I felt then, nonetheless, that I was wholly ineffective because I had little more than duration to play with because the remedy was the same— prison or probation. I longed for a fully integrated criminal justice delivery system, in which all elements worked together, conferred on correction-based sentences, established correctional and thera- peutic goals, then supervised the progress, and accounted for the results. My primary point is that all elements of the criminal justice delivery system must begin to act like a system. From police at one end to parole officers at the other and all, including judges in between, with the same goal of public safety. Preventing crime, ideally. Correcting offenders, hopefully. But, containing offend- ers when necessary.

During a recent year citizens reported that 35 million crimes had been committed against them, but only about 500 thousand, or fewer than 1.5 percent of offenders, were actually put behind bars. Yet from these statistics, (or perhaps ignoring them) our legisla- tures have determined that the appropriate course was to compel longer sentences by establishing guidelines and mandatory mini- mum durations for sentences, build more prisons and hire more law enforcement officers. In other words, beginning with 35 million crimes at the top of the statistical funnel, and ending with 500,000 offenders incarcerated at the bottom, legislatures have nonetheless chosen to expand the bottom of the funnel. This is an approach that guarantees crimes, victims, and, unfortunately, more arrests, more trials, and more sentences. I submit that this is madness. Victims, policemen and courts aside, how many new cells do they think will be sufficient to make us safe? What percentage of growth in prisons will do, 200 percent, 500 percent, 1000 percent increase in the number of cells? One hundred percent increase in cells will enable us to incarcerate 3 percent of offenders. Our current national cost for our failing systems exceeds $75 billion dollars. It is painfully obvious, even to the least sophisti- cated, that we cannot afford to make the scheme now enacted by our legislatures successful. And the top of the funnel is growing. The goal must be refocused on earlier events, to prevent crimes, not just incarcerate offenders. We must begin to work on the top by preventing crimes, diminishing the number of victims and saving money. In other words, working on the intake end of the funnel. Our current penology ignores that end.

Another problem we fail to recognize or confront in mandatory minimum sentences and the promulgation of sentencing guidelines is that there is no commonly accepted national standard or cultural ethos by which to impose or legislate as serious a remedy as a criminal sentence. This is what H.L.A. Hart called "the fallacy of speaking of the United States as if it were a single country."[9] We simply cannot realistically punish or remedy a metropolitan offender by the same standards as may be valid to punish or remedy one convicted of the same crime in rural America. Nor, of course, the obverse. This great land is where the best in the world are united and diversity is our strength. But, the United States Congress has transformed diversity into the weakness of America's approach to crime control. Congress has adopted a "weak-link" formula and by the survival of the weakest, the formula has transmogrified criminal penology into something that is applied everywhere and works nowhere. The sentences are more uniform, if all we want to consider is the crime. They fail, however, to address that which must be changed—the individual.

Norwegian criminologist, Nils Christie states that, "a system that allows itself to be directed solely by the gravity of the act in no way contributes to a satisfactory set of standards for moral values in society."[10] In our penology the crime itself is considered so important that it overshadows all other considerations of what must be done to protect society. The individual is secondary, each of us within the system knows it and consequently, so does the offender. I am not content with this scenario. We treat everything except the problem, the person. A CBS, on the other hand, would emphasize the character and potential of the individual when determining what must be done with him to protect society; and, it requires that **he** do something which is account for his transgressions and improve.

I believe it incumbent upon we judges, who have been endowed with great authority and yoked with great responsibility, to consider Plato's admonition and challenge that "Until the kings become philosophers or the philosophers kings, we shall have no justice." Of course, America has no kings. We do, however, have leaders such as judges, whose solemn responsibility it is to become and remain knowledgeable of not only what they do, but why they do it. I do not view Plato's oft-quoted statement as elitist. It is to me, instead a awesome challenge. The promised land is one wherein "life, liberty and property" are protected. That is the cornerstone of American thought. Society and culture and safety must be the first building-blocks of justice. And, the judges are the fulcrum upon which the system that delivers these rights to the people rests. The judiciary is too important to the proper operation of our democracy, to have its sentencing options so circumscribed by the legislature. Judges must become philosophers. As De Tocqueville stated:

> The existence of democracies is threatened by two principal dangers; namely, the complete subjugation of the legislature to the will of the electoral body, and the concentration of all the other powers of the government in the legislative branch.[11]

The story of legislatively mandated sentences, illustrates both dangers.

Stephen R. Sady argues that the probation officer must not be viewed as just an advocate (what he calls a "second prosecutor"). "Eliminating the Adversarial Role of the Probation Office," *FSR.* Vol. 8, No. 1, (July/ August 1995), p. 28. I quite agree. But, I suspect they will be so viewed as long as we continue to conceptualize the sentencing process as a procedure for rationalizing a punitive scheme, rather than as a remedial opportunity. I suggest that we shift from the *adversarial* procedural posture of the guilt phase of the trial to an *inquisitorial* procedural posture at the sentencing hearing, with the probation officer serving as a counselor to guide the court in imposing a corrective based sentence, and to the offender to help guide him through it.

The law enforcement officers, the probation officers, the prison staff, the counselors and, most of all, the sentencing judges are what Peter Drucker calls the "knowledge workers," who should be endowed with the authority to formulate an appropriate CBS sentence for the offender.[12] Knowledge workers are persons who bear some on-the-job responsibility for actions and decisions. They are the persons who must be empowered and supported in their role as decision-makers, not supplanted as Congress and many legislatures have done in the sentencing guidelines and mandatory minimum sentences which cripple good judgment, not support it.

By enacting Draconian guideline and mandatory sentencing schemes, legislatures have turned their backs upon what each of us knows of productive decision-making. Instead of educating, supporting and "tuning" on the unwise or even biased judgments, legislatures have simply removed the function from the courts and judges and centralized it in commissions and committees that are supposed to respond after-the-fact to the need for changes in sentencing. This scheme, by design, will produce a significant number of unwise and unjust decisions, because the commissions and the committees cannot change the individual sentences that the courts have already meted out. No matter how costly, unproductive or unjust the sentences are, the committees can only change the guidelines and minimum sentences for the future offenders. This is an antiquated executive model of leadership, and it is destined to be unsuccessful with horrible results to our culture. A shorter mandatory term, followed by an indeterminate correction based sentence, and a hearing before release, would provide a needed post-sentencing look at the offender and the productivity of the sentence.

After having said all that, I hasten to reiterate that I am opposed to neither the *concept* of mandatory minimum sentences nor am I opposed to the *concept* of guidelines. I am opposed to the *current* scheme of guidelines and mandatory sentences, because it simply adds mathematical formulae, comparativity, and objective, offense-based criteria to a moribund philosophy, and because it is neither behaviorally realistic nor based upon rational penal goals. Correcting disparate sentences is both an illusory and an illegitimate target: I am not convinced that in itself disparency is a negative. Disparate sentences may have the appearance of injustice. The real question, however, is whether in a pragmatic sense, the sentence treats the root cause of the crime. We cannot answer that question in the first place when we fail even to find out why one has committed the crime. Disparate treatment for invidious reasons must be dealt with where it exists. Moreover, the future of no human being should depend upon the mood of the sentencing judge. But people are not the same, why should sentences be so? I think that they should not be. I suggest that the guidelines and sentence minima be retained, but be a part of an overall sentencing pathway to correction.[13]

To become fully functional, sentencing must become "outcome-based." No system has fully come-of-age until it is prepared to account for the quality of its product. And the current scheme of guidelines and mandatory minimum sentences further obfuscate accountability. Everyone can point to others as being responsible for penological failures. The greatest concern expressed today is how to do our components function efficiently. The police department by number of arrests, the courts by managing their backlogs, the prisons by effectively warehousing its inmates. All each cares about is that it does its limited function efficiently. And, none needs to account for the system's failures. The fact that some of our prisons are populated 80 percent by recidivists should give anyone examining the system cause for alarm. But, even if everyone is alarmed, what should be done? There must be developed a mechanism, a procedure and rules which not only enable but require all who are connected with the criminal justice delivery system to grade and be graded on their success and failure.

> "[N]o machinery [now] exists by which the success or failure of particular decisions in reaching the objective may be assessed. In consequences, it is impossible for anyone who passes sentences either to test his own performance or to learn from experience, and equally impossible to test the relevance of any information provided with the object of assisting the court to arrive at its decisions."[14]

This systemic deficiency is no longer either acceptable, nor possible. Good systems management, economics, and soon, the public will demand more.

Ignorance may be blissful, but it is disquieting once recognized. Many beliefs that have been bases of critical sentencing decisions, and once held dear, are now under new scrutiny. Offense-based criminal sentences, and the belief that punishment alone cure criminal misbehavior, are two such beliefs or premises. Science continues to challenge these beliefs and other unwieldy and inaccurate premises by which law operates. Stability, once a hallmark of the traditional values of law, is being exposed as simply the retrenchment of a penal system that ostrich-like has buried its head in the sands of precedent. Scientism, or the elevation of science, has reached religious proportions in many fields of inquiry and has defrocked their myths.[15] Scientism, and indeed science, have somehow passed the criminal justice delivery system by. Punishment, too, must go through the same "demythification" process and proceed to scientific inquiry. Penology, too, must be subject to the same scrutiny to free it from the traditions and concepts that, although once possibly true, or at least useful at their inception, have become dysfunctional for the scientific thinking so necessary to address contemporary penological problems. Theories in penology rely upon facts and events. They can, however, only thrive or survive on success. The dismal results of American penology are becoming known, and we can no longer ignore a system that in some areas has an 80 percent failure rate. The myth of punishment, I submit, is dead and we must bury it.

A myth is that which rationalizes the otherwise inexplicable event or problem. It must be accepted as true, and cares little for new discovery because it cannot change. Science-based decision making, on the other hand, depends upon a multitude of changes, minute and great, as progressive discoveries help us to analyze problems, find failures and dictate corrections. We in penology can posit little as ultimate truth. Penologists can only give the contemporary answers, which may be different from the answers given yesterday, and, may be different from the answers we will give tomorrow. Yet, too many theorists cling to this systemically immutable myth which is the efficacy of punishment by prison. To punish, we imprison. To deter, we imprison. To contain, we imprison. To rehabilitate, we imprison. Not surprisingly, the criminal justice delivery system does not progress because it continues to be guided by those who only listen to the emotional voices of the public. To progress, however, we must listen to and examine the voices from all sides of the issues and, must expose the myth to reason. We must study our civilization's offenders like dreaded diseases and discover what caused them to err, and devise techniques to assist the individual to change if he wants to, or to contain him inexpensively if he does not. If I am right, both our sentencing theory and our sentencing scheme stand athwart the pathway to progress.

ENDNOTES

1. Barbara Meierhoefer Vincent states that reform in the state of Oklahoma has been "hindered more than helped by the federal experience." "Informing a Discussion of Guideline Simplification," *FSR*: Vol. 8, No. 1, (July/August 1995), p. 36.

2. "Suggestions for the New Sentencing Commission," *FSR*: Vol. 8, No. 1, (July/August 1995), p. 10.

3. Christie, *Limits*, p. 84.

4. Romilly, Sir Samuel, (*Speeches*, vol. I, p. 110-111).

5. Wooton, p. 110.

6. In most guideline schemes, the judge has some limited discretion to vary sentences. In the federal guideline system, that discretion is extremely limited.

7. Wooton, Barbara, *Crime and the Criminal Law: Reflections of a Magistrate and Social Scientist*, Steven and Sons, 1981, p. 111.

8. FSR, Vol. 8, No. 1 (Jul/Aug 1995), p. 12

9. Hart, H. L. A., *Punishment and Responsibility*, Oxford 1968, p. 59.

10. Christie, Nils, *Limits to Pain*, Universitetsforlaget, Oslo, 1981, p. 45.

11. Tocqueville, Alexis, *Democracy in America*, (1838), Henry Reeve text, Knopf, (1945), p. 156.

12. Drucker, Peter F., *The Effective Executive*, Harper, 1966, p.

13. For an excellent discussion of quality management techniques, and, for that matter, vices that threaten quality, see Deming, W. Edwards, *Out of the Crisis*, MIT, (1986). I have carefully studied Deming, and have concluded that most of his quality management techniques would work in, and greatly improve, all elements of the criminal justice delivery system.

14. Wooton, p. 94.

15. Or as Jacob Needleman says, *sinful proportions*. See generally Needleman, Jacob, *Sin and Scientism*, (19).

The Ten Commandments of Behavioral Genetic Data and Criminology

A little learning is a dangerous thing:
Drink deep, or taste not the Pierian spring:
Where shallow drafts intoxicate the brain,
And drinking largely sobers us again.

Alexander Pope

A s you have no doubt read and heard in almost all the media, the era of genetics is upon us, and we seemingly cannot escape it. Every day, or so it seems, a new genetics discovery is reported in the general press. Cloning of sheep in Scotland receives banner headlines one day, and familial breast cancer susceptibility is addressed the next. Recently, more speculative behavioral news was announced: girls with Turner syndrome seem to display more sociable characteristics if they receive their lone X chromosome from their fathers than from their mothers. So it becomes evident not only that the genetics era is upon us but also that genetic research is also discovering traits that go far beyond our basic physical makeup and delve deeper into the core of our individual personalities.

This recent reportage of behavioral genetic data is certainly not startlingly news. Ever since E.O. Wilson coined the term "sociobiology" in the seventies, great controversy about behavioral genetics has flowed to and fro in essays, articles, and speeches. We are all going to have to learn to cope with this new knowledge about the hereditary bases of social behavior, just as we have adjusted to knowledge about the genetic bases of many forms of disease. But you may well wonder what this has to do with those of us who participate in the fields of criminology and penology. This is a question that deserves concentrated attention.

I would posit that our first concern should be whether criminology is going to *benefit* should anything emerge from this new behavioral genetic information. Assuming the data can be put to good use, they must be used it in such a way as to minimize cultural disruptions and to prevent humanitarian violations. With each new discovery, we have the opportunity to advance criminology and penology significantly, and the concomitant responsibility to do so. But the behavioral territory is vast, and opening it to inspection brings immense challenges. Penologists must not only decide where they must go with behavioral genetic data, but having taken the first steps, we must carefully consider what we find, and eventually what we will do with it when we get further along the pathway.

People talk about "entering the public debate" on genetics. I sincerely doubt whether any of us have any such choice. Once a technology is developed, it is used. If genetic discoveries will help inform medical, psychological, and behavioral decisions in any way, they are ignored at our peril. We who are concerned with criminal sentencing must decide how law should receive this behavioral genetic data, cope with it, and use it to inform a systemic, social response to crime. We must also educate legislators, members of the criminal law profession, and the public at large about behavioral genetic data. If we do not, I fear that the laws and rules governing this data will be developed, as far too much law is, on the fracture lines of society, and in the adversarial bouts in courtrooms across the country where all too often the search for truth, and truth itself, get lost.

We must not let this happen. If behavioral genetic data can provide insight into reasons for an individual's behavior (more specifically, a criminal's behavior), we must carefully consider how the data can be incorporated into the criminal justice delivery system. The root causes of crime must be discovered, *whatever they are*, and treated, *whatever that takes*. Something more than our present efforts must be exerted, and I welcome any research whose product might help isolate causes of, or indicate therapies for, destructive behavior. I do not care whether scientific discoveries lead toward genes, neurotransmitters, nutrition, environment, morality, or a synoptic equation comprising all of these factors, as playing the major role in aberrant behavior, and ecology of crime. What *does* matter is that we use the best data available to assist us in developing pragmatic criminal remedies: preventive, interventive, and therapeutic. We can develop an appropriate appreciation of what an amalgam of discoveries, allied together, can contribute to our understanding of human nature. If we appreciate the contributions that physical science can make to behavioral science, we can use this knowledge wisely and humanely. Moreover, it can be used to enhance the public's understanding and confidence that what the criminal justice delivery system is trying to do for offenders, it is also doing for the public safety.

I propose the following ten commandments for using behavioral genetic data. I am obviously not a Moses, nor do I pretend to have received inspiration from any higher authority. However, I do not shrink from, nor apologize for, advocating that criminologists develop some categorical imperatives and guidelines for using behavioral genetic data. I am urging that we use any new data tentatively and with much testing and retesting of hypotheses and remedies, all for the eventual outcome of a greater social good.

THE COMMANDMENTS

1. **Do not use behavioral genetic data to prove guilt. Remove behavioral genetic data from the adversarial battleground of the trial itself, and limit its use to evidence employed in formulating appropriate therapeutic (not punitive) sentences.**

Seldom is there an excuse for a crime; however, reasons abound. To date we have spent but few resources to discover the reasons. Even when we do discover the reasons for a crime, the reasons do little good in sentencing unless we know what we will do with them. Unless we intend to provide therapeutic responses to the cause or causes of an event, knowing *why* (any *why)* is really of no use. Indeed, if all we want is revenge, punishment is an acceptable response, and ignorance serves us just fine. Of course, something more is needed. It is becoming obvious that punishment as a solitary response to crime is ineffectual for all but a few criminals and all but a few crimes. Unfortunately, however, most people do not express much interest in research to unearth the root causes of crime, and politicians routinely campaign in the cheapest market, which now means sounding tougher on crime than the next guy.

Society has built a high wall between *us* and *them*, between the *good guys* and the *bad guys*. This wall is an attitude called denial. It psychologically protects *us* in an illusory fashion, only for as long as we choose to remain ignorant of the other side. We must not only change this attitude, we must replace it. If the wall is torn down, if the psychological protection is removed, if the emphasis is taken off punishment, something new must be offered in its place. If punishment is not replaced, sentencers may feel relieved of their responsibility to do anything productive about crime; they may say, "If we cannot punish, we have no response." Yet for the public, there must be an acceptable method for displaying their revulsion to, and denunciation of, crime. If none exists, society is then tempted to reject any change altogether or to express its revulsion as a form of vigilantism. But the simple fact is that we must change and replace because what we are doing now does not work.

The "twinkie defense" is so-named after an imaginative defense attorney in California. He proffered the defense for his client, who had been accused of a crime that he had so indulged in junk food, namely "Hostess Twinkies," that he was unable to control his behavior, and should not be found guilty. A "twinkie defense" is now shorthand for any of a number of chimeric defenses to misbehavior.

The incipiency, or scope, of genetic data's use in the criminal justice system is not yet known. The system is still so thoroughly steeped in the moral/immoral behavioral dichotomy and punitive theory that to permit a defense of "my genes made me do it" will offend our traditional notions of personal responsibility and blameworthiness. I am also afraid that any "genes" defense will sound to the public eerily like the infamous "Twinkie defense." Then, too, in the face of uncertain scientific evidence, we must be concerned about the possibility that defendants will use unsupported theories as a means of escaping accountability for their actions by faking disorders, or the behavior patterns associated with them.

Behavior is a complex equation, and a behavioral modification formula can be neither fully understood nor fully used without knowing the value contributed by its components, including behavioral genetic data. Permitting scientific explanations to have some persuasive force in the sentencing context is a safer way of introducing new data into the criminal justice delivery system than to permit their use as a defense to guilt itself. Sentencing science can use behavioral genetic data to isolate reasons, to mitigate punishment, and to develop pragmatic remedies, but it need not challenge or rethink the basic assumptions of criminal blameworthiness or upset the guilt-determining process. I suggest that the data be used as one integer in an equation supporting remedial action, and that barriers be established to prevent an offender's status (genetic makeup), from inculpating him further.

We must work from causal explanations to regulative ideals, and neither let transgressors off the hook because they have unsuccessfully struggled against temptation, nor let sentencers off the hook because they have struggled unsuccessfully with appropriate remedies. Whether crime is caused by poverty, joblessness, moral degeneration, greed, genetics, opportunity, or some combination of many factors, should be of little consequence to guilt. These, however, causes are *all* valuable bits of explanatory data to aid in defining a remedial sentence. Any explanatory data offers sentencing science a ray of hope if it can be used to isolate reasons for crime and treat or correct them in an effort to prevent crime. I urge that this be the first baseline for using behavioral genetic data: humanitarian means toward pragmatic ends, no matter how attractive a deviation for other purposes may seem.

2. Do not use behavioral genetic data coercively. Use it to inform sentencers and aid them in developing reformatory and therapeutic sentences.

Technology cannot solve our social problems. It can, however, help to isolate the problems and give valuable aid if *we* have the will to solve them. Likewise science cannot foretell the future. It can, however, help us prepare for it. I have my hopes for behavioral genetic data, just as I have my fears. What we currently do to control crime is not working well. Our sentencing policy is in shambles. What could be houses of behavioral correction are now pitiless institutes of social destruction. Something will have to change. Therefore, as a judge, I look with optimism to the sciences for help in piecing together the behavioral puzzle that each offender presents. Nonetheless, although I think the criminal justice delivery system should welcome what science offers, and listen carefully to its messages, I suggest that it react skeptically and move cautiously.

Are we comfortable with the possibility of coercing individuals into some biological modification program when we are dealing with data that are not connected to some form of objectively determined condition, like addiction? I am not, at least not yet; the therapies for genetic conditions are still too speculative. How we answer this question, perhaps more than any other, affects the potential for abusing science. Indeed, the prospect of our punitive criminal justice system mandating genetic alterations to effect behavioral modification makes me fearful. Such a powerful tool could be horrifyingly misused without the proper safeguards and checks in place. Nor is medicine specifically, and science generally, off the ethical hook. When science becomes detached from its moral implications or attempts to function in a value-free context, there is a danger, because *it* will err. Just as when law pictures itself in a self-righteous sense as so ethically enmeshed that it can ignore the philosophy and science that drives its decisions, *we* will err tragically. Until the purposes of sentencing are more corrective than punitive, and the intentions more humanitarian than vengeful, I am not comfortable with any involuntary behavioral modification through genetic means, even of offenders who have been stigmatized by criminal conviction.

3. Develop a minimum threshold of competence for witnesses proffering expert testimony on behavioral genetic data, and create standards of scientific certainty and proof.

I often used to advise juries, after they had heard the testimony of conflicting *experts*, that "there is nothing smarter than one expert, and nothing dumber than two." Standards for expert and opinion testimony on scientific matters have serious shortcomings. I suggest that any attempted application of behavioral genetic data must be preceded and accompanied by scientific standards that will enable law to determine the stage when an innovation in behavioral technology is in fact certain enough to apply in the criminal justice context. Of equal importance, when the science is sufficiently certain, the law must have standards in place for the introduction of this evidence. To avoid the problem of a battle of experts, the criminal justice system must promulgate standards, based upon state-of-the-science discoveries, and the assistance of scientists, to determine when baseline findings of genetic research have reached a sufficient level of certainty that courts can consider them to be "correct" and acceptable as fact.

Development in science is nearly the antipole of development in criminal law and the legal system. In science, a proposition is only stated as law after scientists study and observe a phenomenon, hypothesize causes therefore, and test the hypotheses. Only then, and if after continued retesting and observation the results are consistent, is it stated as a principle. The principle only becomes law after extensive replication of the phenomenon. In contrast, in the legal system, and specifically the criminal justice system, a legislative enactment or proclamation posits and defines the norm and, hence, the deviations. Hypotheses need not be accurate, only stable or popular. In case law, for example, a decision reached by a court in one case is regarded as law and may control decisions in many other cases, until it is proven to be wrong and overturned by the court, a reviewing court, or the legislature. Instead of the testing and replication to prove or disprove hypotheses before acceptance in science, courts accept and retain their rules until the rule can no longer successfully resist attempts to falsify it. In science, such a methodology would be absurd.

How shall we know when a discovery in behavioral technology is so certain that we feel comfortable applying it to criminal law? Conversely, how can we reassure parties that the base of genetic information that we rely upon remains open to new hypotheses and changes? We must develop answers before we are faced with these questions, or courts risk making arbitrary decisions that will be difficult to correct. I suggest that we tap the expertise of physical and social sciences to help determine the admissibility standards for behavioral genetic data evidence and to help develop certification criteria for expert witnesses. Penology must use behavioral sciences to guide courts and cases proactively, not follow behind and simply analyze and critique how the law has used or misused science. The current standards and rules are inadequate for the scientific data they must accommodate.

4. Insist that the same values that we currently require from criminal law in punitive sentencing be required when behavioral genetic data are used to fashion remedial sentences.

Traditionally, we have required that the criminal law strive to achieve a number of fundamental values including equality before the law, consistency in application and outcome, predictability in terms of public knowledge of what behavior is legally acceptable, and protection of public expectations that the law will not randomly or arbitrarily change. These are vital values to retain as we attempt to add anything to the mix. Indeed, we certainly should not view the introduction of behavioral genetic data into the criminal law as an indication that somehow these values are somehow less important. Rather, given the potential of behavioral genetic data to change both the theories and the system, zealously maintaining these values as essential guideposts makes sense.

Maintaining these values means that, as a first step, we commit ourselves to the idea that genetic information or technology will not be applied selectively among cases or offenders. This is not to say that all scientific data should be currency of equal value in the criminal justice system. Rather, my assertion is that relevant evidence pertaining to a specific disorder should never be applied selectively. If an offender has a genetically-based behavioral disorder, he should have access to the means of proving it. Just as he is entitled to an attorney, a physician, or a psychological exam, he should likewise have access to a molecular biologist. When we create a database pertaining to a particular environment, character trait, propensity, or disorder, that evidence should be equally accessible to all offenders for whom the data are relevant. This does not mean that other factors will not influence whether or not the use of behavioral genetic data results in the mitigation of punishment at sentencing. Instead, it is merely a basic principle of nondiscrimination to ensure equality of access to the evidence, not equality of outcomes resulting from its use. Simply stated, baseline standards should be established for admitting evidence into consideration in a sentencing hearing. If courts are deciding upon a remedy to correct misbehavior, they should not be permitted to arbitrarily limit the offender's right to present evidence concerning the genetic disorder that had an impact upon his behavior.

Similarly, we must remain committed to ensuring that genetic technology does not interfere with the clear functioning and statement of the law: assuring the public's safety. We must also ensure that the public is kept aware of how genetic discoveries are changing the application and operation of the criminal law to make sure that the public's expectations of the law are met. It must be demonstrated that the development of behavioral genetic data will not adversely affect the stability or predictability of the law by simply providing other "loopholes" for offenders to avoid the consequences of their acts. Stability and predictability are essential because they lend the perception of legitimacy, and are what support the public confidence in the law.

5. Where necessary, change the free-will assumptions underlying criminal justice and offense-based punitive penology.

The core, underlying principle of both criminology and penology has historically been that human beings are totally free, rational, and independent actors who exercise their wills and make their own decisions. Our concept of culpability presupposes that individuals are fully responsible for their own actions. Under this theory of free will, guilt generally has a direct relationship to the potential of the individual to have chosen not to perform the actions for which he is being punished. Since the presumption is that every offender has totally free will, the offender may try to demonstrate in his defense that his will was somehow superseded by circumstances that impeded or intercepted his ability to resist temptation (by proving, diminished capacity, or that he was responding to an irresistible impulse, for example), and that he lacks the mental component of the crime.

Although this premise is not wholly flawed, as physical science helps criminal science reach the point where it can isolate causes of crime, the central principle of free will becomes less serviceable, and continues to erode. The history of a person's universe is not wholly written in the genes inherited from her or his ancestors. Nor are individuals entirely the product of temptations and opportunities created by the environment in which their will is expressed. It is becoming more and more obvious that we humans all occupy slightly different positions along a free-will/determinism continuum, influenced in varying degrees by a host of factors, possibly including our genes.

Nevertheless, we continue to ignore the role of behavior ecology in criminal acts (all the factors that may influence an act are its behavioral ecology), content to believe that all transgressions are essentially the result of moral lapses and ethical flaws, entirely curable by punishment. Even at the present stage of genetic and behavioral research, we already know enough to conclude that certain individuals are statistically at risk for certain types of behavioral traits strongly correlated with criminal activity. The fact that not all individuals are equally "wired," (physically, mentally, emotionally, or genetically), to exercise the will necessary to resist temptation or impulse, highlights the fact that human beings are neither totally nor equally free agents. As behavioral research progresses, criminal science is likely to discover even more evidence of why some human beings respond to, and interact with their environment differently from others.

No matter what the balance between genetic factors and the environment may prove to be, or regardless the manner in which our unlearned propensities are led toward certain behavioral expressions by the opportunities presented in our environment, behavioral genetic science is sure to have an impact on the concept of the free will that is as significant as any other explanations of why one acts as one does. Quite simply, we must be prepared to rethink our total reliance on the idea of free will. Free will has a diminished posture whether it turns out that human beings are genetically predisposed to certain criminal behaviors, and/or that environmental factors play the most significant role in those behaviors. Neither free will nor determinism can be a full-service philosophy for the criminal law when science and experience tell us that human beings are not equally capable of exercising free choice. We must search for a new principle upon which to base the criminal justice system, by which we can account for and respond to the myriad of generators that actuate human behavior.

6. Keep the public abreast of genetics and behavioral research, as it enables us to improve upon the traditional justifications for punishment.

I am not at all sanguine that behavioral genetic data, and what it will tell us about human beings or the effect of one's environment, will receive a warm reception in penology unless the science is firmly established and we correspondingly engage in massive public, political, and professional education. Theorists have historically identified four purposes for imposing punishment on offenders: retribution, rehabilitation, deterrence (specific and general), and incapacitation or containment. Although I am skeptical that any one or all of these theories justify what we do to our offenders, they all depend in varying degrees on free will.

Moving away from the free will principle and reliance upon punishment, our justifications do not remain reasonable. Indeed, accepting that behavioral genetic data are already capable of telling us that certain individuals, when mixed with certain environmental factors, are at risk for a particular behavior, the extant theories of punishment are wholly unsatisfactory. To rely then entirely upon punishment and prison makes little sense because the behavior may have many causes, and because no individual may be fully in control of his or her actions, the cause being a confluence of many motives. Moreover, there is little emotional or psychic reward to the citizens of a culture in exacting revenge on an offender when it cannot be said that the offender truly made a conscious choice to transgress the law. Indeed, the cathartic value to society of punishing its deviants is lost when we cannot blame or hate the offenders for choosing to harm us.

Similarly, the idea of punishment as a means of deterrence makes little sense if it will not have a positive effect on behavior. Indeed, punishment will neither *specifically* deter the individual who cannot control his behavior, nor *generally* deter others who do not identify with the punished person. Imprisoning one to incapacitate him seems equally unsatisfactory if the crime is biologically or environmentally driven, because incapacitation amounts to punishment based on biological or social status, a result with which most theorists would be uncomfortable. I certainly am. And, neither ethical nor biological rehabilitation is going to happen as the result of a traditional prison environment. I cannot imagine a worse place to convalesce from a lapse of morality than in prison. I suggest that as science isolates reasons for behavior, sentences are flawed to the extent they are based upon any rationale other than their response to these reasons. Systemic change to our sentencing scheme, however, will occur only to the extent that people are aware of current failures and become pragmatic about results.

7. Require the criminal justice delivery system to account for the results of its efforts.

Adding scientific method and research discoveries to our criminal justice delivery system, requires that it become "outcome-based." It is absurd that each element of the system moves blindly on its own without regard for the product of the whole. Behavioral genetic data will be of little assistance in sentencing unless sentencers are all cognizant of "outcome." They must know what good any of this data did. Although we must condemn the offending act because it is a crime, we must also study it and its consequences, and impose a sentence on the perpetrator that flows pragmatically from what he is, not vengefully from what he has done. The American criminal justice delivery system must become concerned with results, and the system must be accountable for them.

In an address to the New York Academy of Medicine, Judge Benjamin Cardozo predicted "that at a day not far remote, the teachings of biochemists and behaviorists, of psychiatrists and penologists, will transform our whole system of punishment for crime."[1] I say that time is nigh for the system to take his prediction seriously. Indeed, it is long overdue. The consequences of a crime must be a sentence with that I have no quarrel. But, the value of a sentence must not be judged on such facile but specious grounds as its perceived *toughness* or *softness* on *the* or *a* crime. Indeed, the toughest sentence we can impose on an offender may be one that requires real change. I recommend that the criminal justice delivery system and its components be called upon to account, individually and collectively, for results. In my vision of the system, each component of it should be accountable to the others and the system as a whole, and accountable to the society it is ostensibly designed to protect. Criminal justice must become a correction-based, outcome-concerned system, designed around a goal of producing obedient and productive citizens.

I suggest that the experts of whom Judge Cardozo wrote be treated as officers and witnesses of the court, called by the court to assist the criminal justice delivery system in formulating an appropriate sentence; and, not be the "hired gun" *experts* that each party subpoenas to court to duel it out before the court or jury. There can be and are differences of scientific and professional opinion. I am not at all sure, however, that law-trained judges and untrained juries are on any sure footing to sort out and decide which opinion is correct. When behavioral genetic data are added to the sentencing mix, I suggest the time has come to turn the sentencing phase of the criminal proceeding experimentally into a meeting of experts from many disciplines. This panel would be convened to help the court formulate an appropriate sentence, and to follow the offenders progress to determine if their remedy has produced the desired result.

Judge Cardozo wondered skeptically whether "medicine or penology [had] arrived at such a stage as to make a revolution in our system of punishment advisable or possible."[2] I, too, am not sure about a revolution. But I *am* certain we are floundering hopelessly with sentences now, and we are close enough to helpful scientific discoveries that we must prepare to receive them. Cardozo concluded:

> I have faith . . . that a century or less from now
> our descendants will look back upon the penal
> system of today with the same surprise and horror
> that fill our minds when we are told that only about
> a century ago, one-hundred-sixty crimes were visited
> under English law with death . . . [3]

Today, seventy years after he spoke these words, we need not look back to be horrified. We only need to look around us. We have not progressed much at all.

Today, science offers us another reason to rethink sentencing and another opportunity for progress. Sentencing must be freed from the fetters of offense-based reasoning. It is senseless to respond to an event without a predominating concern with the actor producing it. Each crime and each offender must be part of a longitudinal study and contribute to data from which sentencers can study acts, actors and environs, and engage in such activities as computer modeling to develop appropriate sentence remedies, architecture and urban planning to diminish criminal opportunity, educational recommendations to mold young minds, and perhaps a host of other results that might potentially flow from the studies. Each sentence and each offender must be followed closely to determine what did and did not work, and the results must become part of the data for future decisions. I suggest that by requiring the criminal justice delivery system to account for its acts, acknowledge its failures and study the reasons why, the natural systemic processes will migrate remedial methods toward successful results.

8. **Stop thinking of the criminal justice system as relevant only after offenders have committed infractions. Instead, reconceptualize crime as a continuum along which lie the rule, the temptation, the opportunity, the infraction, the disposition, and the remedy.**

In my vision of the 21st century, the criminal justice system will look more like a "Health Maintenance Organization" than the current farrago of functions which operate neither systematically nor accountably for their contributions to safety. It may, as it now does, comprise police, courts, probation officers, judges, prisons, and parole boards. I predict, however, that it will also encompass social scientists, physicians, educators, health and zoning administrators, and other professionals from numerous other disciplines. I also predict that the criminal justice system will rely on other social institutions and professionals for pre-offense intervention and prevention, post-incarceration behavioral modification and post-release observation and support.

Behavioral technology requires that we consider how the criminal justice delivery system of tomorrow will interact with the individual at several distinct times in the criminal justice delivery process. How it will interact with other social institutions and, importantly, how it will interact or interface with the allied sciences. Currently, the criminal justice system does not get involved in the life of the individual until after he has committed an offense. Informed by scientific research about the predispositions of potential offenders, or the risk posed by the influence of certain environments and conditions, this should not remain the case. When behavioral science can predict how a person is likely to react to a situation, it can devise strategies for changing the situation or otherwise intervening between the individual and the temptation. For example, Dr. C. Ray Jeffrey has conducted extensive research into how urban planning and architecture can prevent crime. Pharmacology has developed remedies to assist some individuals in controlling their antisocial behavior. Dr. Roger D. Masters at the Gruter Institute for Law and Behavioral Research at Dartmouth College has conducted extensive research into how lead poisoning has effected behavior. The science of genetics may open other preventive or preemptive doors as well.

Setting out a preemptive role for the criminal justice delivery system (acting before a crime is committed), however, raises a number of issues. Each component of the system must be willing to cede a sufficient portions of its power that a criminal justice delivery system can be developed. The criminal justice delivery system must be willing to recognize the importance of other disciplines and institutions. The criminal justice delivery system must have the institutional capacity or resources to engage in preventive action. There must be a public will to develop preventive measures. We all must be concerned about stigma in the process of targeting would-be offenders and offering therapy, counseling and education. Finally, we theoreticians must explore the constitutional implications of all this.

In my vision of the future system, the role of the criminal justice delivery system in the post-offense time frame will also be different. It will move first toward a theory of sentencing that emphasizes correction and not punishment, and then, toward the ideal, prevention. The components of the criminal justice delivery system and its personnel will be taught to deal holistically with offenders as morally, educationally, socially or biologically deficient individuals. In practice, this means that sentences will be less focused on incarceration and more focused on methods designed to return corrected offenders to a society whose security and safety is not threatened thereby. Clearly, as recidivism rates indicate, this is not a task at which the present system has been particularly successful. Indeed, given the overwhelming emphasis on punishment in today's penology, it would be fair to say that policy makers do not know how to correct offenders; or knowing how, do not have the will to do so; or, nonetheless choose a politically more popular stance, for fear that doing something productive would place them perilously close to the political quicksand of being considered "soft" on crime.

If we want a criminal justice system that values either humanity or its own citizen's safety, the whole scheme must be changed. Neither excessive nor inadequate punishments are just. Because punishment, when therapy is indicated, is unjust to the offender who needs therapy. Likewise, lesser responses, when punishment is indicated, are unjust to the public which needs to see its deviants reproved. And, all of it is both senseless and unjust if with pragmatic and preventive effort we could have superseded and precluded the criminal act and saved a victim in the first place.

9. Do not allow behavioral genetic data to either become the property of, or come under the full control and authority of, the courts.

It sounds like heresy for a judge to recommend that evidentiary data and rules for its admissibility in court proceedings remain partially in the control of others. Perhaps it is! Although I would prefer to think of myself as a philosophical variant rather than a heretic. Nonetheless, I have seen how badly courts interpret and misuse science, and I now see an opportunity for the behavioral sciences to rise above the courtroom evidentiary melee. To do so we must prevent behavioral genetic data in the criminal law from becoming the next "battleground of experts" upon which each side produces its own hired genetic champion to advance its respective adversarial contentions about degrees of usefulness, certainty and predisposition. Shared responsibility for defining the data's significance is a pathway through the thicket.

Rigorous, independent oversight from professionals outside the criminal justice system, and shared control of the use of behavioral genetic data as it impacts upon the criminal law is a must. Such oversight is necessary because neither the American public nor our penology has accepted the fact that crime has an ecology that comprises all physical, moral, social and environmental factors that impinge or have any effect upon behavior. Popular opinion willingly accepts that crime is simply a matter of deliberate rule violation (a moral lapse), rendering the offender susceptible to behavior modification by negative reinforcement. Indeed, most persons fail even to think of our criminal justice delivery system as involved in behavior modification at all. They are content with the idea of punishment as vengeance, that everyone gets what is coming to him. Unfortunately, the winds of public opinion are what currently propel our legislative ship. Until the system is willing to shift its foci, it is doubtful that it can deal responsibly with scientific data that threatens its underlying philosophy.

I am confident that scientific behavioral explanations will eventually destroy our comfort with simple notions of vengeance, and compel us to rethink our basic assumptions about punishment and the criminal justice system and develop the manifold pathways of sentencing. All change, however, is disconcerting to some of us and to some extent, because it involves placing yourself at a point of indecision where you can look backward to the security of something known but ending, and must look forward to the uncertainty of something unknown but beginning.

10. **Use behavioral genetic data in conjunction with all the allied sciences, sociology, psychology, and others, to discover, to understand and to treat the root causes of criminal behavior, whatever they may be, and to explore a gentler, more pragmatic and productive way of punishment.**

There are many who lobby against using any behavioral genetic data in any legal forum. They look to the past, accept genetics' legacy of distrust and fear the future. I do not. The poet Shelley said it well; "Fear not the future, weep not the past." The eugenics of Dalton and Adolf Hitler was not science. It was perverse social policy run amok and masquerading under the guise, and in a costume, of science. Genetics research is science first, and we are given an opportunity to use its discoveries to help inform remedies to our social problems, for which we now employ only failing solutions.

To use a medical analogy, penology has not progressed beyond the leper colony mentality. We have identified the affliction, but shun the afflicted, and are content to let them fester with each other. The causes of crime are undoubtedly complex, but out of neither reach nor reason. The nervous system was once thought to be too complicated to yield its secrets to scientific efforts at understanding. But, no more, the effort to unravel its complexities is succeeding with accelerating speed. Science, too, can begin to peel away the layers of the behavioral enigma. I think that both the science and its technological fallout will produce useable results.

I say beware the *pro's* who give too much behavioral credit to genetics. But also, beware the *anti's* who give it none or too little. It is enough if we are willing to lay aside our preconceptions and the basic belief in the power of an individual's will alone to conquer all temptation, irrespective of whether the laws governing behavior have his support, make sense to him, or, help him. It is enough if we can instead recognize that some wills may need some therapeutic assistance to overcome the combination of immorality, environment and genes to resist temptation. So, let us beware the first error: blaming genes too much: or, blaming them too little.

Behavioral genetic data may inform the law that biology has nothing (or everything) to do with behavior. I am not sure. But that does not matter if it helps isolate the causes of crime to enable criminal science to develop a response. Whatever we can provide to better inform our sentencers and reform our sentencing, will improve the criminal justice delivery system if we take care for the safety of the public and humanity of the person. The current interest in genetic research generally, and behavioral genetic data specifically, is an opportunity to add some science to the sentencing procedure, and what is more important, to add some scientific method to the life and death determinations that courts and legislatures so casually and ill-advisedly make as they respond to our culture's deviants.

CONCLUSION

I have received many letters from prisoners. I have one consistent "pen pal" whom I sentenced to prison years ago. He is now aged and in failing health, has been in and out of prison for about 35 years, and writes to me 15-20 times a year with rambling discourses about daily prison life. I have read every one of his letters, most often with feelings of great sadness. I do not necessarily weep for him and many others who now populate our prisons. I do, however, weep for an America so bound to the desire for revenge and punishment that it will recognize neither the futility of its penal practices, nor that the social cancer it leaves untreated, indeed cultivated within its prisons, will surely metastasize in the neighborhoods of America. I do weep for an America that is unwilling to invest in research and programs to keep the children of today from committing the crimes that will place them in the prisons of tomorrow.

The epigraph with which I began this essay is one of Pope's most known and most misquoted quatrains. Often people will miscite it to caution that "A little *knowledge* is a dangerous thing." That is not so. Pope knew, and when we pause to think about it so do we, that knowledge in any quantity is a positive and assuring thing, if we act upon it. It is *learning* "in limited doses" that is dangerous. To the extent that behavioral genetic data adds to the quality or quantity of our behavioral knowledge, it, too, is a positive and assuring thing. It is to the extent that we ignore behavioral genetic data, learn too little of it, or misuse it, that behavioral genetic data or any data is dangerous.

The genetic revolution is not new. For several decades science has quietly been discovering genetic connections for many old and troubling human problems. As problems are solved, geneticists are sure to turn their attention from the negative to the positive, from diseases to health, from life saving to life enhancing interventions. Criminology and penology must make ready for science's developments by reestablishing corrections (rehabilitation) to be the armature of our sentencing system. Let us try to move from the obsolete philosophy and science that criminology and penology now follow, and not just accept the present, but prepare for the future. Ten commandments may not be enough (whether for the uncharted areas of religion or science) but they do represent points with which we can begin to develop new imperatives. Let us try to break the cycle of crime we now tolerate, even perpetuate. In the criminal law we see people at their behavioral worst. But, we must begin to look to the regions beyond. Let us, like geneticists, begin to look at offenders as they really are. Let us use all the data at our disposal and let us sentence them to what they really need— punishment, treatment, containment, or some combination of all three.

ENDNOTES

1.   Benjamin Cardozo, "What Medicine Can Do For Law," quoted in Bernard L. Shientag, *Molders of Legal Thought*, 39-40 (Viking 1943).

2.   *Id*. at 39.

3.   *Id*. at 40.

The Dawn of
Therapeutic Justice

A s I wrestled through the years with the issues involving criminal behavior, sentencing and punishment, I sought to find something rational in what I was doing *to* criminal offenders and in what I was doing *about* crime. I am still seeking. But I am finding little that is rational. The American criminal justice delivery system seems to have profited little from the philosophical debate about the efficacy of penal methods that has tensed and eased over the centuries. Scholars have mused about the repressive, nondeterministic Hobbsian model lying on one end of the philosophical spectrum to the somewhat more centrist theories of Cesare de Beccaria, Jeremy Bentham and Samuel Romilly;[1] then to the deterministic/rehabilitative Ferrian view, which lies on the other end.[2] Without much regard for the merits of the various theories and penal justifications, indeed, ignorant of them, we Americans maintain essentially a nondeterminist frame of reference and, hence, penal model. This leaves most persons behaviorally on their own and fully responsible for the consequences of their actions. Offenses against the law, whatever the actual reasons and causes, are generally viewed as the result of ethical flaws and moral lapses to which we respond by punishing the offender by our limited form of banishment—prison. The durability of this penal model in American culture results from the ease with which it is explained to the governed and executed by the government and not, however, from its success in countering crime.

> The determinist says simply that what will be, will be: one's behavior is shaped entirely by non-willed events or by God. The indeterminist believes there is room for some autonomy. The nondeterminist says all events are a consequence of an exercise of free will.

269

The criminal justice system also has profited little from the social, biological and medical sciences. Within the past decade research in these sciences increasingly points toward genetic, neurological, neurobiological, toxicological, environmental and traumatic factors as playing significant roles in aberrant behavior. Moreover, the research is also leading us toward help from suitable psychological and pharmacological therapies to intervene between some behavioral actuating factors and their potentially disruptive results. But the help avails us only if we choose to follow the counsel it offers us. Little of this, unfortunately, has found its way into the *correction* that is supposed to take place when an offender's crime places him within the state's control. Nor into the dialogue of legislators and jurists who must decide upon remedial measures to be imposed upon offenders to correct them. Perhaps it is with penology and prison, as Pascal says about life, "Being unable to cure death, wretchedness and ignorance, men have decided, in order to be happy, not to think about such things."[3] And so, we think but little about our equation of crime = punishment = prison. It is just that it is a facile and politically acceptable response to the common and base emotions, revulsion and anger, that we feel towards misbehavior by others. That attitude and response, however, ignores behavioral reality and leaves us sailing well to the lee of the mark which is productive, pragmatic results.

The failures of this equation to deter or prevent crime punitively, or to correct the offenders who commit them, require that we take a wholly different approach and to embrace new theory. This new theory must not simply provide society with a medium in which to express a vengeful response to offending behavior. I fully recognize that anger is a natural and expected reaction by a fearful public, because fear is a natural predicate of anger. Moreover, it is natural for victims of crimes to be angry. As such, punishment may be necessary, both to denounce the act and as a component of correction. But reaction and denunciation are not enough. A complete penology must do more. It must first and foremost, center upon discovering *reasons* for the offending acts, whatever they are, and upon providing pragmatic *remedies*, whatever they may be. I look to therapeutic justice to help us meet these requirements.

A. Introduction

Recently there has been a reduction in violent crime. According to many of us who should know better than to employ simplistic post hoc rationalization, credit is given to the fact that we are finally getting tough on criminals. Massive and extensive incarceration does account for some of the success. We know that empirically and intuitively recidivists account for substantially more crimes than those for which they are actually convicted. But a program that calls for long prison terms for all offenders regardless of reason, is a bit like *carpet bombing* in which the whole landscape is blasted with the hope that sufficient numbers of the enemy are killed along with the non-combatants. My point continues to be that with a little effort we could sort out offenders and decide who needs long incarceration, who needs treatment, and who needs neither, thereby preventing enormous social and fiscal waste.

Under current theory, little thought is given to prevention, and none to preemption of the crime itself. Our system is essentially passive. It is content to await a victim to bestir it into a reaction. And our post offense reaction to a crime is essentially one-dimensional. We incarcerate as a method of, and a venue for punishment. Thus, our theory goes, as the seriousness of the crime committed increases, we should merely increase the duration of the punishment, or perhaps even put the offender to death. But reality is not really that simple. The fact is that most of us do not know why we punish, have no idea of the purpose each sentence serves, and none of us really knows why our violent crime statistics are improving. The consequences of our ignorance are negative, manifold and expensive. Our penal theory and practice are failing our culture, and the social and economic cost is staggering.

Scienter is a Latin adverb meaning "knowingly." Our system shares with most other systems, as a prerequisite to culpability for crimes, that the offender not only have "done" the act that the law forbids, but that he also have a threshold knowledge, mental capacity and intention—a "frame of mind," if you will.

I have a narrow but deep professional passion outside the duties of my court: reformulating our criminology and penology so that it responds to the needs of society, the victim *and* the offender. All this, though, is easier to theorize about than to apply. Admittedly my suggestion that we bifurcate criminal trials (deciding in the first phase whether the offender did the act, and in the second, the reasons why, so that we can develop an appropriate response) has some criminological and constitutional impediments. First, if we continue to insist upon using "guilt" and "innocence" as mutually exclusive moral concepts, to determine whether we may punish the offender, then scienter is a necessary ingredient of the process. Second, if all we want is retribution against offenders to assuage a public's desire to get even, irrespective of whether it leads to positive consequences, then knowing why one performed an offensive act only complicates our vengeful emotion.

I am concerned with rights and individual autonomy. As a judge, I am also keenly aware of the social costs of irresponsibility. I am motivated by public safety as a primary goal of criminal law, and hence, I am concerned with results. So, imprison and punish if it serves a productive purpose. But by all means necessary, we must either correct and prepare an offender for release or decide that we are going to continue to contain him humanely. For everyone's sake, however, let us do something to stop the offender from coming back time and again and to stop the offenses by learning something about prevention, preemption and intervention. Finally, the discoveries about behavior in the social, biomedical and physical sciences are of no value to criminology and penology unless they can become factors in legislative and judicial decision-making, and find their way into remedial use in sentencing, treating offenders and preventing crimes.

A recent United States Supreme Court opinion, however, may well open the constitutional doors to a more positive remedial penology, to CBS (as described in earlier essays), and to therapeutic justice. Near the end of the 1997 Court term, the Court unanimously agreed that a law permitting the civil commitment of persons likely to engage in sexually predatory acts because of mental abnormalities did not offend substantive due process principles.[4]

B. *Kansas v. Hendricks*

1. History and Procedure

Leroy Hendricks has a history of sexually molesting children that dates from 1955. He was charged with several offenses in 1957 and in 1960 and detained in a state mental hospital until 1965, when he was discharged. Nevertheless, by 1967 he was back in prison for molesting an 8-year-old girl and an 11-year-old boy. He refused to participate in a sex offenders' treatment program and remained incarcerated until he was paroled in 1972. While on parole, Hendricks began to abuse his own stepdaughter and stepson. He was diagnosed as a pedophile and entered into a treatment program, which he later abandoned. In 1984, Hendricks was convicted of taking indecent liberties with two 13-year-old boys, and he served nearly 10 years for this offense.

Just before he was scheduled to be released in 1994, Kansas authorities filed a petition seeking to commit him as a sexually violent predator under the Kansas Sexually Violent Predator Act, a civil statute that permits convicted sex offenders who are scheduled for release from prison to be involuntarily committed for treatment if they have a mental abnormality that makes them likely to engage in predatory acts of sexual violence.

The Kansas legislature, in enacting the statute, noted that there exist sexually violent predators who have no mental disease or defect that would subject them to involuntary commitment under extant general civil commitment statutes. Because these sexually violent predators may also not be unamenable to existing mental illness treatments and are likely to engage in sexually violent behavior, the legislature declared the existing involuntary commitment procedure inadequate to address the risk these sexually violent predators pose to society, and the duration of civil commitments themselves insufficient for the long-term care and treatment necessary for these offenders.

Kansas recognized, what most of us intimate with the criminal justice delivery system know, that the prognosis for rehabilitating *anyone* in the prison setting is extremely poor, especially for a sexually violent predator. Indeed, it is difficult to imagine a more debilitating behavioral system than the American prison. Moreover, any therapeutic commitment, unlike current criminal sentences, must be of a duration that is not likely to be determinable at the outset, (i.e., at sentencing) and certainly not by a legislature that determines mandatory sentences, sentencing ranges and guidelines long before the specific crime is even committed. Thus, Kansas found it necessary to establish "a civil commitment procedure for the long-term care and treatment of the sexually violent predator."

The Act's civil commitment procedures as pertained to Hendricks were: (1) a presently confined person who, like Hendricks, "has been convicted of a sexually violent offense" and is scheduled for release; (2) a person who has been "charged with a sexually violent offense" but has been found incompetent to stand trial; (3) a person who has been found "not guilty by reason of insanity of a sexually violent offense"; and (4) a person found "not guilty" of a sexually violent offense because of a mental disease or defect.[5]

Reasonable doubt is the highest evidentiary standard. In criminal trials, the government must prove guilt "beyond a reasonable doubt." In civil trials, a plaintiff must prove his case by a "preponderance of the evidence." Proof by "clear and convincing evidence" is an intermediate level used in other proceedings.

Hendricks requested a jury trial during which he admitted his sexual abuse and further acknowledged that he abused children whenever he was not confined. He testified that whenever he got "stressed out," he could not control the urge to molest children. He agreed with the state physician's diagnosis that he was a pedophile and that he still had the condition. He also expressed his belief that treatment would not be effective, and he despaired that the only way he would be cured was "to die." Upon this ominous portent the jury unanimously found, on the standard of proof "beyond a reasonable doubt," that Hendricks was a sexually violent predator.

The trial court also concluded as a matter of law that pedophilia qualified as a "mental abnormality" under the Act. Hendricks was committed to the custody of the Kansas Secretary of Social and Rehabilitation Services based on the court's conclusion and the jury's finding that he was a sexually violent predator.

2. The United States Supreme Court

The United States Supreme Court held that the Sexually Violent Predator Act met the threshold requirements of due process and did not transgress either double jeopardy or *ex post facto* protections provided by the United States Constitution. In the past, the Supreme Court has sustained civil commitment statutes when they have coupled proof of dangerous propensities with the proof of some additional factor, such as a "mental illness."[6] This Act is different. As the Supreme Court noted, the Act extends "involuntary civil confinement to those who suffer from a volitional impairment rendering them dangerous beyond their control." Hendricks was diagnosed as a pedophile. Psychiatrists classify his condition as a serious mental disorder. Hendricks himself admitted that his sexual desires were out of his control.

The Kansas Act requires a finding based on the offender's history of sexually violent behavior, and on evidence of a current mental condition, which together support the conclusion that the offender is likely to engage in future acts of predatory violence. Because, however, a finding of dangerous propensity standing alone is ordinarily not a sufficient ground upon which to justify indefinite involuntary commitment, the Kansas Act went further, requiring evidence both of sexually violent acts and a present mental condition that creates a likelihood of repetition if the offender is not incapacitated. The Court said that a statute such as this, that is triggered by acts and requires proof of more than a mere predisposition to violence, does not offend either legally accepted behavioral principles, or constitutional due process protections.

Next, the decision refuted double jeopardy and *ex post facto* arguments by holding that the proceeding under the Act was not a criminal proceeding and that confinement under the Act did not constitute punishment. The Court found it significant that the

Kansas legislature labeled the proceedings under the Act as "civil," and that "[n]othing on the face of the statute suggests that the legislature sought to create anything other than a civil commitment scheme designed to protect the public from harm." This, the Court indicated, counsels against "reject[ing a] legislature's manifest intent [unless] a party challenging the statute provides the clearest proof that the statutory scheme is so punitive either in purpose or effect as to negate the State's intention to deem it civil."

The Supreme Court also found several other factors to be significant in distinguishing this Kansas Legislative Act as a civil law and not criminal in nature. First, that the Act does not implicate what the Supreme Court considered to be the two principal philosophical supports for criminal punishment: retribution and deterrence. Second, unlike a criminal statute, no finding of *scienter*, or state of mind, is required for commitment under the Act. Third, although the Act permits commitment to what is potentially a confinement of infinite duration, this in itself did not manifest a punitive purpose because no person can be committed for more than a year without another judicial proceeding. Finally, Kansas's inclusion of procedural safeguards typically associated with criminal trials did not transform the proceedings from civil to criminal.

This opinion muffles some earlier constitutional limitations on involuntary civil commitment by approving language in the Kansas Act that breaks with Supreme Court precedent. Before *Hendricks*, involuntary commitment proceedings required that two preconditions be established by clear and convincing evidence: that the person was mentally ill and that he posed a danger to himself or to others. Here, the Court opened the mental illness definition to include not only the mentally ill but also the mentally abnormal, or those offenders suffering from a *personality disorder*, whether congenital or acquired that creates a *volitional* impairment.

Moreover, the Court simply was not deterred by the lack of an exact calculus of what constitutes *mental illness*. First, it deflected the argument that a finding of mental illness is a prerequisite for civil commitment, concluding that because a mental abnormality or personality disorder justifying civil commitment is equivalent to what is commonly thought of as a mental illness, the generic, non-scientific terms, "mental abnormality" and "personality disorder" would suffice, although they do not describe any specifically identified condition.

Second, the Supreme Court's opinion calls into question the relevance of scientific evidence by psychiatric and psychological professionals, by accepting empirical or behavioral evidence over examination and theory. It thus undercuts the value of scientific or other expert opinion. Indeed, the Kansas legislature had acknowledged in its preamble to the Act that the definition of "mental abnormality" or "personality disorder" would not rise to the level of "mental disease or defect." Hendricks was diagnosed as suffering from pedophilia, which, because one who molests children is likely to be a pedophile, can be a largely fact-driven diagnosis. Other volitional dysfunctions may, however, not be so patent. Third, building on these two premises, the opinion leaves state legislatures with the discretion to define the mental health concepts that have legal implications.

I am skeptical that, given the vagaries of politics, we can assume that legislators will rely solely upon scientific data in their determination. If the legislatures do, the results will be therapeutic. If they do not, I fear we will regress to punitive politics.

Unfortunately, in criminal sentencing, especially in sentencing sex offenders, correction or therapy is likely to be well down on the list of considerations that compete with a culture's desire for revenge. Thus, it should not be surprising that, without regard for the fact that the class of individuals targeted for treatment because they lack volitional control, and, as a result are likely to be dangerous in the future, revenge remains a sufficient justification to commit offenders regardless of whether they "fit precisely with the definitions employed by the medical community." In so saying in this opinion, the Supreme Court rejected the requirement that tests traditionally used by courts to decide whether one's behavior was actuated by the type of mental abnormality or personality disorder that justifies civil commitment be equivalent to what is generally accepted among professionals as scientifically supportable. This, of course, also gives to the legislatures the authority of determining which offenses may be amenable to treatment rather than punishment, and places squarely upon the legislative branch of government, the responsibility for failure if it does not develop an appropriate response to crime. Unfortunately, this also places the response to crime in the arena of politics, and exacerbates the potential that the remedies the legislature prescribes for crime may continue to be driven by popular opinion, whether they are scientifically supportable or not.

Historically, the Supreme Court's approach with respect to due process protection of liberty was built on caution: "Given the lack of certainty and the fallibility of psychiatric diagnosis, there is a serious question as to whether a state could ever prove beyond a reasonable doubt that an individual is both mentally ill and likely to be dangerous."[7] Now with the states' legislatures wide discretion in defining mental health and behavioral concepts that have penal implications, the relevance of psychiatric, psychological and other scientific evidence by experts is depreciated in value, sweeping this "lack of certainty" and "fallibility" aside. Indeed, taken literally, the Supreme Court's new standard could potentially permit other courts to impose an indefinite civil commitment upon many offenders, depending first upon how legislatures define the mental predicates to civil commitment, and second, upon how juries and judges with no scientific training, and with no clinical guidance about risk assessment apply the legislative definition.[8]

In sum, the Court's opinion concluded that because the Act is civil in nature, commencement of commitment proceedings did not constitute a second prosecution. Because commitment under the Act is not punitive, involuntary confinement does not constitute double jeopardy even when confinement follows a prison term. Finally, the Act does not violate the *Ex Post Facto* Clause, which "forbids the application of any new punitive measure to a crime already consummated," because the Act is not a punitive measure. Because Hendricks suffers from a mental abnormality under the Act, and because the state is free within the limits of reason to define the level of mental infirmity required for commitment, Hendricks's confinement under the Act comported with due process.

3. Penal Implications

The Court's decision in *Hendricks* may well have a greater impact on future legal developments in penology and criminology generally, rather than for sexual predators like Hendricks specifically, because the expansion of the due process civil commitment standard from mental "illness" to mental "abnormality" eases another of the rigid distinctions that have jurisprudentially separated criminal and civil commitments. That is to say, merely because one has performed a criminal act, that which follows need not be a penal commitment. A civil commitment for treatment or preventive detention, either as an additive or an alternative, is an option for structuring the sentence, if the offense was actuated by a mental, or perhaps biological flaw, rather than a moral lapse.

> Throughout, I have been addressing "involuntary" commitment and treatment. Based upon experience, I know there are substantial numbers of offenders who want to lead "normal" or "conventional" lives and would opt for treatment rather than incarceration if they had some confidence they would receive therapy, not merely by being indefinitely warehoused in a different setting. Irwin and Austin, in their classic work on sentencing, said, "What may be...surprising is that a majority of all persons sent to prison, even the high-rate offenders, aspire to a relatively modest conventional life and hope to prepare for that while serving their prison sentences." John Irwin & James Austin, *It's About Time: America's Imprisonment Binge* 61, at 143 (1994).

I see little from this opinion that will limit extending civil commitments to dangerous propensity to others in contexts of violent behavior other than *sexually* predatory violence. The limiting test is whether the criminal behavior is caused by a person's mental or biological status. The opinion thus steers us towards the jurisprudence of prevention. The Court held that in certain circumstances one may be defensively detained to prevent one from committing acts of predatory violence. In doing so, it embraced the ideology of *therapeutic justice*. The implications of this are enormous.

No doubt there are myriad behavioral actuators or precipitators that will fall within the label of "abnormalities" and "disorders." Awareness of, and acceptance of this fact in itself will be enabling to a system that wants to affect positive change in its offenders. A therapeutic focus may also lighten the adversarial context that is the unseen specter in criminal law decisions. Honest dialogue over the most productive, acceptable remedy may encourage cooperation from offenders and defense attorneys who now are adverse to prosecutors and the courts. Offenders who are offered treatment may opt for a therapeutic remedy in lieu of a totally punitive sentence. And an offender who is assured of treatment may be more inclined to admit his wrongdoing and seek help that is offered. Detailed admissions, such as in plea colloquies, could help to overcome the ever-prevalent offender denial. The "presumption of innocence" which is the frame of reference in criminal trials, often has a life that lasts beyond findings of guilt, and usually conspires against the cognitive restructuring necessary for correction. Structured pleas, could include agreements among the offender, victims, families, health care professionals, the court, penal institutions and probationary supervisors, and permit the court to fashion consensus and corrective remedies for which there is written record and accountability for the results. A court faced with an offender suffering from a qualifying abnormality could steer offenders toward therapeutic alternatives to prison.

With a focus more on treatment or palliation, the criminal justice delivery system will be forced to look for the *reasons why* a person behaved as he did, not to excuse the behavior, but to discover how to counteract, correct or otherwise impose a useful sentence to provide a remedy for it. When criminal science begins to concentrate on reasons *why* a person has erred, and collects offense and offender-specific data, I am certain the resulting knowledge it accumulates will permit more informed sentencing conclusions and advance the criminal justice delivery system's ability to predict recurrent violence and the offender's violent propensities, and then engage in appropriate remediation. Full accounting by the system for the results of its sentencing decisions will produce data testing hypotheses about the operation of the corrective process and the value of its constituent parts. From this, penology can begin to develop a *purpose* behind each sentence.

> My version of therapeutic justice does not abandon punishment. As any counselor, custodian or parent knows, correction often requires it. Dr. Phillip Q. Roche called the criminal law a "child rearing system for grownups." Roche, "Criminal Responsibility," quoted in Henry Weihofen, *The Urge to Punish: New Approaches to the Problem of Mental Irresponsibility for Crime* 26, (1956). Moreover, the notion of, and need for, valence between a predatory act and the victim's and society's needs, cannot be ignored if the procedure and result are to be cathartic and therapeutic to the most significant presence in criminal sentencing—the general public.

Both the Kansas Legislature and the Supreme Court were addressing "sexually violent behavior" in the context of persons who have been charged with or convicted of sexual crimes. Nevertheless, the argument can be made that if a person has a history of violent and predatory behavior (sexual or nonsexual, and even without a criminal charge or conviction), then that person could be civilly committed if legislatures are convinced that the offender's present mental condition creates a likelihood that the offender will engage in similar violent behavior again. Some hope lies in the fact of this recognition if we concede the existence of behavioral actuators other than moral and begin to speak of *treatment* rather than mere *punishment* for misbehavior.

I fear, however, that political over attention to the collective ignorance of society, the reactionary anger towards crimes and offenders, the comparison of direct costs for effective treatment and research with preventive or preemptive detention, and the popularity of *macho toughness,* will groom the path of least resistance for legislatures which is no change at all. The Achille's heel of the genuine therapeutic progress is also exposed. It is therapeutically rationalized commitment without therapy, or conversely, therapy without boundaries. Neither alternative will withstand the harshest critic of all, the scrutiny of time. Commitment without therapy is penal containment in other clothes. The result is that the offender is being punished without a trial or is being punished twice.

C. Therapeutic Justice

I advocate a criminal justice delivery system that (1) views a sentence as a journey, not an end; (2) retains *detention*, not just for punishment, but also as a venue for change; (3) introduces *intervention* to remove the offender from his milieu, and coordinates and deploys social forces that make crimes more difficult to commit; (4) uses *prevention* to intercede in past and potential offender's lives at an earlier stage to thwart offenses; and, (5) uses *preemption* by employing all civic and social forces to make the commission of crimes more difficult, or at least less convenient. Unfortunately, each social science is becoming professionally more centripetal; driven by the competitive rigors of its own endeavors to concentrate its intellectual energies on an ever-diminishing scholastic *locus in quo*. To accomplish what I advocate the sciences truly need each other (sociologists, education professionals, psychologists, victims and victim support organizations, ministers, priests, rabbis, and even urban planners) to fully comprehend the contours of any situation, discovery or action.

Towards this end, I would transform sentencing into an integrated social and penal response to infractions based on a holistic view of the whole ecology of the crime. The courts work to develop appropriate remedial sentences that present offenders with **real** obligations and **real** opportunities to change their behavior and to achieve the end goal of correcting the criminal offenders at all points on the continuum between preoffense and postrelease. This would remake criminal justice into an interdisciplinary justice delivery system. And, because hindsight is a ruthless critic, each element thereof must be accountable to the others, and the whole criminal justice delivery system must be accountable for the results of its actions to society. I believe that the criminal justice delivery system must, in addition to everything else, become a therapeutic vector and look at sentencing as a behavioral tool, and where indicated, through a mental health prism.

Law, whether we jurists admit it or not, is a significant social force in American culture that will either be a socially corrosive or therapeutic. Seldom is it neutral, at least in the criminal law and penal context. It produces change: positive or negative. Therapeutic jurisprudence, which studies "the extent to which substantive rules, legal procedures, and the roles of lawyers and judges produce therapeutic consequences,"[9] began as a mental health approach to law, but in its brief history has attracted significant attention among jurists. It is particularly attractive because it tackles what we jurists recognize as the primary shortcoming of any movement that begins with what "ought" to be—it fails to know what really "is." Therapeutic jurisprudence is pragmatic and deals with real life situations. Therapeutic justice is a scion of therapeutic jurisprudence. Therapeutic justice, however, is at once narrower and broader than therapeutic jurisprudence. It is narrower because it looks at the therapeutic response as it relates to criminal offenses specifically and not law generally. It is broader because mental health is only one behavioral actuator with which it is concerned. Therapeutic justice, as an interdisciplinary approach to solving the problems of crime, is concerned with discovering causes of crime, segregating offenders who are amendable to treatment, then determining what therapies are indicated for them in addition to the initial punitive response.

It is important to consider what therapeutic justice is *not*. First, therapeutic justice says nothing about free will and determinism or good and evil. Each of us has a different genetic menu that equips us differently for coping with stress, temptation and other social pressures. Moreover, none of us can escape the fact that our lives, in significant measure, have been shaped by antecedent causes (other people, external events, developmental milieu) which combine in some individualized personal equation with the genes our ancestors gave us. We, unfortunately, are not as Immanuel Kant contended, free and rational sovereigns in the "realm of ends."[10] Moreover, irrespective of genetic, environmental or educational factors, and depending upon the strength of the temptation or provocation, each of us is capable of performing acts that lie somewhere along the continuum between the good and evil poles of the moral continuum. Where an offender lies on these continua, however, only assists in determining the appropriate remedy for the offense that he committed.

Therapeutic justice offers nothing to assist in deciding whether a person accused of a crime is guilty. There may be multiple *reasons* why one performed a criminal act (*reasons* assist in deciding upon a therapeutic program), but none may *excuse* it (leading to a finding of guilt, or culpability). The concepts of guilt should not be confused with the need to develop a therapeutic program for to the offender, a deterrent for the offensive act, and some satisfaction for the victim specifically and society generally. Hendricks may have committed his crimes because he is a pedophile but that does not excuse from the social safety equation what he did to the children. Therapeutic justice does not expand the concept of conditional or status defenses by putting "new wine into old bottles" it contracts it so that each offender is held to a scientifically rational and legally appropriate degree of accountability for his actions. To face up to what he has done. When one is culpable and deserves some remedy, then therapeutic justice helps determine it.

In 1994, Lorena Bobbitt severed her husband's penis with a kitchen knife but was acquitted of aggravated assault because the jury deemed her temporarily insane. Psychologists and psychiatrists testified that she suffered myriad post-trauma disorders that resulted from mistreatment by her husband.

The Menendez brother's murder trial ended in a mistrial on a defense that the brothers had suffered mental, sexual and emotional abuse from their parents whom they had killed. Other *defenses* to culpability proffered in other trials, and with varying degrees of success, include insanity, diminished emotional or mental capacity, irresistible impulses, overindulgence in movies and TV, junk food, alcohol and drugs, post-partum depression, attention deficit disorder, age, PMS, and most recently genes, an inherited predisposition to violence, to name a few. Some, or all, may be reasons why the offender did what he did. Nonetheless, these reasons are not, and should neither be, defenses by which one can be excused from accounting to society for an offending act nor lead to the declaration of some degree or form of innocence. These reasons are, *if true*, graphic evidence that these individuals are in great need of help.

Truth *is* stranger than fiction. In fiction we reform and conform the truth to make it more believable than the reality of what we think actually exists, but which we may not wish to believe. So, too, in behavior. The truth truly may be strange, exceedingly complex, seemingly incomprehensible, and, indeed often bizarre. The true reasons why one behaves as one does *is* truth, and, as in the adage, may well be stranger than the fiction we employ in attempts to find an excuse for that behavior. The search for truth about behavior may lead us to facts about nutrition, neurotransmittters, toxins, testosterone levels, brain damage, genes and a host of other variables hitherto unexamined, that explain behavior; hence may explain crime. That is the point! With therapeutic theory one is neither absolved from responsibility for one's act, nor found not guilty by reason of some fiction or another. Therapeutic justice is concerned about what to do, and about doing *something* if someone performs an offending act. Importantly, it is concerned about what to do to prevent offending acts from being performed in the first place. It looks for the true reasons why one misbehaved, so that we can understand misbehavior and those who misbehave. Its goal is to provide a systemic response to treat, to counteract, and to prevent both recidivists and potential offenders from committing acts of misbehavior.

Therapeutic justice does not treat crime as a disease or a pathology. Crime may, of course, be a symptom of both, and each may precipitate aberrant behavior not engaged in by the non-diseased or non-pathological. Moreover, some chronic diseases and psychological or biological conditions, may legitimately ex-plain why one behaves as one does. The crime, however, remains an antisocial act. Therapeutic justice views the personhood of the offender, whatever his health, mental capacity or state of nor-malcy. It recognizes the person's degree of competency, accords him that extent of autonomy, to which degree the offender must endure some opprobrium and condemnation, and face the conse-quences of his offense.

Research reveals that individuals, whatever their intelligence, can think to some extent for themselves and learn lessons to some extent from experience. We are all morally responsible for our actions in varying degrees according to our emotional, mental and biological equipment. To be therapeutic, justice requires that we discover that degree and respond accordingly.

With traditional rehabilitation theory, the purpose of punishing criminal offenders is to modify their behavior. At one time, some penologists believed that rehabilitation was the future of the criminal justice system. Unfortunately, earlier rehabilitation theory was based upon a flawed premise: it supposed that the criminal justice system could impose change upon the offender, regardless of whether he wanted to change. Coerced change, however, usually lasts only as long as the pressure to do so remains. This earlier theory of rehabilitation represents to some extent, what happens when the mental health professionals have an insufficient grasp on the reality of correcting offenders, and the legal theorists have an authority that exceeds the value of their ideas to true correction. Those who were called upon to execute the rehabilitation scheme, the prisons, had neither a realistic view of the goal, nor held a firm commitment to the ideal. Nor did either the penologists who held to the rehabilitation theory or the prison administrators understand either *how* to rehabilitate, or *who* was capable of being rehabilitated. Finally, under rehabilitation theory, punishment was placed in too-shallow a grave, and the idea of rehabilitation as a penal theory was scrapped too soon. Had the system been truly interested in correction penologically and been more tenacious in a search for theories and methods of correction, I think that it would have discovered and could have repaired, its flaws.

A paternalistic notion of rehabilitation, however, is *not* therapeutic theory. Therapeutic justice is about positive change. It is occupied with creating clinical and penal climates in which transgressors are encouraged to change. It is for the offenders who sincerely want to change, and it assists in their endeavors to do so. Prisoners who are correctable or have treatable conditions bear the ultimate moral and personal responsibility both for the change resulting from treatment and for their condition afterwards. This is true whether one has a physical ailment, an addiction disease, a more complex emotional problem, or has committed a crime. The system *can* help offenders do what they cannot do for, or by, themselves. It can restore hope where despair exists. It can coordinate individual and component efforts. It can intervene. But it *cannot* rehabilitate offenders who do not want to be rehabilitated. We have learned that lesson. Change is tough. Therapeutic justice is not a soft, easy remedy.

After presiding over hundreds of criminal trials, guilty pleas, and sentences, I was asked following a speech, "What is the central feature of crime in America?" I replied that I did not know, except that I could not recall any criminal case I had tried or defended that did not in some way implicate the abuse of alcohol or the use of drugs. Statistics on drug-related crimes are but the tip of the iceberg. The statistics are conservative. Drug use is pervasive. A substantial number of arrestees test positive for drugs. A substantial number of addicts support their habits by crime. Chemical addiction in its various forms may not be the central feature of crime in America, it is, however, inextricable from crime.

Nonetheless, I have yet to meet an addict, drug dealer, drug treatment specialist, or penologist who believes punishment alone will cure their, or our, drug problem. Unlike the situation with other crimes, with drug users and drug traffickers the law of our land is not the sovereign of theirs. They are governed by the laws of supply and demand only. And, there is so much money to be made on the *supply* side of the equation that the punishment one offender faces upon conviction is insufficient to deter others who are all too willing to step into the convicted dealer's shoes and continue to sell drugs. Limiting *demand* is the key to controlling the drug problem. And demand can only be controlled by a massive therapeutic effort. Unfortunately, all too many Americans seem to want war, not therapy.

The *war* on drugs, although it sounds exciting and dramatic, is a flawed metaphor. It is flawed because they who use or accept the concept forget that in any war both victor and vanquished sustain battle casualties. The battle concept is a dramatic, catchy slogan, but does not describe reality. For we have declared war on no one. We are not shooting down planes that smuggle drugs into the U.S. We mine no harbors to sink ships carrying drugs. We do not shoot drug dealers nor invade drug-producing countries. Iindeed, we continue to give economic aid to some countries that we know just wink at the drug trade. There is *no* war.

Drugs and alcohol, however, are but two *reasons* why some persons commit crimes. There are many others. I recall a tearful telephone call from a mother, distraught because her otherwise decent son at times performed bizarre and violent acts. She had nowhere to go and could not attract anyone's attention to get help. She was told that unless her son committed a crime, the authorities had no opportunity to intervene. She was able eventually to get help but only after her son assaulted a police officer. In the custody of the courts it was determined that he was suffering from schizophrenia, a treatable condition. By taking medicine that controls his condition, he is a peaceful and productive citizen. This is therapeutic justice in action; but for him and for the police officer, it came a bit late. Perhaps justice to the victims of crime requires that we try therapy, not to excuse the acts the offenders have performed, but because we will thereby discover how to intervene and to prevent offensive acts, and, other victims. That is therapeutic justice.

If we are able to diagnose a physical, biological or emotional condition that may precipitate violent behavior, and then can treat it, it makes sense that we do so. The most humane response to crime is to try to prevent the trauma of other persons becoming victims of crime; and to prevent the trauma of being accused and convicted of crime, and prevent the solitary negative experience of prison. Moreover, because we can do all this while guaranteeing to the subject individual no fewer rights than those afforded to the criminally accused, we should do so. That is the essence of therapeutic justice.

D. Conclusion

Although criminology is about behavior, our criminal law pays little attention to the behavioral sciences. Penology is about mental health, but our sentencing policy pays little attention to the medical, biological or social sciences. Correction of criminal offenders is about change, but our penal system is content with punishment alone. Although science has much to tell law, law is not listening.

The *Hendricks* opinion may represent the first light for including therapeutic concepts as alternatives, complements or supplements to our criminal justice delivery system. But, I fear that it will remain just that: a dawn on the horizon, in sight but always out of reach. The criminal justice delivery system must advance hand-in-hand with civil responses to misbehavior and deploy remedial measures that improve with the discoveries from research in all the allied sciences. Punitive criminal incarceration and therapeutic civil commitments are not a "them" (the bad who commit crimes and deserve punishment), and "us" (the good people who have erred and deserve therapy), proposition. The two parts must operate as components of a justice delivery system focused on correction.

Defensive confinement to protect the public (a common denominator of civil and criminal statutes) is constitutionally acceptable. I suggest that although incapacitation is a goal common to civil and criminal confinement, were the criminal justice delivery system willing to set retribution and deterrence aside and reembrace confinement for correction, it too could gain by considering confinement as a tool for correction and treatment.

The *Hendricks* opinion will have a great impact on future civil commitment laws and the durability of therapeutic justice. One caveat, however, is a clear warning that civil commitment/treatment laws cannot be used simply as surrogates for punishment. Civil commitments cannot be a mere pretext for criminal incarceration. If civil confinement becomes a mechanism for retribution or general deterrence, or alternatively, if it is shown that mental abnormality is too imprecise a category to offer a solid basis for concluding that civil detention is justified, I could not validate it. Civil therapeutic commitment is here to stay if we offer therapy to the persons thus committed and effect change in offenders' behavior.

I am constantly amazed that we Americans, who give with unprecedented generosity to charity and count ourselves as a humanitarian conscience among other governments and cultures of the world, are so content with a vengeful and unproductive criminal justice delivery system. We can treat each other with such dignity and respect until some one of us whose legal flaws may have been well known to all is declared by charge and verdict to be "guilty," then we turn our backs. The criminal justice delivery system should be an instrument of social harmony rather than discord, and prescribe remedies for offenders that are not socially corrosive. We have an obligation to each other and to our culture to be humane, and our government, which after all is *all of us,* has an obligation to set a humanitarian standard for our culture to follow. Whether by imprisoning the criminally rebellious, or in committing the violent and mentally abnormal predacious. In either case, however, I doubt that we can effect change by perpetrating senseless emotional cruelty upon, or indignity to prisoners. I suggest that we explore a gentler way. We must prepare those who are now incarcerated or committed, if they are ever to be released, for a functional life in society. If we fail to do so, if we fail to care for each other and to keep our sights therapeutic and treat the treatable, the dawn of therapeutic justice will not only produce little morning daylight, but will simply result in another nonspectacular sunset.

ENDNOTES

1.   See generally Coleman Phillipson, *Three Criminal Law Reformers: Beccaria, Bentham, Romilly*, Patterson Smith, 1970.

2.   N. Kittrie, *The Right to Be Different: Deviance and Enforced Therapy*, 29, (1971). (Cited in David Wexler, "Therapeutic Justice," 57 *Minn. L.R.*, 289, (1972). Enrico Ferri believed that criminal responsibility and moral guilt should be wholly abolished.

3.   Blaise Pascal, *Pensees*, para. 133.

4.   *Kansas v. Hendricks*, 117 S.Ct. 2072, 138 L.Ed.2d 501, 65 USLW 4564 (1997).

5.   § 59-29a03(a), § 22-3221 (1995).

6.   See e.g., *Heller*, supra, 314-315, 113 S.Ct., at 2639-2640.

7.   *Addington v. Texas*, 441 U.S. 418, at 429 (1979).

8.   Justice Kennedy, however, raised a red flag about future implications of the Court's analysis, saying: "If the civil system is used simply to impose punishment after the State makes an improvident plea bargain on the criminal side, then it is not performing its proper function... [because] incapacitation is a goal common to both the criminal and civil systems of confinement." *Hendricks*, at 2087 (J. Kennedy, concurring).

9.   David Finkleman and Thomas Grisso, "Therapeutic Jurisprudence: From Idea to Application," 20 *New. Eng. J. On Crim. And Civ. Confinement* 243, 244 (1994) quoting David B. Wexler and Bruce J. Winick, "Therapeutic Jurisprudence as a New Approach to Mental Health Law Policy Analysis and Research," 45 *Miami. Rev.* 979, 981 (1991).

10.   Immanuel Kant, *The Metaphysical Elements of Justice*, trans. John Ladd, Bobbs-Merrill, 1965, p. x.

Some Concluding Thoughts

"Forbear to judge, for we are sinners all."
Shakespeare

It is so easy to hate. Each of us in our unguarded moments finds someone we can hate, if we are willing to surrender our consciences a little and if we want to be unkind. I recall the fearsome way our nation's enemies were portrayed in my youth. The Japanese soldier, depicted with squinty eyes and rounded glasses displaying a hateful, hideous, toothy leer, and brandishing a bayoneted rifle. The square-jawed, cruel-looking, jack-booted German Nazi soldier with his helmet pulled down nearly covering his eyes. They glowered menacingly at me from War Bond posters on the post office wall. I feared *them*. And my fear, as fear usually does, came out in hatred.

They were the "Japs" and the "Krauts" whom we children routinely shot and killed in the neighborhood war games we played. Even though I was taught from my earliest years to "love thine enemies," these people were different. No one condemned me for hating these enemies. I hated not just those who bombed Pearl Harbor, not just the demonic minds who conceived the monstrous evils inflicted upon the war's victims, not just those who committed other horrid atrocities and whose names have become charactonyms for indescribable evil, nor those who turned a blind eye while others did their heinous deeds; I hated all *Japs*, all *Krauts*.

Soon after the war, we were given a new object of official hatred, the communists which included the citizens of Central and East Europe, China, and anyone who sided with *them*. It felt good to hate *them*. Hating *them* was acceptable. They were the "commies" and "reds." After all, just as with hating our World War II enemies, it was patriotic to hate our cold war enemies. Indeed, we were unified against and bound together by our common hatred of *them*.

I later learned that another common and unifying theme of our culture is in fear and hatred of criminals. They, too, became pariahs in society. I also learned that this hatred for the criminal, even when it reaches the pitch of paranoia, is socially acceptable. It is accepted as a normal, and even an admirable, quality of a culture to loath its deviants. Those who violate our accepted societal behavior are reproached, feared, and that which follows are hated. They have betrayed us by violating the tenets of our cultural faith, threatening what we accept as good. This hatred for criminals, too, has developed a life of its own and an economy to sustain it.

I have often wondered how a culture that produced a Bach, a Mendelssohn, a Beethoven, and a Mozart, bequeathing to the world such beauty, could also produce a Hitler, an Eichmann and a Mengele, thereby leaving the world such a bequest of evil. This same land of such natural alpine splendor and grand architectural beauty also produced such unspeakable ugliness as death camps. How could a culture that produced such great thinkers as Kepler, Einstein, Schiller, Nietzsche, and Kant, allow the development of science and politics as mindless and bereft of shame, compassion, and morality as Naziism? It is because in all cultures, and in all peoples, there exist the seeds of beauty, compassion and the hope for life, as well as the germs of evil, hatred and the capacity for death.

I have also wondered how our culture, which is producing unparalleled comfort and wealth, leads the world in scientific discoveries, has the best medical facilities, and has the finest universities, could remain satisfied with a penology that thrives on retribution and punishment, and gives little consideration for finding the causes of and cures for crime. Perhaps it is because what we become culturally or individually depends upon the side of human nature that we cultivate, or antithetically, that we exploit. Law and justice must have some absolute point of reference, because justice is compromised and surrendered by adapting itself to its environment. I suggest that we should use *humanity* as that point of reference to critique law, justice and its system of delivery. All official actions and reactions to crime must employ the most humanitarian means and instrumentalities available to achieve penology's desired ends. Our point of reference should always be humanitarian, whether we are dealing with rights violators, killers, or mass murderers. Like the Germany that spawned Naziism, our culture, too, is not immune from evil if it fails to nurture hope, the love of wisdom, and compassion, and resigns itself to inhumane treatment of its citizens—even criminals. It, too, will suffer if we underestimate the cunning minds of those who plan evil, or allows our leaders to exploit despair, hatred, and revenge, at the expense of humanity.

Hating, blaming and rejecting a group of people does, however, ensure that we do not have to take the risk or responsibility of looking more honestly at the individual members of the group, nor, for that matter, looking honestly at ourselves and at our deeper feelings. Hatred, however, creates a blind spot in our personal awareness, the result of which is that we fail to see that although some offenders are violent and entitled to no systemic sympathy, others are not. Some offenders are basically good, but have erred. Some offenders are basically bad. Some are predators. Some are prey. All are offenders, but, some are victims as well. We err when we lump them together.

The trouble with thinking of all offenders as *criminals* is that there really is no such concrete, well-defined, and all-encompassing category. Criminals are not just the murderers, rapists, thugs and drug dealers we love to hate. Nor are all crimes committed by people who live in the slums of which most people have heard of, but have never seen. Many crimes are conceived, not out *there* somewhere, but in well-lit, clean, carpeted and air conditioned offices, by quiet people with trimmed nails, cut hair, who wear suits, ties and shined shoes, and who live in neighborhoods like yours and mine. Criminals are not a clear-cut and insular group of persons whom we can condemn with collective judgments, then ostracize and hate.

Criminals, are for the most part surprisingly like you and me. They are human beings with wants and needs, they love, and are loved, they are someone's parents, they are someone's children, their bodies function like yours and mine. Genetically, we differ little. Nonetheless, we are quite content to hold *them* to standards many of *us* do not meet. And, we subject *them* to penalties that many of *us* could not endure.

The usual stereotype of the criminal is the prison inmate. We come to believe that criminals are criminals *because* they are in prison. That is not the whole story. The moral quality of an act does not depend upon whether one is caught doing it. How many among us can honestly say that we have never committed an act that is, or may be, a violation of the law? If you have, you are a criminal (albeit not a convicted criminal) for you have performed an act that society has declared to be illegal. Nevertheless, it is more comfortable if we can place the focus elsewhere, so, we target others— *them*.

Once we have focused upon the faults and highlighted the defects of a target group, it is easier to perceive them selectively, assume they will all behave a certain way, and cognitively absorb only what is consistent with the judgment we have already formed of them. It does not work. As a sailor in the U.S. Navy stationed in Japan in the 1950's, I met some of the gentle people whom we had earlier condemned as *Japs*, and whom, as a child, I had hated. I discovered that the evil leaders and warriors of World War II Japan were not accurate representatives of all the Japanese people. None of the people whom I met were political ideologues. Indeed, that many were victims of the awful war perpetrated by their leaders and warriors, just as we were. There was no longer a unitary *them*, whom I could comfortably hate. They were just ordinary people, most of whom I liked.

Three decades later I sat in a boardroom of the Russian White House helping a ranking member of the Russian Parliament draft an Ombudsman proposal for the new Russian Constitution. Days later I dined with leaders and judges of the emerging democracy of Ukraine; in Kiev, a city that still had forty American nuclear warheads aimed to destroy it, and us. I listened one-on-one to a Ukrainian judge tearfully tell me why he opposed capital punishment while explaining how that very day he had applied the law and condemned an individual to death. He explained that in Ukraine, at least until 1993, the condemning judge was responsible for making sure the sentence was carried out, usually by a pistol shot to the back of the head when the condemned person did not suspect it. He tearfully said, "I am tired of violence. I am tired of killing. I am tired of death." I both agreed and identified with his feelings. I, too, am tired of the violence and the killing. In Romania I listened to a citizen's fervent plea, as he clasped my hand in both of his with the grip of a vice and said, "I do not know what democracy is. I only know that I want it." No longer the feared and hated members of a monolithic Soviet Union, the Russians, Ukrainians, and Romanians had made themselves vulnerable by asking us for help. The "Evil Empire" was gone, and in its place are human beings. They desperately wanted a role in their own destiny. Just like you. Just like me. I laughed with them. I cried with them. It was no longer *them* and *us. We* had come together.

I have learned that no matter whom you really wish to hate, whether on the basis of race, gender, religion, politics, nationality, or a myriad of motives, eventually you get to know one of *them*, and you find out that *they* are not much different from *us.* Treating criminals as such a class, targeted for hatred, is no different, and the results are the same.

A classic confrontation in literature occurs in *War and Peace,* between the Duke of Eckmuhl (Davout) and Pierre, who stands before Davout condemned to death. But Davout hesitates, and Pierre is spared. Tolstoy writes:

> Davout looked up and gazed intently at him. For some seconds they looked at one another, and that look saved Pierre. Apart from the conditions of war and law, that look established human relations between the two men. At that moment an immense number of things passed dimly through both their minds, and they realized that they were both children of humanity and were brothers. [Until then] Pierre [had been] only a circumstance, and Davout could have shot him without burdening his conscience with an evil deed, but now he saw in him a human being.[1]

Davout discovered what every compassionate and fair judge knows. That it is easy to be harsh and uncompassionate in the insular halls of some legislature. In the theater of the trial, and the reality of sentencing, everybody is human.

Culture is not made up simply of bad and good guys. Culture is *us*, each placed by nature, events, and actions somewhere between polar positions of irredeemably corrupt and wholly incorruptible. We are all there, someplace, and the line separating *them* from *us* is blurred, faint, and in some places it has become indistinguishable. The fact of the matter is, perhaps the difficulty of the matter is, that some of us simply do not know how to behave. Some of us know how, but do not. Some of us know how, but cannot. Some of us simply have never learned the basic notions of civic or social duty. Whatever the category, when caught and convicted of some act of criminal misbehavior, these are the citizens who become *them*—the criminals. The concept of criminals as a separate, or at least separated, genre of human beings prevents consideration of an appropriate remedy for the individual offender. The concept is wrong.

Perhaps as a society we cannot care fully if some offenders, who have reached a certain degree of chronic culpability are injured by systemic punishment. Even if we do not care for the offenders, however, we must care that our culture thrives. The notion of *us* against *them* is no longer functional and may threaten cultural stability. Fear and hatred are no longer useful emotions by which to guide our penology. These emotions are at odds with both our current state of psychological awareness, and that which we know to be morally proper. Fear and hatred are like bacteria or viruses lying latent, but sure to break out at the time of greatest social weakness.

Our moral lens, and the view we see through it, are like a split image that blurs our vision and prevents us from focusing on the real issues which are how to prevent crime, thus saving our citizens from becoming victims, and how to correct offenders and interrupt the criminalization process itself. It does not help our analysis to lump offenders together and then give them the same sentence, prison. There are too many of *them*, and some of them are *us*. We need more numerous, smaller, well-defined lumps, because some offenders are salvageable and can become productive again. Were I to sum up the goals of sentencing as I see it, but in another person's words, I would quote Goethe, who said:

> If you treat a person as he appears to be, you
> make him worse than he is. But if you treat a person
> as if he already were what he could potentially be,
> you make him what he should be.

An offender's sentence need not just punish, nor should citizens be satisfied with mere punishment. Sentencing can do more, and I would require that it do more. It can, in some instances, facilitate the healing process as well. What William James calls the "whole phenomenon of regeneration" is the sum of "subconscious incubations and maturing of motives deposited by the experiences of life." I suggest that we have little to lose by using the opportunity of a criminal sentence to expose the offender to experiences of life from which the criminal justice delivery system can help to regenerate or create solid citizens out of our cultural offenders. Let us require full restitution, a face-to-face apology to the victim, and that the offender achieve an acceptable level of social competence. It is time for government to follow Goethe's admonition and exercise its leadership to help us reach toward our civilization's potential for greatness. This is the sentencing goal we should reach for. This is what sentencing *should be*, as I see it.

ENDNOTES

1. *War and Peace,* Leo Tolstoy, 51 Great Books 549 Chicago (1952).

America's Most Popular
Practical Police Books

Becoming a Police Officer $14.95
Criminal Law 2nd $44.95
California Criminal Codes 2nd $44.95
California Criminal Procedure 4th $44.95
California Criminal Procedure Workbook $19.95
California's Dangerous Weapons Laws $9.95
Community Relations Concepts 3rd $44.95
Courtroom Survival $16.95
Criminal Evidence 4th $44.95
Criminal Interrogation 3rd $19.95
Criminal Procedure 2nd $44.95
Criminal Procedure (*Case approach*) 5th $44.95
Effective Training $29.95
Exploring Juvenile Justice 2nd $44.95
Encyclopedic Dictionary of Criminology $19.95
Evidence and Property Management $29.95
Florida's Criminal Justice System $14.95
Fingerprint Science 2nd $19.95
Gangs, Graffiti, and Violence 2nd $14.95
Getting Promoted $29.95
Informants: Development and Management $19.95
Inside American Prisons and Jails $19.95
Introduction to Corrections $44.95
Introduction to Criminal Justice 2nd $44.95
Introduction to Criminology $44.95
Investigating a Homicide Workbook $14.95
Legal Aspects of Police Supervision $24.95
Legal Aspects of Police Supervision Case Book $24.95
The New Police Report Manual 2nd $14.95
Natl. Park Service Law Enforcement $19.95
Paradoxes of Police Work $14.95
PC 832 Concepts $24.95
Police Patrol Operations 2nd d $44.95
Practical Criminal Investigation 5th $44.95
Report Writing Essentials $14.95
Research Methods $37.95
Search and Seizure Handbook 6th $19.95
Sentencing: As I see it $14.95
Traffic Investigation and Enforcement 3rd $31.95
Understanding Street Gangs $19.95

Shipping costs: $5.00 for first item and 50¢ for each additional item.
Price subject to change

*All prices are quoted in U.S. Dollars. International orders add
$10.00 for shipping.*

Credit card orders only, call:

1-800-223-4838

*Nevada Residents add 7.25% Sales Tax
Unconditionally Guaranteed!*
www.copperhouse.com